Beyond the Reach of Ladders

*My story as a therapist forging bonds
with firefighters in the aftermath of 9/11*

Elizabeth Goren, PhD

OPEN GATE PRESS

incorporating Centaur Press

LONDON

First published in 2011 by Open Gate Press
51 Achilles Road, London NW6 1DZ

British Library Cataloguing-in-Publication Programme
A catalogue reference for this book is available from the
British Library.

ISBN: 978-1-871871-72-2

Printed and bound by Lightning Source.

This book is dedicated to the men of my firehouse – you guys know who you are – as well as to the memory of all those lost on September 11th and those after who died for the cause.

A portion of the proceeds of this book will go to the New York City Firefighter Foundation

Everything in this book happened. However, in order to protect the privacy of the individuals concerned, I have, as is customary among psychoanalysts, disguised all the protagonists, creating fictionalised composite characters in order that no person may be identified from the information given in these pages. As a consequence, anyone who thinks that they can recognise anyone in this book is mistaken. The fundamental story, however, is one hundred per cent true. That is precisely why it needs to be told.

Contents

Acknowledgements

Thanks first to my writing group – 'the ladies', as our leader Carole Maso refers to us – the seven analyst writers who have striven alongside me to find a new language for expressing who we are and what we do. This book owes its existence to her, for Carole was the first person to see the writer in me and the book in these stories. Her originality of mind and spirit, her steadfast and fearless approach to writing has been a source of inspiration through every point in this book.

I am indebted to the Fire Department of New York for giving me the opportunity to work in its organization, and to its Counseling Services Unit for making our program possible. The fellowship grant awarded to me by the Psychoanalytic Society of the Postdoctoral Program in Psychotherapy and Psychoanalysis of New York University in preparation for this book is gratefully acknowledged. The insight and support of Bob Wool and my agent Stephanie Ebdon early on in this project was invaluable. To my editor Jeannie Cohen I am forever appreciative for believing in this book and nourishing it in its many incarnations over the years.

My story owes itself to my family. To Annie, Barbara and Sue, my commune sisters, who have watched over me since I began taking paper to pen in this effort. To my husband Michael, my life partner, for his unerring love and faith in me and my work. And to my daughters Abby and Dannie, who are the wellspring of my life.

I am a New York City psychoanalyst, a professional decoder of messages from the unconscious, guardian of memories and stories. I am an explorer of the vast world of inner life, plying my tools, an understanding of the human heart and mind at work, on journeys of self-exploration and discovery. My patients and I bond in a way that eases the pain and isolation of human separateness, as we search together for the unforeseen ways that the past wends its way into the present, and create new paths for a more fulfilling future. As the leader of the expedition, it's my job to recognize, remember and make sense of what they bring to me, as I guide them through their pain and hurt, their sorrow, laughter and tears, sharing moments that really matter between people. Together we travel over landscapes of pathos, defeat, survival, and triumph, and weave meaning into life, within the privacy and safety of my 18 x 20 room, twenty-three storeys above Manhattan's streets.

I've had the good fortune to be taken into the lives of persons from nearly every corner of the globe and every walk of life, in the many mottled shades of race, age, class and lifestyle that make up the palette of New York City. This has made me into a witness of how culture and history inform an individual's life story and a society's spirit, and passes from one generation to the next. But in the time right before September 11th I was becoming concerned that I was turning into the kind of jaded and hackneyed over-the-hill 'shrink' in long skirts you see in the movies. My last journal article had brought a few comments of 'interesting' from those who bothered to read it. I'd just spent another summer in Vermont tending to my empty nest garden without many visitors to notice its brief organic bloom.

In the last thirty years a steady stream of people has entered and left the secluded world of my one room office. In that time my children have grown up, and I was now growing old. I kept going over the numbers. Could it be thirty years since I started out as a young radical psychologist working in community mental health? After all the time I've put into doing therapy and being in therapy, I was still struggling with vestiges of the same pesky unresolved conflicts of mine. There were still the occasional feelings of frustration over being the behind-the-scenes woman, the invisible mover and shaker of other people's lives that is the life of private practice. Were there no more new or exciting challenges ahead of me? Nothing more to learn about myself or life?

Then, in a split second, when life in lower Manhattan became a theatre of the unimaginable, everything changed for me, my fellow New Yorkers, Americans, and ultimately, for the world. The terrorist attacks that have come to be known as '9/11' to the world at large, while forever remaining 'September 11th' to its victims and survivors, transformed the American if not the global psyche. It has led to the wars in Afghanistan and Iraq, in which thousands more lives have since been sacrificed in addition to the three thousand persons who lost their lives on that day. Trauma researchers estimate that for each individual directly involved in a traumatic incident, roughly two hundred more people are directly affected. So it's probably no exaggeration to say that what happened on the morning of September 11th has changed the face and heart of the world.

I worked intimately with many of those directly involved in the attack on the World Trade Center – the first responders and other eye witnesses, survivors of the collapse, and victims who lost loved ones. Through my experience on the couch, in makeshift therapeutic settings, in the streets and in a firehouse that lost several of its men, I have learned more than I would wish to know about how trauma becomes embedded in the human psyche, and infiltrates into the next generation. I have also learned more than I could ever have anticipated about the extraordinary ways people can and do band together in tragedy, and the profound ways we can help one another heal. While the events of 9/11 carry different meanings for each one of us, as a society we now share a collective history, anxiety and sensitivity, indeed at times even dread, of 'the next one'. As we commemorate the tenth anniversary of 9/11, I invite you to look back with me at that personal and world-altering moment in time. Perhaps in listening to my story you will retrieve and embrace your own memories. For capturing and sharing memory is the psychoanalytic road to understanding, learning, and change.

PART I
New York City 2001
'The new normal'

On the morning of . . .

September 11th was a Tuesday, primary election day in the city. The second day of the first full week after Labor Day, the unofficial end of summer. I no longer had a dog to walk or young children to awaken, dress, feed and get out the door with lunch in hand. I knew I would even have the luxury of voting after work. But did I still have it in me to for a 6.30 a.m. jog before work?

Contemporary psychoanalysts believe that insight and personal change is brought about through the unique interaction between patient and therapist. To guide the patient and therapy process, the analyst must be able to empathize with every emotion and thought known to humanity. To do this, she must be able to access the most petty and trivial concerns that can occupy an anxious or depressed spirit, the silly, incongruous and absurd thoughts that come to an imaginative and neurotic mind, and the most terrifying, horrific and shameful feelings and impulses that we all know but keep buried from consciousness for sanity sake. So each 'fifty minute hour' (or forty-five minutes in today's faster-paced world), requires the therapist to wander through the deepest recesses of her own as well as her patient's heart and soul, to mine her own unconscious in order to bring to bear those of her own feelings and thoughts which are relevant to the patient and prevent those that are not from being imposed on the patient and therapy.

A tall order for a day's work, that made me question whether I had it me to take a morning run before I headed in to work. Though it was hard to resist the pull of the early morning lingering summer sun for a run, I doubted I'd have the energy to feel prepared for whatever might be asked of me in the day ahead. So I turned my focus to deciding which subway line to take, the less crowded but painfully slow one or the swifter but sardine packed subway line. For the life of me I can't recall which one I came in on that particular day.

But I'm sure that on that morning I did what I do every Tuesday morning. I'm sure I watched another younger mother holding her daughter's hand as they walked to school, just as I had done for so long. On the subway platform I might have had to ask someone if he or she could make out the static announcements from the loudspeaker, and maybe I read the headlines of someone else's newspaper on the twenty minute ride into Manhattan from Brooklyn. I'm sure I crossed paths with some of the men and women in the rainbow coalition of uniformed people whose job is to keep the behemoth running, to keep us safe – a subway conductor, a school crossing guard, a police person directing traffic. I may even have nodded good morning, but I'm sure I didn't stop to think about what these people do for the public every single day.

Before that fateful September 11th that came to be known as '9/11', my only reference to 911 was that it was the national telephone number for personal emergencies.

Before 9/11, I never thought much about firemen. I never knew there were different kinds of fire companies, or for that matter, different kinds of firemen. My image of firemen was that they wore big black hats and boots, shimmied down gold poles, climbed ladders and rescued people and pets. Before I met Firefighter Jack Smith I had no idea that a fireman can carry up to 80 pounds on his back when entering a building on fire, and how many injuries a fireman typically incurs over the course of his career. Until I worked with Officer Steve Holland I didn't know that since 1996, thousands of New York City's firemen are actually fully trained Emergency Medical Services technicians. I never knew, that is until Lt. Patrick Darby made sure I knew, that the fire truck ladders cannot reach my office on the twenty-third floor. Nor did I know that the oxygen in their protective gear lasts only eighteen minutes.

I never gave more than a passing thought to where the emergency exit signs were. Or to what those red buttons on large elevator display panels marked 'For Firefighters' were for. Firemen were just there, one part of the pulsing noisy fabric of New York City. I assumed I was safe.

Climbing the subway stairs into the bright morning light at 8.30 a.m., I turned my cell phone back on. Decided the coffee better be a regular, not decaf. I had a heavy schedule of patients lined up. How else could I be sure to remember all that I would be entrusted with?

* * *

When Firefighter Jack Smith, or Smitty as he's known around the firehouse, pulled his rig up to the North Tower of the Trade Center, he could see this was big. It was not chaos. There was a system, there's always a system. When his group got to what Smitty later recalled to me was the twenty-eighth floor and opened the first office door, he was met with the strangest sight. Dozens of people were still sitting at their desks, as if they were still working. Smitty couldn't believe it; it almost made him laugh. One man was gathering papers and putting them in file folders! The civilians started talking all at once, one person saying they'd been told to stay there, to return to their desks. Another one said that some had left anyway, most planning to try to make their way down, and a few followed the guy who insisted they were better off trying to go up to the roof.

At this point no one, not even the firemen, knew exactly what had happened, and no one, in or outside those buildings, had any idea that the edifice of the World Trade Center could and actually would, less than an hour later, collapse in a matter of a minute or two. As for those workers who decided to evacuate via the roof, though their strategy was sound, given that the 1993 bombing was in the basement garage of the Trade Center, they did not make it out alive, while those who went down were among the 15,000 successfully evacuated, thanks in large measure to the extraordinary rescue operation of the FDNY.

Smitty and his partner George quickly organized the people in the office into lines, instructing them clearly that they were to go down, not up, reassuring them they'd get out. They began moving the people to the stairwell, where they joined others who were filing down in an amazingly orderly fashion, considering the situation. One man in his forties dressed in suit and tie, was not moving. At first Smitty thought he was just being a wise guy, but then realized the man was frozen to his desk. He immediately grasped the situation. He'd seen this many times in his career – absolute terror inducing the primal instinct to fight, flight, or freeze. Within seconds, with a mere glance at George, they reached around him, put their arms under his shoulders, lifted him up and got him moving on his own steam. All the while the man kept repeating in a robot voice, 'But they came over the loudspeaker and told us to stay.' Understanding that universal need for authority in such frightful moments, Smitty and his partner kept talking to the folks as they showed them to the stairwell, reassuring them they'd be okay, that all they had to do was follow people going down. Once everyone was out, they went to check out the other offices on the floor.

'It was a series of random events, that killed thousands and saved hundreds . . . not many did anything right that day, but not many did anything wrong that day either.'
New York Times, July 7, 2002

Afterwards, Smitty couldn't remember how many floors his group cleared out before they started down. He remembered meeting lots of other firefighters. Despite the darkness and the smoke clouded masks, Smitty was able to recognize some guys he'd worked with over the years. The firefighters were guiding people, calming people down, carrying people, like a normal operation. Then things became confused. Some firefighters began to tire with the constant climbing under the weight of their heavy gear and oxygen tanks, and some had to stop for a breath at a landing. At some point in the smoke filled darkness, Smitty and his partner got separated from the group. Exactly when, on which floor, or what happened after that, Smitty couldn't clearly remember. He distinctly remembers at some point turning to George and saying something like, 'Guess it's you and me now.'

* * *

Both rigs from another lower Manhattan firehouse were among the first to respond to the call. When they arrived on the scene, the ladder company or the 'truck' as it's called, left the engine company near the water hook-ups of the South Tower and headed back to the northern end of the massive World Trade Center. The captain of the engine company saw men from another engine about to hook up their hoses. He stepped down from the rig, and in what would turn out to be a fatal decision, Captain McNeil pulled rank and ordered the smaller engine to pull back, so his guys could set up. Reluctantly, the men from the other engine company followed his orders.

The men from the ladder company headed back to the NorthTower. As Firefighter Sean Foster came to tell me when I became their firehouse counsellor, what they encountered was nothing like anything they'd ever seen before or would ever be able to forget.

'When we entered the building suddenly Bobby Walsh appeared, out of nowhere. He wasn't on duty but happened to be in the area, and there he was. How he found us, I don't know. And Danny, the probie was there with us. He and the other probie, Lebowski, they just graduated from the academy and they were only on the job a few weeks. Danny was supposed to be with the engine, but somehow they got mixed up. At first we all stayed together. Me, William, Walker, Lieutenant Ross, and Walsh and Danny. It was on the tenth floor maybe that Lt. Ross decided we should split up. Bobby Walsh offered to take Danny with him. Danny had never been with us on the truck, he'd only worked the engine, so he wouldn't have a clue what to do. Walsh wasn't officially on duty, so the Lieu told Danny to go with William.

'I stayed with the Lieu. After we checked out the offices in the middle, we went to the hallway between A and B exits to wait for the other guys to return. It seemed like forever. Lt. Ross's radio was still working, sort of. He kept calling, but couldn't reach anyone. Finally William and Danny came back, but there was no sign of Walsh or Walker. The Lieu decided we better keep moving. So we started back up, checking each floor to make sure everyone was out. People were filing down the stairs, pretty orderly actually. There were some disabled people. We kept running into other guys everywhere on the floors and in the stairways keeping the people going. There was no sign of either Bobby Walsh or Ben Walker. Somebody said he'd seen Bobby Walsh, so we figured he must've hooked up with some guys. I remember recognizing this guy from another company I'd worked with in the battalion; he was trying to get this lady down in a wheelchair. I asked him if he needed help. He said he was OK. I don't know if he made it out. Guys I'd worked with, from other companies over the years, we'd ask if they knew anything. They just shook their heads. A few of them had radios, but communication was sporadic. The lieutenant's radio had given out altogether. The civilians were still going down, I remember seeing this one older guy, and somebody was holding his hand; funny the things you remember. People were pushing, pulling, trying to get everybody down, but trying to keep the situation under control. The guys were helping the slow ones, carrying some of them. It was clear the situation was beyond containment; we knew we had to evacuate the civilians as fast as possible, and we had no idea about the other tower. Once we got them out we knew what to do in the smoke and darkness. We had to stay with our group, keep each other's back, and follow orders.'

'No other agency lost communications on Sept 11 as broadly or to such devastating effect, as the Fire Department' New York Times, 7/7/02

'By the time we hit the thirtieth floor, Lt. Ross could see we had to give it up. He said we better go back down, check floors on the way down for anyone still there. Next thing I remember, things changed. The guys were getting tired, from, you know, the smoke, the climbing, carrying people, the weight of the oxygen tanks. That's when I started to think maybe we weren't gonna make it out. The smoke – it was hard to see, and to breathe. That's when I think our group got separated. I was with the Lieu, but I couldn't see William or Danny any more. Next thing I know, I'm losing oxygen. Those tanks only got so much in them. My kids and wife flashed through my mind. Why? I kept thinking. Like why was I a fireman, but it was just a split second, then there was no time. Time, I don't even know how long anything was, how long it took really to get down. We met up with some guys maybe on the eighteenth floor; told 'em we hadn't found anybody on the floors above. They told us the B stairway had given out. We looked at each other; nobody said anything, we didn't have to. We knew the last we'd seen Bobby Walsh and Walker, they were headed in the direction of that staircase. I hate to say it but that gave us back that extra adrenaline boost to hightail it down before this one gave out. I don't know how long it took to get down. We had to stop at each landing. They'd been up there a while.

'When we got to the lobby there were guys everywhere. So many. Like I said, somehow our group had gotten split up. But I was still with the Lieu. We were just trying to get our bearings. Wasn't like we didn't know exactly where we were, which way the exits were. But the falling. It wasn't safe outside. I'll never forget that sound – falling bodies. No one was saying anything; we just kind of looked away, acting like we didn't hear. Bodies were falling on bodies. Blood was everywhere. It all happened so fast. We couldn't figure out what to do. We were, like, stunned, you know. Some guys started heading for the exits. 'Suddenly I see William coming to us. He's got Danny who's looking out of it. Next thing I know we hear this screaming. We turn to see this lady running out of the elevator, her hair's on fire. That's when Marino went running over toward her. Will starts looking around. He says we gotta get out of here. But what about Walsh and Walker? So we waited, a minute, two, maybe five, I don't know. Guys were leaving in droves by now. Some were going around to the far side of the building, away from the window side. Other guys were making a dive for it, you know, trying to avoid getting hit by the falling. We're just standing there waiting for Marino and praying Walsh and Walker'd show up. Nobody'd seen or heard from either of them since we first split up. We didn't have radio communication. But we didn't hear anybody call mayday. Seemed like hours, I don't know, but maybe it was a minute, honestly I can't say for sure, Doc. But then Will says 'Dammit, we gotta go.' How could we leave without our guys? Lt. Ross, he's in charge, and we're waiting for him to tell us what to do, but he's not saying anything. Will says again 'I don't care. I'm leaving and I'm taking Danny,' and he turned toward the exit. Just then Lt. Ross orders us to go and says he'll wait for Marino, Walsh and Walker to return. That's when Thomasini said he'd stay back and wait for them to return. After all, he was Marino's partner, and that way the Lieutenant could lead the way out. And you know the rest, Doc.'

The rest is that Bobby Walsh and Walker, Thomasini, along with every other firefighter and civilian still in the towers, were killed in the mere minute or so it took for the tallest buildings in New York City, that icon of American ingenuity and invincibility, The World Trade Center, to collapse.

Marino, who'd taken the burn victim out of the building to the medical triage at the far end of the plaza, survived by rolling under a nearby truck that was miraculously not buried in the collapse. The engine had no such luck. All four men from the engine company were buried, along with the rig itself. In the countless ironic twists of fate that day, the smaller engine from the outer borough was still standing. Bobby Walsh, like so many other firemen and police officers not officially on duty, did what first responders do and sacrificed his life to rescue others. Danny's uncanny error in leaving the engine and going with the ladder company saved his life. The guys who left the lobby survived without getting struck down by the falling people, glass and metal, while those like Thomasini who waited for their brothers in the lobby did not.

* * *

The cloud of death had passed over Jack Smith and his partner, George. They were sitting by the curb alongside the West Side Highway, trying to catch their breath and register the reality that they were alive. Smitty removed the kerchief a stranger had given him in the melée from over his face. As he stuffed it in his pocket, he felt something, his cell phone. Quickly his fingers flew across the keys. It took several tries, but he made it through to his home. Hearing his daughter's voice all he could manage was 'I'm OK.' The signal died as inexplicably as it had appeared. Though still thick in the head, thoughts began to congeal. He should go home. But he was still on duty.

For years afterward, Smitty struggled to remember everything that happened that day. No matter how many times he tried to recover the details in therapy with me, he couldn't retrieve certain facts, like how he got back to the firehouse. He figured that he and George must have just started walking northward like everybody else on the western side of the collapse.

* * *

In my office, a dozen or so blocks away, on the twenty-third floor, I heard myself ask Linda, my '8:45', 'Did you see that plane?' as the session was just getting under way. It was an inappropriate thing to say. She had begun talking about something I cannot recall now, but that certainly had nothing to do with the plane flying right outside my window down Fifth Avenue. Linda responded how she sometimes did when I'd make a comment or ask a question about which she was unsure how to respond. She just flashed an uncomfortable smile at me, stopped for a moment or two then picked right up where she left off. As though by her ignoring what I'd said she was gently protecting the two of us the embarrassment of addressing the absurdity of my comment. Now in 'regular' life, at this point in the conversation the other person might say something, like, 'You act like I hadn't just said something, I don't really appreciate that.' Or, 'Didn't you hear what I said?' But this is psychotherapy, and I was the therapist. I made a mental note to explore this protectiveness on her part at a more propitious moment, and redirected my attention to the subject on Linda's mind.

But even the most conscientious therapist is a real person with human vulnerabilities. So when the building shook seconds later, I couldn't stop myself from interrupting her midstream and pressing my own rising concern on her with 'Oh, it must have broken the sound barrier.' She nodded in agreement, once again pretending to not notice my momentary lapse in therapeutic focus, and perhaps finding reassurance in the poorly developed scientific knowledge I offered as a rational explanation of what was happening. At 9.30 a.m. I opened the door to let Linda out, and discovered my office partner in the waiting room, anxiously jiggling the dials, trying to pick up a signal on an old radio that didn't work well when I plopped it there temporarily some twenty years ago. All we got was static. Whatever happened to that 'emergency broadcasting system' that always came on as a test? Finally we heard the familiar voice who periodically chimes in with 'this is CBS news, give us 22 minutes and we'll give you the world.' Now he was stating with calm tension that the World

Trade Center had been struck by a plane which had knocked out much of the radio and telephone service in the listening area.

I ran to my phone. Dead. I couldn't get online. My mobile phone emitted a continuous busy signal. The intercom to the lobby was jammed. The radio announcer then reported that a second plane had hit the towers, that phone service was disrupted and uneven, and some subways weren't running, and informing listeners to 'Stay tuned for further updates.' I went to the hallway. No one. With a methodical calm uncharacteristic for me, I systematically attempted to reach the outside world by making my way through the various telecommunications instruments available, while my partner and I took turns sticking our heads out the window to watch the two buildings ablaze, black smoke billowing to the sky. Curiosity alternated with the need to reach my family.

The streets below my office window were empty. The eerie quiet was broken by the abrupt sound of my phone ringing. Back in touch with the world! It was my husband informing me that they were evacuating his office building in case of another attack. Another attack? Only much later did I realize that I was, like people around the globe, in a kind of muted state of shock. My sensations were blunted, my thinking slowed and my perception narrowed to the singular vision of the smoking towers blocks away.

As I was trying to wrap my mind around the possibility that more danger lie ahead, I was startled by the phone ringing again. This time it was my niece in Philadelphia. Now I had to wrap my mind around the idea that people outside the city knew what was happening. As soon as I heard that everyone in my family was safe and accounted for, I left my office. The elevators were out, leaving me no option but to walk down the twenty-three floors As I made my way down the dark stairwell, I became aware of feeling simultaneously in an altered state and clear as a bell. It was as if I had I had finally gotten 'it'. That realization of what life is really about, the lucidity of understanding that eludes us most of the time but can come when faced head on with death. The folly and senselessness of the petty preoccupations of my daily life, the small time frustrations, disappointments and injuries that had managed to mar my appreciation of being alive – all of it, disappeared in a flash.

Once out on the street, I was struck by how deceptively fresh the late summer morning air felt. I walked to the end of the street. At the corner, I had to make a decision. Left to the west, closer to the disaster, and to St Vincent's Hospital where I knew they would bring people? Or to the right, to the east, to the subway and a chance to make it home?

I was at a fork in the road and I turned left. With no idea of the collisions and connections that I would make, and the lives with whom I would become so entwined. In my thirty years as a psychologist, I'd seen my share of patients in every stage of trauma, doing 'crisis intervention' and therapy in hospitals, clinics, community settings and private practice. But none of the training and experience I had accumulated could have fully prepared me for what I witnessed and for what I was going to be called upon to do in the next twenty-four hours and in the months after.

The need to question motivation, including one's own, is the gift and occupational hazard of being a psychoanalyst. What made me walk towards the disaster rather than away from it, as most people instinctively did? To this day I wonder. Theories abound about what draws people to disaster like moths to a flame – the seductive fantasy of the grand rescue, the counter-phobic impulse to deny or overcome fear, the primitive arousal of disaster, as well as genuine altruism. But to invoke a theory of motivation implies causation. I know that my behaviour at that moment was surely determined by many forces at play, internal psychological as well as those external forces we think of as chance, fate, divine intervention, and of course free will.

How do we grant external forces their due without robbing self-determination its importance in determining our actions and the course of life? Whether it is just another ordinary late summer day in the city or whether it is one of those extra-ordinary moments where one wanders into the apex and nadir of man's relation to his fellow man. All behaviour is multi-determined, subject to the intractability of lifelong patterns and our momentary openness to change. Much of the mystery and magic of life lies in how we respond to the challenges that present themselves to us at such unexpected moments in time.

It would all too easy to proclaim that even if I had known what was in store for me I would still have done what I did that day. I'll never know. But of one thing I am certain. When I watched those towers come down, I felt like I was watching a movie at the same time as I knew full well that this thing we were in was all too real. At that moment I had neither the time nor the inclination to think through or analyze the situation. I just knew I had to move, to do something.

I was aware of being shaken, but I was sure that every other New Yorker at that moment was just as shaken and uncomprehending as I was. I thought I'd long ago relinquished my child self, but a small part of me was probably thinking that there would surely be someone older and wiser who could swoop in, take charge, and guide me. What most strongly propelled me forward was the odd sensation of feeling the reality that neither I nor anyone else would know all that might be needed, and the palpable sense of God watching to see what we humans would do.

I only knew there would be need for help. And that police, firemen and other emergency services would be tending to the injuries of the body, not of the heart. So I headed down 8th street, one of the central arteries in Greenwich Village, in the direction of the nearest hospital, where you go to get help, to give help. It was a Tuesday morning yet I saw no one and heard nothing. Not even the sound of fire or ambulance alarms, a staple of New York life, something you can count on in an emergency. As I crossed 6th Avenue a US Army truck in full camouflage colours sailed unobstructed through the traffic light at the intersection. When I arrived at the official entrance of St Vincent's Hospital I was met by a phalanx of stretchers and dozens of reassuring blue green uniformed personnel waiting in weary tension.

Several ambulances were at the ready by the curb, their sirens aching to rush down Seventh Avenue to come to the aid of the hundreds, thousands of expected injured. The numbers game had already begun: how many would have been at their desks at 8.45, how many could have gotten out, how many burned, injured, dead? No one had a clue whether the injured would number in the hundreds, or thousands. No one as of yet had any idea by day's end you could count the number of ambulance calls on your hands. For with few exceptions people had either escaped physically unscathed, or never made it out alive.

A thick long line of people indistinguishable in colour, age, size, had already formed. No one was talking, there was nothing to say or do. But wait. To donate blood. To do something. We were in a minimalist still-life Hopper-like portrait. People were walking and talking in slow-motion fluidity, with the slightest nods and barely perceptible turns of the head. Collective communication, starkly brilliant in its silent simplicity: death and something more. The inexpressible clarity of our mortality and acceptance of our shared vulnerability that comes at those rare moments when life stops moving, but its pulse continues.

— Even when the next one strikes, it will not be the same.

— To someone whose face is lost to me, I said, 'I am a psychologist.'

— That someone replied, 'I think they're setting up over at the New School.'

— Back in the direction where I had just come from . . .

And so I walked back over the still deserted 8th Street, re-crossed 6th Avenue, again without having to wait for the pedestrian signal, past another subway station that I could have gone down into to go home, but didn't.

* * *

If I am not for myself, who will be for me?
If I am only for myself, what am I?
If not now, when?
Rabbi Hillel
Mishnah

* * *

'Now this is the life!' Sal whispered to himself as he slipped out of bed and stood to stretch under the whirring fan. It was going to be another hot one. He could feel the heat of the Caribbean sun streaming through the tilted shutters. It's been great so far. No fighting. She never once brought up the marriage thing. Glancing at his watch, Sal couldn't believe it. It was almost 10! His internal clock was still on New York time. Tiptoeing to the door he carefully slid the 'Do Not Disturb' sign over the knob and headed for the hotel breakfast bar.

When he got there, he couldn't make heads or tails out of what was going on. A dozen people were gathered around the bar, silently staring at the TV. He needed his coffee. Spooning the sugar with one hand and pouring cream with the other, Sal was shaken awake by what he was hearing – 'Trade Center . . . not sure . . . firefighters . . . Pentagon . . .'

There was no question in Sal's mind. He had to get a plane out of there immediately. He jumped into his rented jeep and hightailed it over to the airport at the far end of the island. 'Don't you get it? I'm a New York City fireman. I'm supposed to be there,' he tried to explain to the person at the ticket counter roughly at the very moment when the first tower began to collapse. The man, whose English was at best fair, stared blankly at him. Sal went on, 'My brother's a fireman.' 'I'm sure he's okay,' replied the airline representative with that tone of distant professionalism, then added, 'But you see sir. It's your country . . . Ah, you see . . . no planes in or out right now. There's nothing I can do.'

'Nothing you can do?!' Sal was getting more agitated by the minute. 'You mean I'm stuck here?' The supervisor came over and reassured Sal that they would let him know as soon as planes were able to take off for the states again. There was nothing Sal could do but drive back to the hotel, try to reach his family and the firehouse, then wait. And keep watching the hotel television replay over and over the burning towers collapse, without knowing that seven of his brothers from the firehouse had just died.

Later when Sal Gerardi talked about being so far away and unable to do anything, he was frank about how fortunate he was to not have been there. Secretly he wasn't sure whether he felt more relief or regret about being stuck 3,000 miles away from the catastrophe. In his heart of hearts he thanked God for sparing him from the things he could see reflected in the faces of his buddies and that Sal knew would plague them for the rest of their lives. But Sal could never give voice to the guilt he had for feeling relief because having those feelings, in Sal's mind, made him a traitor.

Later that evening

In firefighting terms, the stairway gave way when the floors 'pancaked', shortly before the entire structure collapsed. Trapped, but still alive, Bobby Walsh tried to keep his head clear. He was pretty sure his partner Ben Walker had to be close by. After catching his breath he called out, 'Hey buddy, you there?' Why wasn't he answering? They were together the whole way, since they got separated from the group. And there were other guys with them on this stairway exit. Where was everybody? He called out again, this time a little louder, 'Anybody there?' Nothing.

It was insanely quiet. Bobby Walsh was a seasoned fireman. He knew the score. The others were either buried or, like him, still alive but too weak to respond. He knew he had to wait for them to reach him. The FDNY wouldn't stop until they had rescued him and everyone else. In the meantime he had to control his breathing and his thinking. He had more than ten years on the job; he'd been in some tough ones before. He knew he had to keep his head straight, he had to silence that voice inside that kept asking 'What will become of me?' He had to keep it together till they got to him, but his mind was racing. The thought kept coming, despite his trying to push it away, What will become of me?

Once more Bobby shouted, as loud as he could, 'Hello! Hello?' Slowly enunciating each word, he began to pray. Desperately, in a hoarse quivering whisper one last time he gasped, 'I'm here you guys! Can you hear me?' He stopped talking out loud. He knew he had to save his breath. He decided he should focus on each word in the prayer, listen to the sound of each word in his mind until they rescued him. 'Our Father . . . Who art . . .'

'Cut off from critical information, at least 121 firefighters, most within striking distance of safety, died when the north tower fell, an analysis by the New York Times has found.'
New York Times, July 7, 2002

* * *

A groundswell of prayers from around the world rushed in like lasers to the fallen towers, travelling into the voids of the mound, or 'the pile' as it was first referred to. Chants and prayers from every religion and spiritual tradition in the eighty languages spoken by the occupants of the World Trade Center. Was anyone alive?

Our Father, Who art in heaven, Hallowed be Thy Name . . .
The Lord is my Shepherd, I shall not want . . .
Shema Yisrael Adonai Eloheinu Adonai Echod . . .
. . . In the name of Allah the Merciful and Compassionate . . .
Oh Mother Earth, oh Father Sky, hear us
Asatho Maa Sad Gamaya, Om Shanti, Shanti,Shanti
May all Beings be peaceful . . . free from suffering

Voices hovered over the mound. Death and the divine blurred all assumptions of reality. It was impossible to tell whether the sounds were coming from above or below the mound of man, steel and concrete. Certain voices unquestionably came from the firemen and other first responders who refused to leave that first day:

'We can't stop'

'I won't leave till I find . . .'

'My brother . . . my father . . . my son'

These were the staccato sounds that rose heavenward from the mass grave that was called 'the pile' or 'the mound' – what remained of the sixteen-acre, seven-building World Trade Center complex, and a single skeletal wall leaning like an ancient ruin. Using stage lights borrowed from the Law & Order shoot a few blocks away, men formed lines and passed dirty plastic buckets of mud hand over hand. The spackle and cement construction buckets were filled with pulverized skyscraper, human remains and tears. The bucket brigade.

Lt. Steve Holland and hundreds of his brothers in the FDNY would not leave. Even if all they could do to rescue anyone still alive was to dig one bucket at a time. 'Over here! I heard a sound . . . a thud, a tap, maybe it's something!' brought the rhythm of the bucket brigade to a halt. They walked delicately in the direction of the sound. When someone slipped he was quickly warned in a whisper, 'Be careful!' One misstep could close the tiny pinpricks of light that led to the voids, the air tunnels that formed the only way to reach those still alive.

Lt. Holland tried to piece together the details of those harrowing early morning hours. He remembers kissing his wife goodbye when he left home. The next thing he remembers was being on the West Side Highway, seeing his old friend Bobby Walsh, and telling him to join him in his car. Bobby shook his head, waving in the direction of the Trade Center and saying something Steve couldn't make out. Then seeing Bobby duck into a side street. The next thing he knew it was the first or maybe the second explosion and things went pitch black. He bolted out of the car and squeezed himself underneath just as a sea of white passed through. And he remembered doing something he hadn't done since a child, something he hadn't even thought he remembered how to do. Praying.

An occasional sound could be heard in the light summer breeze as it passed between the metal columns and skeletal traces of building structure still standing. All of a sudden, Steve could have sworn he heard a voice. 'Quite distinct' were his words later to me. He looked around. No one acted like they'd heard anything. Tentatively he asked to no one in particular, 'You guys hear anything? I could have sworn I just heard someone, or something.' Someone responded, 'Are you sure your mind's not playin' tricks? We're all real tired by now.' Embarrassed, Steve nodded in agreement. He could have sworn it was the voice of his friend Bobby Walsh. But he knew this was crazy. For all he knew, Bobby wasn't there when it went down. Maybe he got out in time.

Steve Holland was a lieutenant in Emergency Medical Services. He knew to observe himself and monitor his reactions. He decided the toxic fumes and dust were getting to him. He better get his head back on straight. There were hundreds of his brothers, thousands of civilians buried here, some still alive, that they needed to save. But he couldn't get his mind off of his friend Bobby Walsh. He willed himself to concentrate on the task at hand, taking the bucket from the guy on his left and passing it along to the guy on his right, finding a strange comfort in the simple movement of passing the bucket. He only faltered when the thought came back to him that he could have, should have, saved Bobby Walsh. Then he forced himself to return to the rhythm of the digging, one bucket at a time, for human life.

* * *

I made it home to Brooklyn, calmed by the smooth rumbling subway. Sharing the car with only one other person, a six-foot, two-hundred-plus, black man in his late teens or early twenties. He sat directly across from me, defeated, his hip-hop baggy jeans ballooning to the floor. His head hung down, partly hidden inside a baseball cap with the visor turned to the back. We took note of each other in that New York exquisite second's glimpse, imparting a sensitivity and comfort beyond non New Yorkers' understanding. Swaying in the rhythm of the 'fabulous F train', one of the few lines in the city running that evening.

Around 2 a.m., I was jolted from sleep by the phone. This time it was the Red Cross. The woman on the other end of the line was explaining that because the city was 'still in lockdown' no one was allowed to enter or leave the city. Their disaster volunteers hadn't arrived yet. So when I heard her say 'We really need psych. Can you make it in this morning?' it didn't seem like much to ask.

The next day
When Smitty finally arrived home, he was met by most of his large family, his parents, his three sisters and their husbands, nieces and nephews keeping his daughter busy playing cards around the dining room table. The only one not there was his brother who'd gotten stuck in California and hadn't yet been able to get a plane back. Starting with his daughter, Smitty went from one to another, hugging each one in turn. Unable to get up from the couch because of her bad knees, his mother waited for Smitty to come to her. They were all laughing and crying. All except for his wife. She just sat there glowering, refusing to look at him, acting as though he'd done something wrong.

Smitty called out, 'Hey, Mary!' With his outstretched arms, she turned away and hissed 'You scared me to death'. Because anger had always been Mary's primary mode of emotional expression, it was unclear how much of her boiling over like that was simply a reflection of how terrified she'd been. They'd had a tough time of it. Any couple that had to go through their child nearly dying in a car accident is allowed a lot of leeway. That was several years ago, and thankfully, Meghan was doing great. But Mary's drinking had gotten worse. They'd both been heavy drinkers, but while the trauma of the accident had a sobering effect on Smitty, it made his wife look all the more to alcohol for solace. From that day on Smitty stopped drinking altogether. Whether it was a pact he'd made with his maker or the shock of almost losing his only child, only the Lord knows. But from that moment on, Smitty put all his energy on taking care of his daughter. This only made his wife feel all the more ignored by her husband. Smitty shuttled Meghan to and from school, from one after school activity to another, from one doctor to another when need be, trying to make up for his past failures and to protect his daughter from his wife's downhill slide.

At the moment Smitty didn't seem to be bothered by Mary's coldness. After all she'd always been a bit mad angry and mad crazy as far as Smitty could tell. An easygoing guy, a good provider, a fireman who'd seen and gone through his share of hard times, he had little sympathy for her getting so bent out of shape by things in general and by him in particular. To be bitter on this day of all days! Still Mary hadn't said anything more after her comment about Smitty scaring her to death. Still she didn't move to touch him. Then she said something, something she later regretted. Words which at the time he didn't even know he had registered, but which tore into the core of Smitty's trauma-permeated being.

* * *

Seven men were missing from the firehouse where Lt. Patrick Darby and I, later on, worked. Patrick Darby's military background in land and sea operations made him perfect for the job of meticulously coordinating the operation of getting the equipment into place and digging without disturbing the mound. Darby was a cockeyed optimist or downright fool, depending on who you talked to, the kind of guy who was always on the move. He was convinced there were people still alive they could rescue. They needed somebody to take charge. It might as well be him.

No one questioned Darby's announcement to the uniformed men gathered by the water's edge that as an officer in the Navy Reserves he should be the one to figure out where and how they could haul equipment over from the Jersey side of the Hudson River to get over to the pile. It was hard to tell who was who at the pile. Who was from FEMA, NYPD, Transit Authority, or the FDNY, who was official and who wasn't, like the excavation and construction workers, and no one at this point particularly cared. There could be people still alive in the rubble, especially anyone in the voids, the air pockets. Darby barely noticed the chaos. All he knew was that there was a job that had to get done and he knew how to get it done.

'In the chaos of the first 48 hours after the twin towers collapsed . . . the only types of breathing protection available to people at ground zero were surgical masks and paper dust masks.'
New York Times, June 5, 2006

In those first hours and days Darby acted with a grace and determination in ever-renewed bursts of energy that he later had to struggle to regain. But for the moment standing on the fifteen story high pile of buried humanity and surrounded by men united in purpose, Lt. Darby was moving with the speed of lightning, telling people what to do, where to bring in the forklifts, where not to tread, protecting the hot spots and voids from stomping feet and incoming equipment. For every step, every touch of the foot and hand meant something. And could mean the difference between life and death.

How could anyone move so fast, so carefully, and wear a protective mask too? The masks that were effective were cumbersome, and, truth be told, there simply weren't enough of them to go around. The silly surgical masks they were passing out were a joke. As if you couldn't smell it meant you weren't breathing it in. That undeniably toxic, indescribable odour.

No words could fully capture that acrid olfactory reality, the pulverization of human beings in a fifteen-storey-high mountain. All that was left of those twin towers was the smell of metal, glass and concrete burning with jet fuel, reeking and unstoppable from deep within the core of the mound. Burning with the distinct smell of human incineration. Smell, that most primary of the senses, the first to develop and the last to leave us in life, is that enduringly cruel reminder of our fundamental animal nature. It informs memory like a volcano, lying dormant for decades, erupting without awareness or concern for what lies in its wake, memory rushing over and covering the present in the wash of the past. Long after sight and sound memory fades. Every person at or near the site in those first days after 9/11 was permanently branded, indelibly imprinted with that olfactory memory, many ultimately poisoned by its toxic reality. Each and every one of us who breathed it in have been turned into unwitting carriers of truth, bystanders complicit in the disappearance of thousands of lives.

At the time it didn't seem right to Darby to cover his face with a mask. That would have been a turning away from the dead. How could you refuse your body serving as a portal for those journeying from this life to the next? Not that Lt. Darby had time to seriously contemplate such matters. And it wasn't that he hadn't quite registered somewhere in his consciousness the possible dangers of inhaling the blatantly contaminated air. But for Patrick Darby, like for so many down there in that initial period, time was of the essence – people might still be alive in there.

Commanding the operations down at the site those first several days, not going home, was a blessing in the battle against feeling, against thinking, more than anything against the helplessness that had begun to overtake others. Darby just had to keep moving. Be useful. Work the pile.

'Scorching temperatures on the pile made working in the masks unbearable . . .so they pulled them down and many later kept them off.'
New York Times, June 5, 2006

* * *

It felt like it was still the 11th, but it might have been 9 a.m., or 2 p.m. or 4 p.m. on the 12th. Time collapsed in on itself, taking with it 'life before'. In the never-never land of New York City, those first days, it was them and us. Them – the family and friends voicing the same word: 'missing'. Us – 'mental health', the people with the information, that is, the St. Vincent's staff and the stray mental health professionals like myself who gathered to 'help'.

We organized people and things, sectioning off tables and chairs for quasi-private 'interviews' and shuffled people into lines that snaked around the block. 'We' compiled paper, and made lists, of names, telephone numbers. 'They' hung papers over lamp-posts and police barricade horseshoes—paper photos of faces above the words in large print 'HAVE YOU SEEN' and 'MISSING'.

We ministers of mental health were enjoined as co-conspirators in sealing off death cries from contagion. Part of our job was to catch those few persons who began to sob or shriek, to swoop them up and escort them away. Containment and dispensing of information, then comfort. This was not 'crisis intervention'. We were just people with 'information'. That was all we were. Neither the catastrophe nor we yet possessed names.

The 'list' was the lifeline between them and us. It held the names of those verified as alive, those who had signed into an emergency room or been admitted to a hospital. For the first hour or so there were no more than a dozen people. The list was 'updated' every hour or so, but never approached a substantial number. Thousands of persons were yet unaccounted for.

I was a field guide in a futuristic landscape with a science-fiction topography. What was I supposed to say, do? By this point I was sure they must all be dead, and thought that the families and friends should be notified. But then I questioned myself. I only saw the towers collapse from a distance. But what about that unbelievable smell that wafts in every time they open the door? That smell that we were not yet able to admit was human life incinerated with the buildings. Are we really helping these people to placate them with this sham of going over the list? Who am I to say?

It was good to have orders to follow. 'Just tell them if the name is on the list, and that they can come back in two hours.' Words not to be spoken: 'bodies', 'morgue'. 'Dead'. Anyway, no one seemed to know where the bodies were being taken. We assumed, we had to believe, that there were bodies. Unmarked freezer trucks were still waiting to be called to pick up bodies. Yet so far there were no bodies. So we spoke 'information'.

And we spoke of the missing as though they were alive. Or should I say they, the families and friends, spoke of them as though they were possibly still alive. 'Here's her necklace. Maybe somebody found her matching bracelet.' One photo after another, of graduations, weddings, and family gatherings, were set before me, with pleas, 'I don't know what to tell the family. I came here for them. What should I tell them?' I, in turn, had no idea how to respond. I looked around me and saw that no one else had answers to their questions. Nor to why or how this could have happened in New York City in 2001.

It was black Oxfords that I had chosen for the day, adequately professional, sombre, but outfitted with my athletic orthotics just in case there was another attack and I had to run for my life. Ridiculous as this may sound, at this point everyone in New York City believed absolutely that anything was possible. The world of certainties, the ability to take daily life for granted – going to work and coming home to your family being there – had evaporated with one stroke on the morning of September 11th. Footwear became the talk of the day. 'It was a good thing I keep a pair of sneakers under my desk' – 'I lost my shoes somewhere running up Vesey' – 'Some nice woman came out of her house and gave me a pair of shoes'. Something about footwear that could be spoken of, whereas the rest, well, the rest was somewhere, not far away from consciousness but not yet really registered.

I was staring down at my Oxfords and trying to wipe my sweaty palms on my slacks to gather myself for the next 'interview' when I heard an authoritative 'Next' from the 'supervisor' as she guided three men toward me. Two were in their forties or early fifties, and the third no older than sixteen. They were dressed in faded work shirts and jeans; possibly, I thought, construction workers. The one in the middle took charge and explained, 'It's our brother that's missing. We're firemen.'

This would turn out to be my introduction to the devastating loss suffered by the families of New York City's firemen. In our isolated little rescue world, removed from the media, we had no idea yet of the extent of what had happened to the FDNY, or that at that very moment the city's firefighters, along with other first responders, were in the desperate search for any signs of life in that mile high mound.

'My brother, he's got a wife and three kids. This one here's his oldest, he's a good kid,' the uncle explained as he put his arm over the shoulder of his nephew. In the course of our short meeting I watched the child self of this 16-year-old, with eyes full and lip quivering, depart, leaving in its wake a grown man with a mask of impenetrable grief. Folding his hands tightly across his chest, the son of the missing fireman nodded his head slightly as our eyes met. Then he looked away. His uncle went on, 'It's my mother. I can't go home and tell her we don't know where her son is. You gotta understand, I have to . . .' Before he could finish, his brother handed me a photo, and then sat on his hands in silence. His brother began again, 'Martin. My name's Martin. Five of us in the family. Three of us are firemen. There was a fourth. He died on the job at a fire a long time ago. My mother. You see, I need something to tell her. It couldn't be that two of us . . .' he trailed off.

I was struck by a fresh wave of shock. Silently I screamed, How could you strike at those who have already been struck? Out loud, I calmly asked whether they had checked in with the Fire Department. Of course they already had. The older brother replied, 'We just don't know what to do, where to go. Can we wait here?'

'If you like, you can come back in a few hours. Have you checked the other hospitals?' I asked in a strained effort at hopefulness.

'Like where do you think we should go?'

'Try Bellevue, they brought some people there,' I responded, trying my best to maintain my function as a person dispensing 'information'. Knowing, but deciding there was no need to state the fact, that Bellevue is the transfer station to the morgue.

Days Later

I joined the army of Red Cross disaster volunteers flown in from around the country. More than a few had never set foot in New York City before this. Donning my official disaster volunteer vest with its signature red cross and my 'Mental Health' badge, I went to my first assignment, one of a number of Family Service Centres set up around the city. This one had been set up in Battery Park City, a residential complex built right along the far side of the West Side Highway by the Trade Center, at the edge of the Hudson River, a stone's throw from New Jersey.

With few exceptions, those few who were unable to move or be moved in time, everyone still at home in the 92-acre residential complex had been successfully evacuated on September 11th. Smoke, dust, bits of clothing, parts of planes and people had been strewn over the grounds, even blown into some apartments. On this day residents were finally being allowed back into the area, and certain buildings were being officially cleared for re-opening. Using a bullhorn, organizers drove through the empty streets telling them to come to the Family Service Centre for help.

We found displaced residents wandering the ghost town in a daze and dropping fragmentary images of that morning into the air:

'My wife and I got separated. She was in her slippers when the cloud came.'

'I couldn't see but I managed to crawl to the boat which took us to Jersey.'

'A policeman gave me money and told me, 'Get on that boat lady.' Now!'

Mental Health's job was to assist the displaced residents in filling out the paperwork to register for emergency aid – money, food, clothes, and places to stay as the top priority. Second, we were to distribute masks and home cleaning supplies. And lastly, we could apply our mental health skills as needed. Within the first hour we ran out of the paper surgical masks. At best only mildly muting the stench, the only purpose they served was to assuage fears about the effects of inhaling the impure air. I'd already given mine away.

I didn't much mind the mask situation. But the prêt-a-port cleaning packages were another matter. These boxes of ready-made cleaning supplies might work for natural disasters like floods and for the kind of environmental disasters that have occurred, but nothing quite like this had happened before. There was no way that they could do the job – the poisonous dust may have stopped rolling through the area but jet fuel was continuing to burn in the core of what was about to be named Ground Zero, and it was still actively releasing toxins into the air. We were acting as though some nasty virus had temporarily infected a community and we were going to help our fellow citizens wash, wipe and vacuum it away. They even had set up play rooms for babies and children while the parents filled out forms.

I couldn't stop thinking that this whole exercise was futile and ridiculous. When I questioned the supervisors I was repeatedly told 'Read them the latest printout from the EPA (Environmental Protection Agency) and give them the package', with the implicit 'just follow orders'. I did not openly express my objections. Those cleaning packages were all we had, so we dutifully handed them out and residents dutifully expressed their appreciation. Who could admit it was all beyond imagination or cure? We wanted to believe it was safe.

For the first hours I participated in the farce. I did as I was told; something I will live with for the rest of my life. Despite the fact that I was registering the choking acrid smell; and that I could see with my own eyes the plume of smoke coming from the burning core through the glass walls of the building lobby of the Family Service Centre. Somewhere in the back of my mind I knew that was more real than the sunny sky and the promise of protection from the paper hats, boxes of super-size Mr. Clean, and the cheery blue and green printouts from the EPA claiming that the air quality was 'safe'.

In the back of my mind I knew that no one, not even Christine Whitman, head of the EPA, really knew the truth about the air quality. But in the midst of the unimaginable chaos and disaster that had taken over our lives, we all longed to believe there was still reason and truth; and that it was only a matter of finding and listening to that someone in possession of it.

One family after another marched in. As morning passed into afternoon, the supply of 'cleaning packages' was running out, as was my willingness to follow orders. It was something about one family that finally awakened my conscience. It was a French couple in their thirties, with two boys, one three and other barely a year old. They had moved here only a few months before when the husband was assigned to a job in the financial district. The older boy ran right away to the makeshift day-glow gym. With one hand the mother was holding her toddler's hand and covering her face with the other, trying to hide her tears and telling her older son to be careful as he climbed up the slide. Her husband kept shooting her looks, and turned to me with embarrassment, 'I'm sorry, my wife, I don't know, she gets hysterical and just can't stop crying.' As though there was something wrong with her for being upset. This made me ask myself, Who's the crazy one here – the 'hysterical' mother, the frantic father grasping at straws by trying to assume a rational demeanour, or me for going along with this pretence of safety. He looked at me, waiting for me to tell him it was fine to move back into their apartment. I mumbled something about the EPA statement of reassurance but then suggested that they might just consider waiting, 'Just in case, with the kids and all . . .'

Once they left, I could no longer continue to pass out the latest EPA bulletin suggesting the air was adequately safe for people to return home. There was no way I could hand out one more prêt-a-port cleaning package. It was already nearing the end of tour of duty, sparing me from having to declare my unwillingness to go on with an intervention that I knew in my heart was wrong. That family, along with many families I saw later, who lived or whose children attended the schools right near the Trade Center, were in such a state of shock at that point that they simply couldn't think clearly. Their perceptions and cognitive capacities were narrowed. Paradoxically, in moments of crisis like this we can also be granted an extra-ordinary clarity about life, as many did at that time. But for those families to be fully aware that they weren't their normal selves would have threatened their ability to cope as well as they were with what they were facing. In a crisis, our very physical and psychic survival depends on not fully registering what is happening to our own being.

But what excuse did we volunteers have? Even the devastating reality of the fifteen-storey mountain of civilization gone awry and the undeniable reeking smoke rising above it – right in front of us – failed to break through the protective barrier our minds insisted on. Our minds simply refused access to our body knowledge, as a way to unconsciously insulate ourselves from being fully traumatized ourselves. But the visceral knowledge remains buried within us all.

'A statement made on Sept. 18, 2001, by Christie Whitman, the Environmental Protection Agency administrator, that air sampling done by her agency showed that the air was safe to breathe. The agency . . . concluded in 2003 that Ms. Whitman's statement . . . could not be scientifically supported at the time she made it.'
The New York Times, June 5, 2006

No one commented on the shift in nomenclature from 'rescue' to 'relief' by the end of the week. My next assignment was the Respite Centre for the hundreds of firefighters, police officers, construction workers, and emergency service specialists, in the search for signs of life. It was set up in a converted hotel on the southern edge of the site. The disaster trainers had emphasized that we had to be prepared to leave our professional training and egos behind and be willing to do whatever might be needed, which meant hauling water bottles, shuffling paper, standing around 'doing nothing' and be ready to offer the men and women coming off the pile something that might be needed: a phone card, candy, a comforting smile, a chance to talk.

It was immediately obvious that there was no chance of healing the oozing wounds of any recovery person spending a substantial amount of time at Ground Zero. Many could sense what lie ahead. More than one saying things like 'I know it's going to hit me later . . . so I can't stop now.' All we mental health volunteers could do was to convey our steadiness and our willingness to listen, and help shore up whatever scraggly defences the individual had left to call upon before going back out to the pile.

They were hesitant to speak of the horrors of what they were doing, but found themselves unable not to relay 'the fingers, feet, torsos we're finding' in telegraphed flashes to those of us in the relief centre. When they were able to put words to the images that haunted them, 'torn pieces of shirts', 'somebody's eyeglasses', flickers of aliveness were temporarily restored to their frozen faces and dull eyes.

Those who witness atrocities struggle with an inherent conflict between the need to expel the horrors within them by communicating them and the humane impulse to not subject others to the horrors they have witnessed. Because we mental health volunteers were within the radius of exposure, the disaster workers considered us fellow travellers in this nightmare reality. Our shared numbness and sense of separateness from the world beyond Ground Zero was palpable to them, and enabled their need to connect and talk to outweigh their hesitation to speak. Perhaps it was simply the ultimate power of the emotional and moral imperative to tell one's story to someone prepared to listen. And for me to tell you some of what I saw and heard there.

One afternoon I was manning the station outside the massage therapy area. A young man from Emergency Medical Services approached. He was wearing a thick rubber protective suit with the large white letters EMS smudged black across the back. Taking a seat, he dropped his arms down between his legs, and began by explaining what his job entailed, 'We go into the voids.' Then he sputtered, 'Just fingers, toes,' his eyes darting to avoid direct contact. I could feel his fear of spreading the horror of all that he had seen. Without saying anything I put my arm on his shoulder. His head fell into his hands, and he told me about going into the child care centre of the World Trade Center.

Entering this once-upon-a-time child world, and exuding the stench of human incineration, he came upon a half-eaten McDonald's egg-McMuffin breakfast sandwich abandoned in its opened Styrofoam box on a table. The room was filled with child-size chairs, lots of toys and books and a dozen or so cribs. In one lay a teddy bear that caught the worker's eye. It was dusted in pulverized concrete-human powder but still wearing the manufacturers' sewn-shut grin. He found himself almost secretively picking it up. But as the man left to return to the sanitized world of insanity penned Respite Centre I, he thought better of what he'd done and carefully set the dust covered bear back in its place.

The young EMS worker began weeping. Gathering himself, he apologized, 'You see, I have a three-year-old at home.' I did see – that lone child care centre and lone rescue worker were emblazoned in my mind's eye, and would return to me against my will for days, reminding me of the reality I had been brought into. I, too, was now tainted by exposure to the raw truth of what humans are capable of, at their best and worst. No matter how diligently I, like everyone else, made sure to wash my hands and hose my shoes on leaving the site, we would never be able to wash ourselves free of the chemical and psychic contamination. No one spoke of it; it was simply a shared reality that we had to conspire to hide, our defiled innocence that would forever separate us from those who could still believe.

The EMS worker seemed momentarily relieved, but my body now felt thick with the smell and the sounds around me, and I couldn't think straight. Just then a perky out-of-town Red Crosser who'd been professing her scorn for this 'depraved city' to me hours earlier bounced toward us. Handing the man a phone card, she cheerily reminded him 'Don't forget to call your family!' She then thrust a perfectly coiffed untainted stuffed animal into his lap and jaunted away. A six year old's scribbled message, 'Iowa loves you' hung from its neck. This teddy he stuffed in his side pocket. Minutes later the massage therapist came for him. When he was gone I noticed the broken-hearted bear on the floor.

You might question my endowing an inanimate object, a 'stuffed', fake animal, with feelings. But people gleefully embracing mass murder makes me question what defines humanness. In willfully inflicting suffering and destroying the life of a fellow human, the murderer deadens himself, severing his own humanity and basic bond with the living. If living humans can be deadened, who's to say 'things' can't have life?

Walking through the sealed glass doors to go home at the end of the day, the first thing I noticed was the putrid smell. Yet I was so relieved to be outside, away from all that was inside. The air almost seemed fresh. I looked over to the wash station, with its hoses dangling into the industrial sinks and the bars of disinfectant soap lined up in a row. On other days I'd found the ritual of washing our hands bizarrely comforting, a validation that basic principles of health endure. Even though I was fully aware that this ritual of cleanliness wasn't going to prevent the damage from seeping into our bodies and souls, and thereby spreading beyond the perimeter of the disaster site. On that day, however, I didn't have it in me to participate in this surreal pseudo-containment.

Heading straight for the subway, I looked around at the dust-coated canyon. The afternoon sun was descending behind the skyscrapers. The stillness in this never before deserted section of the city was paradoxically peaceful though undeniably post-apocalyptic. Walking past an open air parking garage full of abandoned cars thickly covered with the dust from crushed people and their creations almost brought me to tears. Each of those cars belonged to a person, some of whom would never return. I wasn't ready to cry. Trying to shake myself back into that protective frozenness, I picked up my pace and stared at the thin film of dust around me on the swept clear empty sidewalks and streets. Then I noticed something on the sidewalk, a lone scrap of paper. Like a thief, I picked it up and shoved it in the pocket of my Red Cross uniform 'apron'.

Once I was on the reassuring familiarity of the dank and filthy subway platform I dared to take out this stealthily snatched-up thing. It was no bigger than the palm of my hand and had no apparent significance. I wasn't sure whether I should consider it more as evidence of a crime committed or of a piece of someone's life. I examined the scrap of frayed cardboard, trying to figure out exactly what it was and imagining whose hands it might have passed through. Faint grey markings gave a hint of print. Looking for clues, I ran my fingers over its smooth surface, and thought I could decipher a smudge. A finger print?

It was nothing more than a frayed scrap of paper, but to me this little remnant of humanity was a treasure. A symbol of the paper that marks a way of life, and a period of time, before the electronic era had fully taken hold, before 9/11 changed the world. It signified a city of boundless paper, a city where lives are spent shuffling paper, fortunes made and broken on paper, hopes and dreams inscribed on paper. Before I could decide what to do with this thing, the train rolled out of the dark tunnel and into the station. I couldn't just toss it into the trash. So I placed the cardboard fragment of history inside the pocket of the Red Cross apron. As the doors were opening I took off my volunteer uniform with its bright red cross and shoved it into my bag, so I could re-enter the world as a civilian like the rest of my fellow strap-hangers.

Though I couldn't admit it at the time, something in me knew I wouldn't be returning to volunteer at Ground Zero. I stepped into the air-conditioned subway car, blocked out thoughts of the day, and rejoined the rest of the city. The 'new normal'.

Two months in

It was nearing the two-month mark since medieval mentality merged with modern technology to catapult jumbo jets into the fortress of the American Empire. Things had changed. President Bush declared we were at 'war on terror'. As happens in catastrophes, distinct groups began to develop – who was down there that day and who wasn't, New Yorkers and outsiders, groups with identifications that united and separated people from each other. Those more distant from the devastation were beginning to relate to it as a 'thing' that had happened but was now over. Those most directly affected and those in the relief effort were still very much in the grips of this inchoate 'thing' that had happened and could easily happen again. It seemed wrong and foolish to us to treat the catastrophe as a singular event of the past. Yet those of us inside felt comforted by the idea that there was a world outside the disaster. If the world beyond was going on as normal again, then maybe, just maybe we were safe from another attack, and would eventually come out of this. At the same time we felt separated from the outside world that seemed intent on restoring what felt like a pretence of normalcy.

I was back at work. Some patients couldn't stop talking about 'it'; most people were trying to integrate this stark new thing into their sense of reality and find a way to make sense of it in their own way. A few, out of sheer defensive denial or narcissistic proclivity, went right back to talking about the things they were talking about before. Some of which was feeling petty and trivial. City life had resumed its routine. The buses and subways were running normally again. Businesses and schools re-opened. After all, we'd just crossed into the new millennium, a new era. It was so good to be back to 'normal', that is, what passes for normal in the crazy intense unique life that is New York City.

My next assignment was located about a mile or so uptown from Ground Zero. Alongside the Hudson River, a commercial tent for trade and fashion shows had been converted into a gigantic service centre for the victims and their families that was a study in contrast to the bleakness of Ground Zero. I arrived to throngs of people having their bags and IDs checked by blasé security personnel outside the bright white tent, with the casualness of going to a sports arena or the circus. Inside, the football-field-size tent was decorously divided up into a series of red-carpeted aisles and various booths cordoned off with neon blue curtains and large signs, and lit by a massive fluorescent system hanging from the big top. Altogether the scene conveyed an insistent presentation of order and sanity to the very people who knew better. For them it was still all about information and paper – a death certificate, a money voucher, a list of job opportunities. These were the things that mattered, and a conversation or two that maybe made a difference.

The assignment for 'Mental Health' was to provide the comfort and relief of small talk, nothing too deep, to both visitors and relief workers. Told to wander the site and administer mental health 'where needed' in the various sections of the paper-pushing tent for the traumatized, I began my peripatetic shift exploring the aisles of vaguely-defined categories of help. The rest area for relief workers caught my eye. It was dotted with men and women of many coloured uniforms – the blue of the NYPD, the distinctive military brown of the National Guard, and the bright green of the city sanitation workers, along with various professionals with badges describing the services offered. There were even a few therapy dogs sitting patiently by their masters.

In the back was a lounge where weary workers were slumped on cushioned couches, reading newspapers, watching TV or just sitting sleepily, sadly. I overheard some people, apparently from outside the city, expressing their astonishment at the solidarity and warmth they saw New Yorkers showing in this trying moment. A young New York State Highway trooper, of the sort that one only meets when getting pulled over for speeding, was sitting by himself in the corner, looking forlorn. I introduced myself and was surprised how quickly he opened up. 'I'm used to driving sixty miles along roads lined with cows. Not this.' Then with sadness mingled with a trace of lost innocence, he talked about how strange he'd found working back home these last few weeks with the anthrax crisis, how so much of his time had been spent responding to requests for the police to check the safety of the powder in the bottom of cereal boxes.

I made my way over to the eating area, and sat down at a table where several sanitation workers were eating lunch. Upon seeing my badge they began grumbling about their position in the civil service hierarchy. 'It's our job to unload the trucks at Fresh Kills', the garbage dump. Another man went on, 'Yeah, we're the ones got to sift through the waste for body parts.' The image of wading through human waste and sifting for parts of human beings cut through all the coping mechanisms I'd marshalled since the attack. Painfully reminding me of how many of the notions I'd held about civilized life had been blown apart with those buildings. Including my assumption that the skyscrapers of New York City, in the United States of America, couldn't be brought down and people torn to bits in a matter of minutes while the world stood by helplessly watching.

Here I was, sitting at a lunch table listening to my local garbage collectors dealing with their own trauma of having to search for remains of our fellow New Yorkers by acting the role of disgruntled city employees. Feeling utterly incapable at that moment of a therapeutic response, I took my cue from their stress-induced apathy. With effortful nonchalance I said 'Well, guess it's time for my lunch,' and left the table.

I didn't really want to eat, but I couldn't think of anything else to do now but to go to the food table. Nothing made sense. All the people here who've lost their jobs, homes, not to mention all those who've lost the people closest to them in the world, and all the rest of us here in this thing together with them. Feeling the impossibility of moving forward but having no choice but to go on. With the knowledge at the edge of consciousness of one of life's basic facts – One minute you're here, the next you're not. I felt the basic truth that I was alive. And so I nodded 'no' to the Red Cross server for the meat, 'yes' to the pasta and salad, picked up some plastic utensils and a napkin, and made my way over to an empty table.

Two women police officers asked if the table was free, then signalled to a third patrolwoman to join us. Unaware that my badge only meant that I was a provider and not a possessor of 'Mental Health' at that moment, they began telling me how the Police Department recognized the stress they've been under since 9/11 and provided counselling services but then kept sending them back out on extra tours of duty. One officer explained her situation. 'That day (9/11), it was lock down, I was stuck in Manhattan. I couldn't get back to my daughter at school in Queens. All the other kids' parents came to pick them up. That's when I decided I've had enough. Soon as I can, I'm getting the hell out.' Her partner shook her head in agreement. With her blond pony tail bobbing beneath her cap she proceeded, in seeming explanation for their demoralization, 'Heard they've only been finding fingers, toes, scalps, no faces.'

Clearly, body parts had become lunch room talk for the relief workers. Back at Ground Zero in the initial aftermath of the catastrophe, these words were uttered in hushed whispers. With their insides full of the holiness and horror of life, people ate only to keep going. They moved between the living and the dead. 'Body parts' were reduced to one- or two-word transmissions in fits and starts as people needed to expel the unbearable images from their minds, and struggled with the dual concern for sparing the listener and for speaking up for those individuals who were now 'body parts'.

Today felt different. Things had changed not only around us, but within us. I looked at the young patrolwoman's face for clues to understand why she brought this up. Her rosy cheeks and sprightly demeanour did not suggest she was callous or dramatic. The other people at the table were continuing to eat as they took in her words. It was as if they were hearing a story. A way to make manageable the surreal facts of the situation. That a person is a person, not a sum of body parts.

Believing the policewoman needed to talk, I encouraged her to continue. Looking me in the eye, she went on, 'I heard they found a child's hand, with the mother's wrapped around it.' Another woman, trying to help, offered an explanation, 'Must have been from the airplane.' The words hung like disembodied ideas in the air. Fiercely the woman picked up her fork and pierced the pasta on her plate. I wondered if she was at all connected to what she was saying. Almost immediately someone picked up where she left off, 'Yeah, I heard they found a boot with just a foot in it.' I looked down and began fiddling with my plastic fork and knife. Suddenly I felt a sensation that had eluded me since this began: hunger.

Passing these terrible word images back and forth was a way to feel less alone with the traumatically implanted pictures in our minds. The people around the table were eating, yet engrossed in the conversation. Listening carried none of the morbid fascination that such ideas can have when they are the stuff of imagination. We felt totally immersed, but at an odd distance from what was going on and from all that had happened. It was as if this was a movie or a book. A certain degree of detachment had begun to set in as a coping mechanism. Two months had passed. None of us would ever be the same again, a bit of our own selves had also shattered. Yet the fact remained, we were alive. And so we ate.

We were a typically motley group of New Yorkers sharing lunch around the table, trying to digest it all. Collectively shaping the fragmentary memory of a lived through nightmare into a story. A psychologically manageable narrative. Making a story of human body parts was not an expression of heartlessness or voyeuristic perversion. It was a way of trying to come to terms with the reality of the murder of three thousand persons, each one of whom could have been one of us, in the first major international terrorist attack on American soil. Together we felt and did not have to say out loud that we were fortunate to have been spared, this time. All of us at that table were at that moment at one with the living and the dead, torn inside like so many scattered pieces of paper or bits of bodies.

PART II
Therapy on the run, 2002
My year in a firehouse

The Red Cross army of volunteers departed and I returned to my office. Grief and terror still possessed us, but we did our patriotic best to follow the advice of our leaders, President George W Bush and New York's Mayor Rudy Guiliani – 'go back to normal life'. This wasn't so easy in lower Manhattan, where the smell of death and destruction still permeated the atmosphere. Baby-faced men toting rifles from the various military services did their best to hide their fear and confusion as they stood wide-legged and arms crossed at blockades set up to control downtown access.

It was impossible to walk any distance in the city without being confronted by the sight of a black draped firehouse, for virtually every firehouse and fireman in the FDNY had been affected, with 343 firefighters and 2,823 civilians dead. The Brotherhood, as the Fire Department of New York City is known, had always prided itself on its ability to take care of its own, but the scope of the disaster's effects necessitated the department accepting outside help for the first time in its history. In the first days after the attack and catastrophe a deluge of self-proclaimed helpers and professionals, myself among them, had descended on the firehouses around the city. Warren, the leader of my travelling psychologist squad, cooked up an innovative idea that he, along with our friend Laura developed with the Fire Department's Counselling Unit. The plan was for a group of specially-trained psychoanalysts from New York University to run psycho-educational groups inside firehouses and function 'like the family doctor' for the men to look to for help. The 'in house clinicians', as we were called, were to introduce counselling to the house and encourage the men to utilize the various confidential counselling services available to them, including therapists in private practice and the department's own counselling services located in and around the city. It was left up to the individual clinician to figure out how to get the men to first accept an outsider and then to get them to magically open up while maintaining readiness to respond to an alarm, that is, to be in full gear, on the rig and out the door in sixty seconds. This was the sum of my introduction, mandate and guidance to the FDNY.

Convincing the Counselling Service Unit of the FDNY of the merits of introducing civilian psychotherapists turned out to be the easy part. In retrospect, we were naïve, with little idea of all that was in store for us and the ingenuity it was going to take to get these men, accustomed to being the helpers, to accept help. Just exactly how we therapists managed to reach beyond our couches, answering machines and tissue boxes and how those firemen reached beyond their ladders, axes and fire trucks to find each other around a kitchen table will remain forever a mystery. But when the impossible happens, anything becomes possible.

* * *

January
I was brought into the 'kitchen', as the multi-purpose lounge/TV/ dining room is called in a firehouse, by a peer counsellor from the counselling unit, and given a seat at the head of the table. I looked around. On one wall of the fifties-style dreary wood panelling was a collection of various awards, framed certificates, and plaques, hung in a very particular order to a set of rules that to an uninitiated eye, like mine, seemed casual if not haphazard. Newspapers and automobile magazines were strewn around. From my seat, I faced the photo gallery: 8 x 10 head shots of each man in his helmet and number in bold relief, and adorned with scraps of hand-written notes and cartoons scotch taped to the glass. As in most living rooms, a large television was the focal point. On the floor next to it was a poster board, I later learned,

for making wagers on that season's sports. At the moment all bets were off and there was no interest in playing the odds. Instead, someone had printed in heavy black ink, 'KEEP IT IN THE HOUSE'. The men were sitting around the heavily lacquered pine table but avoiding looking in my direction, and several more were slouched behind them on some overstuffed couches. A daytime re-run of 'Survivor' was playing in the background. The only sound in the room was someone flipping through the pages of a newspaper. I set out the bagels and cream cheese I'd brought as a guest to their home. They passed everything around in polite formality as per strict firehouse code for proper treatment of a visitor. A few picked up a bagel, lamely smearing it with cream cheese. No one was eating, talking or even looking at me. They didn't want to be there and they didn't want me there.

This was turning out to be nothing like the days right after 9/11 when Warren and I drove around the neighbourhood firehouses, and after endless searching for a parking space, were openly welcomed in by the firemen who openly expressed their shock, grief and helplessness. Nor did the hushed room feel anything like typical first session group jitters, when people often wait for others to start talking first. Nor was it your run-of-the-mill half-hearted 'hello' with an anxious look of 'What did I get myself into?' in a first therapy encounter when a person suddenly realizes he's signed on to telling a perfect stranger about the most painful personal things in his life. It wasn't even the sullenness of the skeptical husband coerced by his frustrated wife or the teenager dragged into therapy by parents. This was a case of clear-cut compliance with orders in the paramilitary system of the FDNY. They were acting like schoolboys summoned to the principal's office. And I was playing the part of the well-meaning civilian, assuming I could help the anointed heroes of September 11th with little comprehension of the situation. All of a sudden, ashamed of my hubris to have presumed I knew how to help, I couldn't think of anything to say.

There are lots of moments of silence in the 'talking cure'. Though I'd certainly had my share of working with patients who were unwilling or unable to communicate, I felt something deeper and darker in the stillness and barren speech that pervaded the room. This was the deafening silence of full-blown trauma, for which there are no words or sounds. Massive loss and trauma drain vitality from language and interacting. The men and I were speaking English but we weren't yet speaking the same language. Not because I was a woman and not a part of their masculine world. Because they were in a state of traumatic grief. Seeing these men washed out in shocked disbelief and massive loss broke through a certain post-disaster numbness I'd been swathed in with little awareness. This silence was louder than words, and breached my own defences to make me face the reality that I was going to have to surrender a natural resistance to fully enter the world of trauma if I was going to honestly communicate and reach these men.

Grasping for the right thing to say, I kept waiting for the alarm to go off and put an end to the meeting. A few of the men made a comment here and there, though I don't remember who they were, or what any of us said. Vague generalities of 'Yeah' on their part, and equally pointless expressions of therapeutic consolation like 'I know it's been rough for you guys', failed to breach the wall of silence. They knew and I knew. It had all been said before. After a year-long hour, we broke up, unrelieved by the bell that never rang.

* * *

It was a long time after I left the firehouse before I came to understand the full meaning of the powerful memories that arose for me that first day at the firehouse. The feeling of the men around the firehouse kitchen table that day brought back vivid visions of life around the kitchen table of my childhood. It was always around the fake mahogany oval table that whoever happened to be in my house that day would gather for dinner and find a place setting amidst the stuff that was scattered aimlessly about – newspaper clippings, usually of the Ann Landers advice column sort, and a stray fork or knife. Standing at kitchen sink, at 6 p.m. sharp, with a precision odd for a woman whose very being defied order, my mother let out a sigh of resignation to domesticity, then in a flash mood shift, cheerily hollered in her thick Boston accent, 'So who's eating here tonite?' This was Boston, Massachusetts in the nineteen fifties.

Forty years later, my mother was not in her usual place commandeering the conversation. Earlier that day the phone had been ringing off the hook, with continuous calls of shock and consolation. It had all happened so fast. Tuesday Dad was fit as a fiddle on the tennis court playing doubles. Twenty-four hours later, as required by Jewish law, he was laid to rest wrapped in a shroud in a plain pine box, and we were back at my childhood kitchen table surrounded by piles of food, friends and family. I can't remember who was sitting around the kitchen table with me on that day in the winter of 1997. I do remember that I was sitting in my father's chair. Why his chair I can't really say. Nor can I say that I was even aware that it was his chair that I was sitting in as I received the steady flow of people into my parents' home for the post-funeral meal. Through the din of the doorbell, phone and the sounds of people coming together, I only remember thinking that people wanted to console me, just as I was doing a few years later with the firemen. But then, as later for the men, really what was there to say? The words of solace were filling the empty space in that room but my broken heart couldn't take them in. Despite their best intentions, I was not to be reached. I sat on the chair my father had sat in for as long as I could remember, running my palms over the smooth polished surface of the fake wooden kitchen table.

* * *

There I was in the winter of 2002, sitting around another kitchen table, surrounded by the pall of death. The men didn't really want strangers there, but they understood that the visitors were needing to give support to them as a way to comfort themselves. They wanted to be left alone, to grieve in private, with each other. And

I was a stranger thrust on them, as much of an anomaly to them as they were to me. My curly reddish-blond hair and freckled face, my give-away accent, and my telling them about my cousins who were firefighters in Boston, all seemed to suggest that maybe I too was Irish, but then again, I was a shrink in New York, and aren't all shrinks Jewish? They couldn't put a finger on just who I was as a person. And I couldn't make heads or tails of who they were as individuals. To me they looked like the very same group of boys, mostly Irish, and a few of Italian and Polish backgrounds, that I had gone to school with, dated in provincial Boston, and thought I'd left behind me for the anonymity and limitless possibility of New York.

I couldn't even get their names straight. Though only ten men were on duty at a time, there were fifty men altogether, and trying to remember who was an EMS (emergency medical service) man on the engine company, and who was a FF (firefighter) on the ladder company seemed impossible. My memory, not unlike theirs, just wasn't working quite right. So many men had the same first names, and so many weird nicknames! Me, overwhelmed? Impossible. Unwilling to consider that I too was in a state of shock and grief, I stubbornly attributed my anxiety to how the groups were going, or more to the point, not going.

Group therapy had never been my thing. The idea of so many eyes on me all at once gave me stage fright. Early in my career in hospitals and community settings I had no choice but to lead groups, and I was happy to leave it behind when I went into private practice. I was in my element with individual and couple therapy, able to forge connection and communication by looking and speaking directly with each person. I dreaded taking charge with this resistant group of men who were clearly there only because they had no choice in the matter. I tried to remind myself that groups were just not my forte, but in hindsight I didn't want to admit that as a New Yorker also affected by the disaster I wasn't in the best of shape myself.

There was no getting around the fact that the group meetings just weren't getting off the ground. No matter what I brought up, I was met with ten silent blank faces. Even when I'd say something about how hard I knew it was for them to have to come to the group meetings, the most I'd get was a nod of agreement or a comment like 'Yeah, we've talked about it,' meaning 9/11. Followed by 'counselling's already been here,' meaning 'don't you get it, lady? There's nothing more to say.'

I looked to the officers for help. A few had privately expressed their support for the program, but warned me that the men might not talk about anything 'personal' in a group situation. Officers had their own out – most didn't come to the meetings, claiming it would interfere with the traditional boundary maintained between officer and firefighter. I appealed to a few of the more approachable officers who seemed to be the most interactive with the men. I explained that the Counselling Unit had made up their minds that group meetings was what we had to do. I enlisted them in finding ways to get the guys to feel more at ease with me in the house and how they might utilize me in any way that they thought might be helpful. Then I waited for someone to come forward in or out of group. I waited for inspiration, for something, anything to happen, someone to call upon me. That's where officers Lt. Patrick Darby and Lt. Salvatore Gerardi came to my rescue.

So far the guys and I were only sharing our discomfort facing each other and ourselves across that kitchen table. Till I joined them in an unspoken collusion in finding creative excuses to avoid starting Group. No one could force a guy to come to the table, and no one could tell me exactly when to call the group to the table. So after I signed in with the red pen for Visitors I told the man on house watch, the entryway to the firehouse, to wait a while before announcing my arrival on the loudspeaker and calling the men into the kitchen for Group. I lingered there in watch, chatting with whoever was on the equipment floor, before slowly heading back towards the official group gathering place at the table in the kitchen/lounge.

On one particularly bone-chilling morning somewhere near

the end of my first month, the comforting smell of onions frying beckoned me into the back kitchen behind the lounge area where I recognized the face of the man at the stove – Phil. I'd been told about his magic hands. He was known for his gift with fixing equipment, tying knots, and more than anything else, for his culinary talents. So whenever on duty, Phil was inevitably assigned the job as the chef of the day. Standing by the stove, Phil nodded hello with a face that smiled without lips moving as he waved a spatula with the flair of a conductor at the guys standing around in the room. Two or three of the guys were just hanging around in a sort of circle, as I was beginning to learn was their custom, one leaning against the counter, another sifting through the pile of cookie boxes and bags of chips, in the great American tradition of snacking. Men talking and being together without having to look like they want to talk.

A tall man in officer uniform I'd never been formally introduced to suddenly darted into the room and sidled around a guy with his head in the refrigerator to get to a blackboard wall. As he was writing in big letters 'April 16th SPRING RUN', the guy in the fridge called out, 'There's nothing cold to drink,' to which somebody replied, 'Just look, will ya, or go to the other refrigerator,' with a mix of brotherly affection and disdain. No one seemed to be paying attention to the muscular man with bright red and blue tattoos on his arm who began jabbering something as he put the chalk down. Picking up a metal bucket from the counter he turned to me and asked, 'Hey, Doc, wanna contribute?' letting me know he knew who I was, and letting the guys know I should be included. I asked what it was for. The lieutenant, or Lieu as all lieutenants in the fire department are referred to, as he swayed back and forth with bucket in hand, explained that it was a run in honour of fallen firefighters with a picnic for the families afterwards. Before I finished asking for details, Lt. Darby changed the subject. 'You guys hear about how Mahoney got smashed last year?' So I grabbed one of the brochures and learned that it was only a 10K race and thought maybe, just maybe, I could do it. Before I had a chance to say anything the Lieutenant flitted out saying, 'Come, why don't you come, it'll be fun,' and then, as if suddenly registering what I'd said a minute ago, he asked, 'You run?' To which I responded in embarrassment, 'I'm really slow, I haven't raced for years.' Before I finished, he pulled a Lone Ranger, disappearing out the kitchen door. I heard his booming voice in the apparatus room call out to the man on watch, 'Call the guys down.' Lieutenant Darby, the officer in charge, called Group to order.

The goal of Group was to educate the men on post-traumatic stress reactions and the benefits of individual counselling. I was supposed to encourage discussion, and most importantly, to get the men to take my business card so that they would call for a referral or come see me in my private office, or go to the counselling unit. But to get to that point I was going to have to get them to start talking. So far none of my standard tricks of the trade had been working. I'd talk for them, 'I know you're all feeling this and that' type of thing. I was as non-authoritarian, non shrink-like as I could be, acting more like a maternal party hostess warmly inviting her guests to chat. Then I'd stop and wait for someone to speak. More often than not all I got was zilch, nada.

That day was like every other day there in the month since I'd started in the firehouse. The men on duty, four from the ladder and four from the engine, and took their seats around the table, slumping in some combination of compliant defiance. I needed them to say something. They weren't talking. At my wits' end, I resorted to my tried and true eyebrow raiser. I raised the one subject I'd held out as my last ditch strategy – sex. I opened my sex schpiel with an affectation of playful confidence, 'Well, ya know, I'm a sex therapist, so I know how all that's affected too. Either you can't get enough or you can't get up for it. That's what stress does.' I said no more, and waited with a plastered-on therapist knowing smile for someone to speak up. No eyebrows rose, but then slowly one by one the sad sallow faces in front of me began to blush, and some nervous laughter broke out. Still no one said anything. Then out of nowhere, I heard a voice from the doorway. I hadn't even noticed that Lt. Darby had come in to check on how Group was going. Being the officer leading his men in a mock groan, he said, 'Jeez, wait till my wife hears about this.' I went on, keeping it casual, general, 'Well you either can't get enough or can't get into it, that's the way it goes with stress.' Someone then piped up, 'Hey, Doc, can you get us Viagra?' And so it began. The call for Viagra was the Group icebreaker. A doctor may have been foisted on the men, but they could now claim their firehouse had their very own sex therapist.

And so we sat around the kitchen table, and talked about sex, sometimes never getting past the titters and jokes. As uncomfortable as the guys were about admitting how disrupted their sex lives were, it sure beat talking directly about the really upsetting things. But I still wasn't having much luck getting them past the banter about Viagra and who was getting it and who wasn't, to talk about anything important. I'd try to get them to open up about how their kids were doing, how they felt about being made into heroes, how they were bearing up under the stress, how grief shows itself. I brought in newspaper articles, but after a few minutes of polite response nothing went any further. I just couldn't seem to get the therapy off the ground. I had to get them to feel freer to talk. How was I going to get them to take the plunge and talk about the things that really mattered, and to consider going for counselling? As luck would have it, another officer came to my rescue. Lt. Salvatore Gerardi.

With a nature prone to ponder the metaphysical, Lt. Salvatore Gerardi considered himself lucky on a number of counts. He's the kind of person who wouldn't hesitate to say how fortunate he was to have not been down there on September 11th. On vacation in the Caribbean that morning, he couldn't get a flight back to New York for almost two weeks, though once back, he did his stint just like everyone else down at Ground Zero. Because the department had lost so many officers on 9/11, Sal, like so many others, found himself getting promoted from rank-and-file Firefighter to the officer position of Lieutenant.

Sal considered himself especially fortunate to be able to work as an officer in the same battalion that he had worked in as a firefighter for the last several years. A lot of firefighters prefer transitioning into the role of authority and responsibility as an officer in a setting where they don't have so much history. But not Sal. Being a straddler of multiple worlds, moving from firefighter to officer with guys he knew and worked with was right up his alley. Between his job on the side as a fashion model and his penchant for clowning around, Sal was open game for ribbing, even with his newly raised status as lieutenant. His natural ease as an officer and his winning ways with women earned him the respect of his brothers, and the envy of more than a few.

Like Darby, Sal was unable to tolerate silence. While Darby was so mesmerizing he could bring the conversation to a standstill, Sal's playful chattiness and self-denigrating egotism had a way of getting the other guys going. One day, as group was flubbing its way along, irrepressible Sal piped up, 'It's rough . . . I don't know about you guys, but when that alarm sounds, I feel like I get all charged up, and not in a good way, I tell you . . . You don't know what it's going to be any more, 'specially when you hear the stuff on TV, and the terror alerts and shit . . . I feel my heart racing . . . coming to work just doesn't feel good . . . my girlfriend says she wants me to quit.' To which one of the group cynics reliably quipped with a tension-relieving chuckle that was easy to join in on, 'Yeah Sal, so she can get you to you-know-what.' Even I got the drift – get him to marry her. 'I'm not ready for that,' Sal boasted, 'Yeah, we got a good thing goin', I don't want to mess it up by tying the knot.'

As the meeting was breaking up, within earshot of the guys Sal said, 'So since I told Julie about you comin' here talking to us, telling us about counselling and stuff, the groups and everything . . . she keeps pestering me to ask you, Doc . . . I know I gotta see somebody, Doc.' He paused, as did I, and then, insistently, loud enough to make sure everyone around would hear, Lt. Sal said the magic words I'd been waiting for, 'Can you get me a name of a counsellor near my house?'

Sal paved the way for the men to talk about real things. The guys started talking about things like how tired they were getting with the whole hero thing. To them the true heroes were the men who sacrificed their own lives trying to save others. They talked about people using them as a vessel for their own pain, and were convinced it was only a matter of time before they treated the firemen like they were 'zeroes not heroes'. They were fixated on the mantra that had taken hold in the house of 'Everything's changed. Things will never be the same.' They couldn't fathom what was going on with them or imagine that they would ever feel better.

One day Lt. Darby came up to me and asked if he could talk to me. He walked me over to the corner of the apparatus room. With a dramatic flashing of those blue tattooed arms of his, he attempted to whisper that he was worried about one of the senior guys, William. 'He's just not acting like himself,' going on to say that if William of all people was in trouble, this was simply unfair, unacceptable, and didn't bode well for everyone else. For it was William who the guys were convinced had been the living hero of that day because he had been the one to first sense the impending collapse and insist they leave the building right before it came down.

Darby reiterated what I'd already gotten from the scuttlebutt. That things had gotten out of hand a few times at one of the neighbourhood bars where the guys went to decompress when they got off duty. Someone had to stop William from getting into a fist fight with one of the guys, rumour had it, over how one of the guys was talking to one of the hero-worshiping girls hanging around the bar looking for a fireman. Darby went on. 'William's a good guy. He can be rough I know, but believe me, if you knew Will, you'd know what's he's really about. He was just protecting the girl.'

Darby said that the drinking and carousing wasn't what was worrying him. 'That's just letting off steam, especially these days. But what got to me was the way he took off in that truck. And things he said that night. But maybe it was just booze talkin'

Doc, I don't know, it's just . . .' I pushed him to finish what he was going to say. Finally he said he knew William owned a gun. That William had told him he didn't want to keep it in the house, because of his kids, so he was keeping it in the glove compartment of his truck. Darby shook his head and grimaced. 'The way he gets into that truck and gasses it. He's just not himself.' Was this just Darby's anxiety about the rough housing getting out of hand or could William's short fuse be a sign of something serious that needed attention before someone got hurt. I'd heard a snicker or two in Group about William's tension flaring up and I could feel a certain edginess in William, but I had no relationship with him.

Since the very first meeting in January which he had to attend, William managed to never once sit down for Group, and I never forced it with him. Typically he disappeared altogether when Group was called or when he felt compelled to show his face, he stood by the doorway with his arms crossed and smirking in a way that I took as smugly dismissive. No one, including me, dared to challenge William on this, or anything for that matter. For besides being their hero, he was one of the leading senior men in the house now. The death of Captain McNeil, the Engine captain and official head of the firehouse, and Bobby Walsh, who was the head of the firefighters, created a vacuum of leadership in the house, which left senior men like William, Phil and Robbie Taylor to pretty much run things these days.

No one said anything, yet everyone seemed to think he was in trouble. Was there more to William's skittishness and taking things a little too far than meets the eye? As much as they may have been bothered by Will's irritability and sometimes taking advantage of his seniority to get out of things he didn't want to do, they didn't seem annoyed with him. Perhaps they were too afraid to confront him or they simply sympathized with his situation. They knew that he didn't consider himself any more of a hero than they did.

The fact that he was the one considered most responsible for the men's survival did little to ease the rage and guilt of incomprehensible survival that seemed to grip the soul of

Firefighter William Kingsley. It may seem irrational to feel responsible for those who died, or ungrateful to feel bad about the fact of having survived, even though in doing so he helped save the lives of so many others. But survivor guilt isn't rational. It's human, an all-too-common reaction to the experience of going on living after surviving mass murder. Will's brothers knew full well from their own experience the self-destructive impulses that can consume a man's hurt, sorrow, and fear. But William, always doing things in such a big way and in his own inimitable fashion, was taking the things they all struggled with to a whole other level. What would it mean for the men's confidence in their own recovery and for my credibility as a therapist if I couldn't help the man who they saw as the most indomitable of them all and he ended up self-destructing?

I knew that William's avoidance of me and Group suggested something more serious than the brash indifference he affected. It bespoke of a pain and fear so great it had to be avoided at all costs. What was this fearless man so afraid of? Was he more afraid of breaking down and falling apart or of exploding and harming someone, perhaps himself, as Darby implied? As the kind of person who lives out the extremes of experience, he was simultaneously frightening and fascinating. William, who could go to any lengths to save a life one moment and be compelled to destroy it the next, embodied the contradictions of human nature. So when Lt. Darby pleaded, 'Will's one of our best men. Please talk to him. Would you see what you could do?' I couldn't refuse.

This was the first test of my clinical wherewithal in the firehouse. Could I reach William in his post-traumatic self-destructive behaviour and prove myself in the bargain? How was I going to win William over, when the tools of my trade and personality had so far fallen flat on this man? The only way I could think of to approach him, and to protect his dignity as well as my own, was to assume an off the cuff approach. When I saw him around the house I casually asked to talk to him and if I managed to wrangle him into my orbit, I ran some general question or suggestion by him. This tactic got me nowhere.

His fear of what I represented, the depth of the anguish he was running from, was so palpable I couldn't take his avoidance of me personally. But I still hadn't found a way to reach William.

I came up with a new strategy. One that proved to be helpful with other men as well, once I came to better understand the firehouse culture of mutual responsibility and fellowship. I enlisted the firemen as therapeutic agents. I spoke to the guys who had a close relationship with William and gave them advice on how to help him. In Group, I pushed the subject of how trauma affects not only the libido but, as they could now more easily admit, other emotions as well, especially anger. I talked about how anger and aggression, even violent impulses, can arise out of pain and grief, as a way of releasing feelings that have no other outlet for expression. I suggested that aggression, like sex, can function as a distraction from pain. And that anger can mask and ease feelings not only of frustration but of the helplessness that is part of sorrow and trauma. Who actually spoke directly to William I'll never know. Certain things are kept in confidence in the firehouse. But through the firehouse grapevine I learned that William eventually settled down.

He never did come to Group, but he was less of a time bomb in the firehouse. And from what I could make out from the guys he rarely went to the bar after work, and when he did he was steady behind the wheel when he left for home. Though less of a moody curmudgeon, William still avoided me like the plague. It became a kind of running joke between us that I'd have to chase after him, and the most I ever got was a word or two. But it apparently did something, because more than a year after I left the firehouse, I got a call from William. When I reached him he was sitting in his truck in the breakdown lane of the highway. For the next half an hour, with cars and trucks whizzing by, William and I finally talked.

There was no mask of anger, no sign of a major breakdown. There was simply a man who knew he was in trouble. They say time can heal all wounds. But not before it catches up with you. And time has a way of dulling memory. But one thing I remember as if it was yesterday was what William said that day over the phone with a half-laugh that nearly made me cry – 'I know I can be a stubborn SOB. I need help.'

* * *

February
We were a few months into the program. The men were warming up to me and to the idea that post-disaster distress is normal. They were coming to the group meetings, but didn't think of it as therapy and weren't considering going for therapy outside the firehouse. One day the guys were getting going, complaining about how 'crappy' they were feeling but not getting into anything of substance. Lt. Sal interrupted them, 'I don't mind talking about this stuff. I don't mind saying I got my own therapist. It's good, you guys should try it.' A nervous silence fell around the table. Then one of the back seat attendees sitting on the sofa broke the tension, 'Sure Sal, you love to talk.' This was followed by another guy asking in a mocking tone, 'Hey Sally, you quitting? Is it getting to your head?' This sent the guys into gales of laughter. I had no idea what they were talking about and playfully demanded, 'Hey someone tell me. What the heck is so damn funny?'

'You didn't know? Sal's famous.' They continued their banter, enjoying having me as their audience. I gathered from the snippets that Sal had just been chosen as the Fireman of the Month for one of those post 9/11 pinup calendars of New York City's Bravest. Enjoying the attention, he made one of his characteristic Sal-like comments that are simultaneously self-effacing and boasting. This was the perfect way to gracefully end 'Group'.

As we dispersed I asked him how his therapy was going. He replied, 'She wants me to go two times a week.' He was clearly interested in my opinion on this but I wasn't sure if 'she' was referring to his girlfriend or to his therapist. Before I could inquire, he went on, 'Julie wants me to go, next thing you know she'll want to get married.' Turning to the guys hanging out in the kitchen he bragged. 'We got a good thing going, but I see these broads, ooh, 'scuse me,' then, looking around to see who might be within earshot, he went on. 'I mean I see lots of ladies, I ain't ready to give that up. The idea of NEVER AGAIN, that's it. I'm not ready for that!'

Later, when no one was around, he elaborated on his situation. 'She thinks I got a commitment problem or something but I tell her, leave well enough alone. This stuff's got me on edge.' This vague comment I knew referred to his wavering confidence not only in being marriage material but in being an officer, with the spectre of further terrorist attacks. Sensing his need for encouragement, I reminded him, 'Sal, I hope you know you're a real leader in the house. The guys look up to you, they take their cues from you; I see it all the time.' Incredulous, he responded, 'Yeah, you really think so?' and his mood immediately perked up. Sal and the men played at the fine line between officer and firefighter. He clowned around, they teased, but he had their unquestioned respect as an officer.

Just then the alarm sounded. Sal invited me to go with them. I jumped at the chance to go on a run with them. Barely able to reach the step of the truck, someone pulled me up and the next thing I knew we were flying out the door with the siren blaring, and I was sitting up front next to Lt. Sal and the driver, or chauffeur as he's called, in a shiny red fire truck honking its way through the city streets. On our way down the block, a voluptuous young Puerto Rican girl was coming out of a bodega and smiled up at Sal. He called out to her, 'Hey what's up?' and waved to her with unexpected familiarity as we sped away. 'You know her?' I teased. 'Yeah I know her. She comes around the house.'

Then Sal being Sal, started talking. 'People think we're dumb wops, dumb micks, dumb Polloks, but some of the guys are real smart. They're engineers, teachers, we got an architect, electricians, plumbers, you name it, we got it. We even got a philosopher. Lot of guys with degrees here. Not me. I made it through college by the skin of my teeth, 'borrowed' a few papers . . . I did a lot of stuff back then. Used to be you didn't have to go to college to be a fireman. My dad, my brothers, they were firemen and they never went to school. Now to be an officer you got to go to college. These guys, they may act like they're dumb, but don't be fooled, they aren't. Not me. I had a lot of things happen'. The chauffeur didn't say a word. Nor did the guys in the back who sat still as church mice. The next thing I knew the rig was turning around. A false alarm on my first run in the truck!'

On the way back no one else seemed surprised when we stopped outside the grocery store. Sal explained that they needed frozen vegetables to add to the lunch. When the guys returned and we were rounding the next corner, Sal suddenly said, 'Hey you want some coffee? I need some coffee. Stop here,' he ordered. The chauffeur shook his head disapprovingly but did what as he was told. Sal returned two minutes later, with a fresh donut in his mouth and two cups of coffee. 'Wasn't sure how you like it, so I told them to put cream and sugar, but I did remember to tell him decaf. Here you gotta try these fresh donuts. They're great!' Then he added, 'I shouldn't be eating them,' as he patted his stomach, acting more like a jolly Santa than the stud-ly Romeo I imagined him to be. When I offered to reimburse him once we got back to the firehouse, he acted insulted. As we drove back Sal told me his story while sipping his coffee and looking out the window. 'My brother, he died on the job, but I'll tell you about that another time, it was a long time ago. I got two sisters and three brothers, one's still on the job.' His need and talent for standing out in a group was now beginning to make sense.

Despite his stated wish to drop the topic of his family problems, Sal couldn't stop. He let it slip that his father had suffered a fatal heart attack within a year of his older brother's death on the job. His effort at self-containment aborted once more, he went on,

'That's what clinched it for me – to go into EMS. I'd been thinking about it, it's a family thing, but with my brother and all, my mother she didn't want me to. But then, I was with my dad that day. They came fast, did their thing, but it was too late. That did it for me. You'd think it'd be the opposite, wouldn't ya? When I watched what those guys did. What they can do . . . Who knows, if I'd already had the training.'

That was enough. Sal changed the subject. 'I've been having knee problems, may have to have surgery. They got me on all these drugs for the pain, but I don't use 'em when I'm on the job.' Then he turned to face me and asked in a challenging tone, 'So Doc, What do *you* think of all these drugs for depression, stress? They keep pushing drugs on us for trauma and all that shit. Some of the guys, they're taking them. I don't know . . .' Without giving me a chance to respond, he went on, 'I don't think it's good, especially when you're working.' Stunned over learning of the multiple tragedies in his family history, I was thinking more about Sal's survival rate among his siblings than of the risks of medication. Gripped in his own state, Sal continued without me. 'I just don't believe in all these drugs.'

Several weeks later when I hadn't seen Sal around, I asked one of the guys about him. 'Out, on medical' was all he said and walked off. Darby happened to be on duty and explained, 'Knee problem . . . not sure Sal will ever come back,' with an enigmatic abruptness that was unlike Darby. I gathered that the guys weren't sure what to think about Sal's medical problems. How much of Sal's complaints of knee problems were really his fear talking? Did he want to get out altogether? The men didn't know what was going on with Sal, and I wasn't sure either. A few of the guys in the rank and file had gone 'off line' for the two-week medical leave that was devised as a kind of post 9/11 R & R, with guarantees of being able to return to active duty. Other guys were starting to talk about early retirement, a few had already put in for it. But so far Sal was the only officer going out on medical leave. This was a sign of the emotional and physical sickness taking hold of the men.

I knew I was really in when Group got its own nickname – 'Bitch Sessions'. The men and I were floundering together along in a mirror image of the faltering state of the FDNY. Once they were all at the kitchen table they went on their now familiar roll – a string of complaints about the department being unresponsive to their situation, not so different from the management employee conflicts typical of any large organization. Voiced amidst expressions of sadness, confusion and disillusionment. Laced with a bitterness fed by a rising fear and sense of helplessness staring in the face of another terrorist attack. Mostly, what came out was resentful griping and an occasional burst of outright anger, for anger was the one catch-all feeling it was okay to expose and share in front of each other. Their favourite resentful complaint was 'They knew about the radio problem from the last bombing and they still haven't done anything about it.'

Every once in a while a reference to the dead broke through the griping. 'The Cap was always saying that'd be a problem some day.' It was quickly stopped and followed by a hushed silence around the room. Their grief was too massive to be directly touched. It had to be channelled through that reliable expression, anger.

'Did you hear? None of the chiefs showed up at Moriarty's funeral!'

'You know why, 'cause there was no press there.'

Then, one after another, the mantra, 'Nothing's going to change', from which there was no place to go, but to dead silence. Someone would try to get things going again by moving back to sex. While the dressed-up locker room humour relieved the tension all round, the jocularity and tough guy cynicism was also a defence – a way to avoid talking directly about their pain. Accustomed to reading the many disguises our darker emotions assume I could hear their thinly cloaked expressions of anguish, but I knew I had to be careful about which words I used for emotions like anguish and sorrow. Group hit a dead end when they became struck by unacceptable feelings of vulnerability. They had no language for their helplessness and sorrow. They were having to confront a sense of hopelessness and doubt about themselves and the world that was beyond anything they had known before 9/11. Their shaken faith in the world included me, and expressed itself in doubts about whether I was like everyone else – the department, the government, and even like their caring family and friends – who needed to 'do something' for them in a way that put them in the position of having to take care of the consolers.

There's a delicate balance between support that's beneficial and that which is detrimental. It's a natural tendency to want to comfort the traumatized and grief-stricken person, but it risks leaving the victim feeling responsible for relieving the other person's distress and thereby un-recognized and un-responded to himself. Knowing how much their wives, parents, siblings and friends had also suffered from the disaster, the guys were already having to try their best to spare their loved ones the bleakness of what they were thinking and feeling. They needed one place where they could safely let out their darker side. Unconsciously they were testing, as patients do, whether I possessed the skill and wherewithal to endure and respond to their needs.

When gathered together around that kitchen table, they began to unfetter themselves of the burden of taking care of others. Taking me at my word that I could handle their feelings, they stopped being so concerned about what they were saying. The key, I knew, was finding it within myself to stay with their despair but not join in it, a balance that's easier said than done. In Group, where they were told they could express any feelings, the men became hell-bent on venting the emotions deemed ungentlemanly or insensitive. Mostly they were intent on defending the one thing they felt they could still successfully safeguard – the grim reality of the disaster's effect.

When we weren't holding Group, I developed a method I came to think of as therapy on the run. It was creating moments of therapeutic connection and intervention while standing around the firehouse with our feet on the bumper of the rigs, hanging around the kitchen, or sitting at the table with the TV on low in the background. Speaking in a matter-of-fact way, I made a point of telling them that it was normal to not feel normal, and that it was impossible to live up to their hero image. As one guy put it, being a national hero was 'a yoke and a joke.' It was therapy in an office without walls, in the middle of a big red firehouse, surrounded by boots, helmets, rubber coats, and sirens going off.

Conducting therapy in this way was similar to, but different from, my volunteering in the initial crisis period. That also involved being spontaneous and improvisational, but those were one-shot therapeutic interventions, with therapists functioning like mothers in public, mindfully guarding the privacy and dignity of those in their care. But here I got to follow up with the guys. One of the best things about our therapy on the run was that it had none of the self-consciousness of our formal Group meetings.

Over the next month or so a new pattern emerged. Enough time had passed since the disaster for me to gain my footing and for them to get to know me. Their sensing that I was no longer feeling out of my depth helped them to start taking more risks with this therapy thing. As Group broke up, a guy would linger around the table, then two or three more would join us. Or I'd help the guys prepare the meal and others might join in, forming informal groups which dissolved organically in firehouse fashion. The men were beginning to really communicate. In these brief encounters, these snatches of serious conversation, they confided in me about the changes they were going through, especially about the frighteningly strange ways in which they felt betrayed by their bodies and minds:

— 'Hey, Doc, I got this strange thing, I'll be just standing around and every once in a while I get dizzy. I went to the medical office; they said there's nothing wrong. Could it be mental?'
— 'What's it mean, Doc, I get this feeling in my chest sometimes?'
— 'Headaches'
— 'Stomach aches'
— 'I can't breathe sometimes; I went to the clinic, they say it's nothing, they say it's nerves.'

I tried my best to put them at ease by explaining the connection between psyche and soma. I told them that what defines something as traumatic is when the situation exceeds the brain's normal capacity for filtration, absorption and integration, leaving the body unprotected from invasion. I did not tell them how impressed I was at the mysterious ways I was seeing stress take its toll on the body.

Most of thebefe mental and emotional reactions they reported were common post-traumatic stress symptoms:

— 'Sometimes when the bell rings I get this sensation, for a split second, I can't explain it.' I explained that the alarm is a trigger that brings the mind right back to the immediacy of the trauma, and that these triggers will subside over time.

— 'Hey, Doc, sometimes I just think I'm going to blow my top.' I nodded my understanding and reminded them that feelings are not the same as actions.

— 'I feel weird at home but I feel even weirder when I'm not here in the firehouse.' I reassured them that no matter how much their friends and family loved them and tried to understand, they simply couldn't. I told them that being with the people who were going through the same thing requires less effort than trying to be with people on the outside. I didn't say it, but I knew that we all found a strange, almost guilty, reassurance in being together in the firehouse.

And then there was the refrain:

— 'On the way to work, all of a sudden this feeling hits, I can't describe it.' 'Dread' was all I had, all that could be said.

Every once in a while a guy asked me how I was doing. 'Hey, Doc, how is it for you? Must be hard for you, too.' These were the snitches and snatches of our therapy on the run. Now I was able to follow up the generalities I was dispensing in Group with more personal responses and advice. In Group, I talked about spending more time with the kids or playing golf to relieve their tension. But when a guy came up to me and said something like 'I really don't think about it, that's what strange. How could it be affecting me like this? Are you sure, Doc?' I explained how the psyche is imprinted on the body in his particular situation. Over and over I tried to get across the basic facts of how trauma and grief are processed, 'You don't have to be thinking about it.

That's just the way it works. It's in your body. Your body knows, it's carrying it.'

The guys usually nodded in acceptance and looked away. Direct eye contact was too dangerous, but I felt them taking in what I was saying. Their psyches were like panes of glass: transparent, at once strong yet fragile. Their bodies were the site containing the death and destruction they had been part of, and therefore the place where healing had to begin. Gently but firmly I kept repeating my mantra that their bodies were metabolizing and working through their trauma and grief. Teasing them, I said that even I thought it was okay sometimes to just listen to their body and not talk, or maybe just make a joke. For laughter is the best medicine.

Each visit I handed out my business card to any guy that came up to me. I dropped a few on the kitchen table each day before I left. The plan was for the men to call me whenever they were ready, and then I could either meet with them or any of their family members myself or refer them to one of the department's counselling centres or to one of the Counselling Unit's approved therapists in private practice. The private system, sponsored by Project Liberty, was meant to serve as an added resource to the department's over burdened counselling unit and to offer therapy to those men and their families who preferred going outside the system out of concern about confidentiality and putting their jobs at risk. Though the men were repeatedly reassured by the administration that their jobs wouldn't be at risk if they went for counselling, the men were understandably worried that being seen as having emotional problems might jeopardize their position as first responders.

Amazingly, first one, then another began to call. Many of the guys who lived outside the city requested referrals for private therapists nearer home, especially when it was for their wife or child. But over time, a number of men from the house made it into my office alone or with their wives, some for only a session or two, some only after a few false alarms of last-minute cancellations. The women cried, the men stared at their hands, all of them in one way or another expressing the same idea, 'Sometimes, Doc, I don't know what I might do.' I listened to one story after another, hearing the particulars of the tragedies and miracles that befell each family on September 11th.

The accretion of poignant stories was blurring my brain, but the particulars of each case would return to my consciousness with clarity at unbidden moments or when I saw the man involved at the firehouse. At moments I was flooded by the mounting challenge before me – of being the first woman and first therapist in this firehouse. Did I have it in me to be and do all that these traumatized and grief-stricken men needed? To meet these fifty men in the isolation, confusion and sorrow in which they were lost, to bring form and meaning to their pain, to see the hidden self of each man as he was before, and help restore his faith in the future. I knew that I wasn't going to be able to get close to the rent souls of many of these men. But I felt that I just had to try my best to help those men who were reaching out to me, sometimes with boyish awkward warmth. And to try to reach those whose grief and despair was so profound they could not reach out.

I did manage to learn many factoids that pass for knowing in today's world: whether a guy was married, how many kids he had, where he lived and went on vacation, the kind of office talk gleaned from chats by the water cooler. I never got to know a lot of the men with the depth that makes for great fiction or in the way that some therapists or scientists would consider knowing. Nor did I have a private heart to heart, in or outside the firehouse, with certain men from the firehouse.

But through the parameters of kitchen table talk, and our therapy on the run I got to know them and they got to know me. In these brief controlled moments the men could connect with the rawness of their pain, and communicate their visceral wordless reality to someone they trusted was prepared to listen. Standing by the stove or the trucks, guys told me things and asked my opinion as we rested our feet on the engine bumper. They asked me questions about how they could tell if their kids might be reacting to what had happened. They asked me to speak to other guys who seemed to be troubled. These were the easy requests and easy questions to answer. 'Sure I'll talk to him.' 'What you're feeling is a normal post-traumatic stress reaction.' Many of their reactions, certainly the shock and incomprehensibility of what had happened, were similar to, but exponentially greater than, what everyone in the outside world was experiencing. For trauma is like a nuclear bomb; its impact radiates in direct proportion to the proximity and extent of exposure to the site of the disaster. The more directly the man had been involved in the Trade Center, the longer a man worked at Ground Zero, or the closer he had been to the people who died, the more he was at risk of long term psychological damage. As for the possibility of permanent, irreparable scarring, it was far too soon and pointless to think about.

Once the men opened up they couldn't stop. The more they looked to me as their 'Doc' to address the painful emotions they'd been keeping under wraps, the more paltry my responses began to feel. When they said things like 'You know, Doc, sometimes I just don't want to come in, and I never felt like that before,' all I could say was something like 'Of course you feel that way.' This led to the next question, 'Will it last?' to which all I could offer was, 'It takes time.' I knew that trauma and grief obey no fixed course or time line, and I believed in the resilience of the human spirit. I was confident that most men would move past this. They were, after all, firemen, accustomed to bouncing back from trauma and tragedy. But the devastation they had gone through was on such a massive scale that no one could say for certain just how or when these men and the department as an organization would recover. The uncertainty about the future was compounded by the possibility of further terrorist attacks. Each man and his situation was unique. I wasn't working closely enough with most of them to give more definitive answers to their specific situation. Nor could I say their fear of another attack was unfounded.

While everyone in the city at this time was feeling like a

sitting duck for 'the next one', the reality was that these men as first responders would be on the front lines of the next attack. They began to say things like 'Hey, Doc, since what happened, sometimes I think about whether I could do it again,' and 'I'm afraid one day I just won't have it in me to come in.' Having words now to communicate the dread that they could only earlier convey through their body language and dreams, the men started to acknowledge doubts and fears that they couldn't before. They asked questions like 'What if I hesitate next time? What should I do?' – questions about the unknown for which there are no answers.

I knew that giving voice to the un-nameable would reduce their feelings of helplessness, and restore a sense of coherence to themselves and to the world around them. Trying to make sense of it all is painful but crucial for healing. Their questions went far beyond continuing to put themselves in harm's way. They were the questions that come to those immersed in the reality of death. Questions that no therapist, no one person can answer for another. All a therapist, or anyone really can do, is to stay emotionally present, as hard as that is, with a person experiencing the stark beauty and pain of the human condition.

* * *

In less than two hours on a September morning America, indeed much of the world, was transformed. Trauma unites and divides people. It creates friends and defines enemies. It strengthens a sense of community, in which groups form around perceived common needs that feel different from the other groups. We all shared the loss of something fundamental, the vision of America and New York in particular as a place of freedom and invincibility. But the city, in its own inimitable fashion, felt detached in many ways from the rest of the country. Within the city, people like the firefighters, who had suffered personal loss or who lived through the actual catastrophe, felt distant from those less directly impacted by the attack. Like many New Yorkers, I had lost no one close to me. I had witnessed the burning towers collapse, but at a safe distance. Once taken into The Brotherhood of the FDNY, I was set apart from the community at large, and became a traveller traversing between these estranged communities in my new role as a link between their world and the world at large. The men felt that the public was ignoring or disinterested in knowing what they needed – more appreciation of the risks they undertake as public servants, and greater willingness to give resources to effect the kind of changes in rescue and firefighting to prevent or better manage another disaster. They began to look to me to carry their message to the larger community, as someone who might help get the world to look beyond stereotyped ideas of firemen and the FDNY to see them as people and as a group in need. While I was no longer doubting my abilities as a therapist, I was now unsure whether I, or anyone for that matter, would be able to change such deep-seated attitudes as the men felt from and towards the public.

The guys were relaxing more and began looking forward to my visits. There were typically a few at the front of the firehouse ready to greet me when I arrived, making me feel needed and increasing my confidence. I began to see the commonalities between being a therapist and a fireman. Firefighting, rescue work, and emergency medical service, like psychotherapy, requires instantaneous assessment of people and situations. It necessitates getting what makes a person tick, anticipating what a person needs and quickly providing it, often without words. There is something in the nature of being a therapist and a fireman that inspires people in pain and fear to reach out to them, that gives people the courage to take a leap beyond what they would normally ever consider saying or doing. In psychotherapy, in emergency medical care and rescue services, thoughts and feelings are transmitted almost automatically, in telegraphed or wordless communication. Sharing these moments brings a knowledge of the other that's often not conscious but magnetically bonds the helper and the helped one to each other. They absorb each other's thoughts and feelings at multiple levels of consciousness.

The more connected to the men I felt, the more out of step and alienated from the outside world I started to feel. The culture was creating a psychological distance from the disaster by abstracting it, trying to make it into something emotionally manageable. But in so doing they were turning it into a thing. 'September 11th' became '9/11'. Treating it as an idea was both emotionally impossible and morally repugnant for those who were living in the after-effects of what had happened every single day. In this deepening chasm I was caught in no man's land. I felt more in tune with the guys, but I was well aware that I was not, nor would I ever be, a fully-fledged insider. Like the guys, I felt that no one outside could understand. Yet I also knew that I did not go through what the men had. I felt privileged to be let in, even protected by them, yet oddly isolated.

Ever the analyst, I questioned how I got myself into this position. People volunteer out of a multiplicity of motives, self-serving as well as purely altruistic. I struggled with the moral implications of my relationship with these men, wondering how much I was using the men as a channel for my own grief, giving and helping them as a perverse way to process my own feelings about 9/11, and my own past. The therapist in me rationalized this with the knowledge that we all learn from relationships and 'use' each other to work through our own issues.

* * *

In the dead of winter, when out of the public spotlight, death immersion held sway over the firehouse. They were feeling the fragility of life, not just intellectually but in the very core of their being. A full comprehension of life, sadly, tends to come only when we face death head on. And this had not been one death. This had been the senseless deaths of hundreds of their brothers and nearly three thousand civilians. Their flatness was the numbness which characterizes trauma and massive grief. This numbness serves a protective function. It insulates the grieving or traumatized person from feeling the need to respond to the people around him and to the other pressures of life. But its enveloping protection can end up isolating the sufferer from others. This can leave the victim locked within his post-traumatic grief and the person wanting to make contact with him feeling rebuffed. In this way the victim and the caring other can become alienated from each other, rendering them both vulnerable to having their isolation congeal into frustration and anger. For anger is an organizing emotion, the kind of feeling that makes one feel much less out of control than feeling the far more disorganizing feelings of grief, helplessness, and pain that exceed description and definition.

But thankfully every once in a while even the most morbidly preoccupied person can find humour to alleviate pain. Like many first responders, the guys used black humour as a coping mechanism. Usually it involved things that happened at fires. Things like 'Did you see Anthony carry that 300-pound gorilla down the fire escape? She was kicking and screaming the whole way, nearly broke his nose.' That would bring out a round of chuckles and ripples of laughter. They used bantering and teasing each other, even joking about mistakes or accidents on the job, as effective ways to manage their frequent brushes with death and serious injury. Their hero status provided a natural outlet for humour. With a cynical edge, they siphoned their pain into humour, saying things like treating them as heroes was a definite sign that the world was suffering some form of temporary insanity. But as their scepticism and alienation from the public deepened, their humour began to sour, with lines like 'Doc, we've been here before; when the dust settles, we'll be as interesting as the next bit on the eleven o'clock news.' They talked about the country using them to assuage their guilt over failing to prevent the attack and as a channel for their own grief.

In spite of the fact that the men bore resentment toward the public, they never turned away any visitor that came to the door. No matter what was going on, if a visitor showed up, one of the guys would stop and chat, and more often than not, the guy would end up consoling the visitor. Any kid who came by was sure to be lifted up into the driver's seat with a hat placed on his head and allowed to slide down the gold pole. But as soon as the visitor was gone, their brave persona and faces of warmth returned to the state of bereft blankness that was the truth they didn't have to hide from each other.

* * *

The man on watch told me when I arrived that the ladder company was out on a call and would be back shortly, but that the guys from the engine were somewhere around the house. He was friendly but I could tell he wasn't into talking. He kept glancing over at the small TV in the corner as he uncomfortably tried to maintain a conversation. Just then the phone rang. I wandered onto the apparatus floor. No one was around, so I made my way to the kitchen in back, and sat down at the long pine table. I was so struck by the fact that the television wasn't on, as it so often was, that I didn't notice there was a man sitting at the far end with a newspaper opened up before him. Without saying a word he passed me the remote and went back to reading.

I didn't recognize him and assumed he must be a covering officer from another firehouse. I introduced myself and waited for him to do the same. He didn't respond, so I asked if I could have a section of the paper. He leafed through the pages until he found the Sports section, which he pulled out for himself, then handed me the rest of the paper. Slowly, with an imposing deadpan voice he announced, 'Holland. Steve Holland. Just got here a few weeks ago.' He went back to reading the newspaper. There was an incongruity to this man who appeared to be in his early forties. Though I couldn't tell at the time, he stood at six feet five. He was a muscular man with a commanding voice and presence but his head of closely-cropped copper hair and a sprinkling of freckles over his arms and face gave him a boyish demeanour.

Almost as soon as I started reading I heard him say, 'Bobby Walsh was my buddy,' as though he was speaking to no one in particular. But since I was the only one in the room I knew he was directing his comment to me, and that he was assuming I knew just who Bobby Walsh was. Which of course I did. Bobby was one of the senior men who had died on 9/11. I had heard the story of how he had been off duty but in the area and how he had rushed into the towers. But I had no inkling of Holland's connection to Bobby Walsh or to the disaster. It was long after we'd both ended our tours in the firehouse, and he was in therapy with me, when I learned that Steve Holland had seen Bobby Walsh on the morning of September 11th, when Bobby was running towards the towers.

Bobby Walsh's name hung in the air between us. His eyes met mine as he finished his brief sentence, and then with a purposefulness he looked back down at the paper in front of him. He apparently changed his mind about not talking, because as he continued to methodically turn the pages, he picked up where he left off,

'Bobby and I, we go way back, even before the academy. We sometimes hung out together in high school, played ball together, then we went off to college. I dropped out. Had always thought I was gonna go to medical school. I joined the reserves, that's how I got my EMT training. When I got out, I don't know, just made sense, the Fire Department had just merged with the Emergency Medical Services. So I went to sign up for the test, and who do I see, my old buddy from Staten Island, Bobby Walsh! Weird, hadn't seen him in years. Then while we were both waiting to take the test, they didn't give it so often back then, we started running into each other, different places on the island. That's how it is out there.' He paused, and added, 'On Staten Island. You know Staten Island at all?' I told him I'd worked in the psych hospital there. This established enough of a commonality for him to continue.

'Somehow Bobby and I, we wound up going through the academy at the same time. We went up the ranks, both of us, even managed to get assigned to the same battalion, so over the years we'd end up working the same job, sometimes even doing training at the same time at the Rock.' The Rock being the official FDNY training site.

I noticed he was wearing a bracelet that looked like the same brushed silver wristband I'd seen on several guys. I assumed it had something to do with 9/11 and was curious about it. I thought about asking him about the bracelet or more about his friendship with Bobby Walsh, but didn't. So we sat in silence, both of us pretending to read. And then Lt. Holland came out with the words I remember to this day, not for their dramatic tone, or elegiac elegance, but for the volumes it spoke about the kind of friend Steve Holland was to Bobby Walsh, and the kind of person Steve remains to this day. The crisp simplicity of what Steve Holland described having done was an ode unto itself. 'So, I just decided, afterwards, that's what I wanted to do. To come here. I asked to be assigned to this house.'

This he could do, perhaps even had to do, for his friend and for himself. Holland could assuage his guilt and perhaps find forgiveness for failing to stop him from heading into death, for not being able to rescue him from the stairway buried in the collapse, for being alive himself. He could honour Bobby Walsh's life and make peace with his death by walking where his friend walked, by sleeping where his friend slept, and feel the presence of his friend Bobby Walsh in the nooks and crannies of the firehouse that he had led and worked in for so long.

* * *

That was the most I'd heard about the actual person Bobby Walsh. The pain was still too raw and the restoration of routine too fragile for the men to talk directly about the men who died on 9/11. But bits and pieces about other guys who'd passed through the firehouse over the years were now coming to the surface, usually in a tale with a little edgy humour in it, like a feat of prowess mixed with some goof or gaff. Spinning yarns, a tradition in firehouse life, seemed to be slowly returning, making its way back into life. But when it came to men lost on September

11th, the guys were more comfortable acknowledging them more with action than with words.

One day I happened to be there on a Thursday at 2.30, which was drill time. That day they were doing knots. There was a hint of lightness to the atmosphere, something I hadn't seen before, but was what I imagined the firehouse must have been like before September 11th. Four or five guys were in a circle with a three-inch thick rope in the middle, taking turns swinging the rope into exquisite knots with confident grace and precision, making it look simple. By now I was almost enjoying being the tag-along and didn't think twice about throwing myself into the middle of things. 'I recognize that one, the boson, I remember it from my Girl Scout days. Can I try?' Accustomed to civilians playing fireman, no one objected or even looked askance at my effort to join in. Phil, the senior man leading drill, handed me the rope. As soon as the tight thick hemp was in my hand, I realized this wasn't a Scouts exercise where you learn knots to earn a badge. I was struck by the chilling reality of the skills these men have that I do not. Seeing me fumbling with the line, at a total loss in making the boson knot, Phil broke into the circle, took the rope, and in mock exasperation, rescued me: 'Here, I'll show you a little trick Captain McNeil once showed me.'

Right there, clear as a bell, the name of the dead captain rang out. You could feel the tension in the air, but no one said a word. Phil broke the moment by getting behind me, putting his hands over mine and the rope, guiding me to form first one loop, then another, and then leading my hands to pull the rope through for a perfect boson knot. All while he kept talking, 'It was the Cap taught me. He said, 'Learn this stuff, it's basic, you never know when you'll need it.'

Still no one said a word. Sean, perhaps to manage his fragile stability, quietly slipped away from the group. But the other guys stayed, almost transfixed. Phil, a natural leader, was teaching me and them how to not get twisted up in knots, how to move forward. In talking about their beloved dead captain in his characteristically understated way, Phil was paving the way for the men to free themselves from the bondage of silence born of guilt-laden grief. He was also making room for the dead to have a place of aliveness in the hearts and minds of the men in the firehouse.

I knew I had to say something. And I knew I shouldn't use words like '9/11', 'dead' or 'survivor', terms that belonged outside the firehouse. I was concerned about piercing the delicate stability the men had built up with anything too unsettling. I ended up shrouding painful reference to the dead in an awkward excess of verbiage, 'Phil, were you close to the Captain? How about you guys? I don't hear you guys talk much about them, or about it.' I heard the hollowness of my shrink-y words, vague with 'deep meaning', as probably the men did too. I was sure I had thrown an invisible wet blanket on any further conversation. But then Phil, with the same ease that he brought to knots merely shrugged. He acted like I was their probie-counsellor, and so only natural that I'd have to be taught certain things.

'Oh we talk about it. Sometimes when we're just hanging out and nobody's around when not much is happening. During the day there's too much going on, you can't think about things then, people coming and going, but there are times. Every once in a while something will just occur to somebody and he'll say, "Remember when Joe did this or that?"' Shrugging the topic off, he then said, 'But, Doc, you gotta remember, a lot of these guys here now, they're new, they didn't even know them. So why talk about them?' But he then quipped:

'You know, Doc, Captain McNeil, I remember he'd say to us, "There's always gonna be new guys comin' in, probies, you gotta teach 'em, show 'em the ropes".' He folded his arms and smiled in self-satisfaction at his own pun.

Phil continued, 'The Cap wasn't one of these officers that would bust your chops. He wasn't that type. He ran this house like everybody was his family, and treated the younger guys like they were his own kids. Not like he was soft on them, mind you. I don't mean that. He knew they had to toughen up, that's what the probies got to learn, how to do the job. But the Cap he taught us we all had to look out for these guys too, not just give 'em a hard time, we had to teach them. He didn't cotton much to the whole bit of putting the new guys through the paces just for the fun of it, like some guys around here get into.'

With tempers flaring more than usual, I knew some guys were unloading their frustration on the younger guys. But he seemed to be specifically referring to one in particular, Robbie Taylor, who was getting a reputation for riding hard on the probies. He continued, 'Somebody has to do all the scut work, the dishes, toilets, wash the equipment floor. It's just that, just like what he said to me one day, I remember. He told me, 'Phil you treat a guy right and he'll learn, and it'll come back to you one day.' He used to say stuff like that. That's the kind of guy Captain McNeil was.'

I looked around, our circle had broken up, the guys had quietly moved off without either of us noticing. Phil was brought up short, 'Jeez, I went on there, you were asking me . . . Don't mind me, Doc, sometimes I can go on. I don't usually talk all that much, I'm not like some around here.' We both smiled, knowing just who he was alluding to. Phil then confessed, 'I'm like what one of the guys said, like one of those wind-up clocks, it sits there quiet like, but once you wind me up I keep going . . .'

'I was asking you if you guys talk about what happened.'

'Like I said, when no one's around, when there's just a few of us guys who've been here a while. Nowadays if you've got five years in you're a senior guy; weird, used to be you had to have at least ten years in. Now suddenly I'm one of the oldest guys in. Strange, huh, can you believe it? I don't feel like . . . it's hard to explain, but anyway, like I said, every once in a while somebody will say something like, 'Remember when Bobby Walsh would do . . . whatever, or ''member how we were doing this or that and how Walker or Thomasini would do this or say that . . . That kinda thing. At night mostly.'

* * *

'This was not a matter of, 'Have you had a nightmare?'
. . . This was "You've had nightmares night after night".'
the Daily News 3/28/02

* * *

So naturally I made it my business to get to the firehouse in the
evening. I happened to arrive right as dinner was being served,
and was treated to a portion of beef stew, potatoes and carrots
befitting my fellow diners, twice my size and appetite. Picking
around the meat, I ate the potatoes and vegetables, and quickly
joined the probies in clearing the table.

Things were definitely quieter here at night. The house had
a different feel. The fluorescent lighting gave off that artificial
white light that makes you feel vulnerable but braced against the
encroaching darkness beyond. On tour that night were men like
Sean, Anthony and Pauli, guys that I felt most close to and that
I knew felt comfortable with me. Lt. Holland was the officer in
charge that evening. I soon figured out that the evening plan was
to watch a video of the big yearly football game between the cops
and firemen.

Fifteen minutes later, I was sitting next to Lt. Holland on the
sofa watching him play football on the television. He wasn't
working at the firehouse at the time of the game but he was with us
now, and that made it even more exciting for the men. From what
I could make out the FDNY team was doing well. The enthusiastic
rooting for their team was a refreshing break from the deadened
atmosphere that prevailed most of the time. Someone called
out, 'Did you see that?' and they all cheered as Holland crossed
the goal post with the football raised high in his hand. Pleased,
Holland flushed with embarrassment, then quickly recovered his
somewhat stern stance and reminded the group that he wasn't the
only man from the house on the team. 'But I never got off the
bench!' Anthony playfully protested, making fun of himself and
perhaps Holland as well. This sent his buddies into contagious
guffaws. As soon as the game was over the guys wandered out of

the kitchen, leaving the last man to rewind the tape. The TV went
back to its fixed 'on' position. Once again I'd missed the social
cues that the guys instinctively grasped, about when to linger
and when to walk away. I was left sitting by myself with the
droning of prime time TV as my sole companion. The men knew
the secret, how to get away from the ghosts.

I was thinking of the guys going upstairs to try to sleep and
how they'd talked about how hard it's been for them to sleep at
the firehouse since the disaster. One man had told me he spent
the night lying on his cot, pretending to sleep, waiting for the
sounds of other insomniacs tiptoeing downstairs to get a snack or
watch late night TV. Sitting by myself there at the kitchen table
in the late evening, I felt momentarily overtaken with that certain
feeling of aloneness that comes with the awareness of people
around but not really there with you. With its distinctly male
décor, at first glance the firehouse kitchen was a study in contrast
with the woman as ruler kitchen of the fifties that I grew up in.
And yet there was something about it that made me feel at home,
and reminded me of home, with the mixture of all the good and
bad, and unformulated feelings that come with family life. There
weren't any Hallmark type 'Queen of the Castle' type signs like
my mother had, but there was a sign up sheet for a firehouse
family trip to Disneyland scotch taped to the refrigerator. This
kitchen, like my mother's and like my own, was at the end of
the day spotless, all signs of the day long feeding and foraging
cleaned away. There was a newspaper open, to the Sports page
rather than to the 'Dear Abby' column my mother was so fond
of. And there was the same damp dish towel hung to dry over the
dish rack in satisfaction for a day's work well done.

The ways of each home are simultaneously strange and familiar
to those outside. Or as Tolstoy put it, 'Happy families resemble
one another; each unhappy family is unhappy in its own way.
As distinct as each of our families are, feeling the unhappiness
of another family reminds us of our own family. There I was, at
a kitchen table in a firehouse, feeling the pain and pleasure of
aloneness that may be the inevitable paradox of family living. I

recalled a night many years before when I'd taken my kids to visit their grandparents. After driving two hundred miles, I dropped my dreamy young children into the waiting arms of my father, who gently sang them back into deep sleep. The house was quiet, everyone asleep. I grabbed a midnight snack like I loved to do as a kid and sat down to read the paper. I heard breathing, which I assumed was the dog in the hallway refusing to choose one bed over another. But then I heard the distinct sound of a voice I recognized, 'Man on first . . . one on third, one out, two balls, one strike.'

Why was my father sitting alone in the dark with his transistor radio for his companion? Had he thought I'd gone to bed? Did he want to be left alone or was he waiting for me to call out to him? I wasn't the young girl any more who stood behind his recliner and combed his hair while he watched TV. He wasn't there any more for me to be near or together with. As much as the days are defined by the absence of the dead, the nights reveal the presence of the dead. Sitting alone with the droning of the TV in the background, the men ensconced upstairs and grappling with the night, I realized I was a middle aged woman, once again by myself at a kitchen table, but less afraid of ghosts. I walked up to the picture of Bobby Walsh that hung on the wall along with all the other men from the firehouse on the job on September 11th.

* * *

The little factual information I had about Bobby Walsh was from what Steve Holland told me the day we first met. All the rest was a matter of conjecture – the stuff of imagination, superstition or faith, depending on your your point of view. I don't know whether there really are ghosts or guardian angels, heaven or hell. But I believe that the spirit goes on once we depart from this earth. Including the spirit of senior Firefighter Bobby Walsh, long-time friend of Steve Holland, whose entire career was spent in this firehouse, who I felt trying to bring the light of knowledge and forgiveness to his firehouse family.

Look at you guys, standing stand around all day, not knowing who to look to, what to think. You're not sleeping right any more. If you only knew, but I get it. You guys think maybe you did something wrong but it all happened so fast. Who the hell thought the buildings would go? They were built to withstand anything, we thought anyway.

Wow, look at the new engine, how's it working out? I know, sometimes you're out on a run, you forget. Hey, it's OK. Then sometimes you suddenly remember that you haven't been thinking about it, you think you forgot maybe . . . You get bent out of shape with these new guys comin' in who don't seem to know or care about 'how it was' . . . hey, that's just the way it is.

Remember, some of 'em are just probies. It's good the way you guys are with Danny, he's really freaked out. Remember he was only on the job a few weeks at the time. What do you expect? Go easy on him guys. He'll be a good fireman, you'll see. He's got what it takes. The other probies too.

I love this house. It's my house. Everything still looks pretty much the same. Black soot lining the ceiling even with the new exhaust hose they jerry rigged. Looks like a giant vacuum sucking away traces of what's in the lungs that nobody wants to think too much about, Traces. Memory. Board's up, chalked in the names for the day's tour. Broom clean, the way it should be. Cruddy can's the way it always was, single stall, door won't shut all the way, crappy disinfectant smell that never really goes away, scum coating the soap.

Ah, house watch . . . smallest one-foot-square smoke glass window I ever seen. Looks more like a picture than a window; not much light but more than enough to see what's going on. Still got the pin up calendar. Nothing too racy, nothing the chiefs would have anything to say about. There's good old Mousey, flipping the pages on the Daily News, He's still the one you know you can get to take watch. Bench cushion's got bits of equipment lying on it. Don't leave that stuff lying around.

Good for you, guys, you finally got it together to get rid of that banged up old couch and do a real paint job. But what the hell

is this woman doing here? Doesn't she know we don't have ladies
here? Things seem to going okay . . . like the way they always
were . . . Taylor pushing his weight around as always. Only now
you don't have me there to put him in his place. You just let him
take over, running the house meetings. Not the way I did. Taylor,
what are you thinking, riding the new guys the way you do? You
think you're a tough guy? Lighten up. Show them by helping
them. You're a senior man, remember. And you Holland, you son
of a bitch. Can't sleep like a baby like you used to? I used to have
to shake you, shout to get you up. But we were kids then. What
the hell you doin' in my firehouse? You know we go way back,
nothing'll change that. Things go down. That's just the way it is.

But I get it, really. Guys, it hurts to see you feelin' so bad.
Stop goin' around blaming yourselves. It was nobody's fault. Me,
what was I doin' rushing in like I did . . .? Who knew? Seemed
like it was like any other big job . . . you guys know. Hey, some
of you guys did just what I did that day . . . only you made it. But
you know the deal, when you see something happening whether
you're on duty or not, you gotta go in. Quit it with the guilt
already. It's like what I always told you guys. You do the best you
can. And then you gotta let it go.

Can't stand to see you guys like this. You gotta keep goin', you
know that. You know what me and the other guys need, just look
after the wife and kids, that's all. Wish I could tell you. It's not
what you think. Wish you could hear me.

* * *

'The mythological hero . . . encounters a shadow presence
that guards the passage . . . beyond the threshold, then the
hero journeys through a world of unfamiliar yet strangely
intimate forces, some of which . . . threaten him . . . Some give
magical aid . . . At the return . . . the hero re-emerges from the
kingdom of dread.'
Joseph Campbell

* * *

Where do those sounds and shadows come from in those hours of darkness when you're not sure you're dreaming or awake? Could it really be that Bobby Walsh was somehow there with them? I knew some guys really felt they could sense the presence of their brothers who had died, but few dared to admit it openly. Are the Bobby Walshes merely figments of our imagination? Do we create ghosts so as to not have to feel our fundamental aloneness? The answers to such imponderable questions are best left with the Joseph Campbells and Carl Jungs of the world. But one thing I do know, those who responded to the call on the morning of September 11th and who returned alive were given a visionary glimpse into the essence and meaning of life through their encounter with death. They were granted a kind of understanding that eludes most of us and cannot be imparted. It can only be learned, as they learned it, by living through the experience. Leaving them blessed and cursed with the power to hear their brothers' voices, to see their faces and sense their presence in the middle of the night. Whether apparitions, tricks of memory or glimpses into the beyond, they were something beyond scientific explanation or psychoanalytic interpretation, and as real to these heroes as anything else.

* * *

March
Despite its image of vibrant immunity to the vicissitudes of life, until now New York had remained in the dullness of the disaster's aftermath, and in the moral commitment to 'never forget'. But with spring in sight talk began to float about it being time to 'move on'. With the pall of grief and anguish thoroughly seeped into the atmosphere of the firehouse, the wall thickened between the world inside and outside the firehouse. The National Guard departed from the city. Locals who had fled after September 11th had slowly begun the return home to New York. Barricades blocking off whole sections of downtown were removed one after the other. The Trade Center site was cordoned off with hurricane fencing into four neat clean corners. The

massive gaping hole was now barely visible from the 'viewing' stage set up at a comfortable distance for the increasing numbers of people coming to pay respects and see for themselves this unbelievable reality. Ground Zero was, or at least appeared to be, fully contained.

And miraculously, just when we'd come to think it would be with us forever, the smell that pervaded downtown Manhattan, that smell that was unlike any other, was finally gone. Leaving New Yorkers with such a restoration of normalcy that left us wondering, Did it really happen? Perhaps that neighbour, colleague, friend who disappeared just might return tomorrow. When we pick up the messages on our phones, maybe, just maybe we might hear the voice of that loved one that we know is gone but can't believe we'll never see or hear from again.

There comes a time in mourning when the suspension of life and time no longer works. When you're needing to get back in the game, resume the life you've been living. But life isn't exactly like a board game; there are no 'Free Passes' to 'Go', no 'Get out of Jail' cards. All we can do is toss the dice, hold our breath and see where we land on a particular day. Some days are just not good days, and some days you've actually forgotten, for the briefest of moments, but then you wake up the next day and it's back. It makes you fear you'll never come out of it, that there is no other side to sorrow. You know there must be. That's when another truth hits you – neither you nor anything about your life will ever be as they were before.

It is often just about at this point in the glacial process of grief relentlessly working its way through the body and spirit that people start to lose patience with mourning, whether it's their own or others'. They begin to turn away from active manifestations of sorrow. This is reinforced by the western cultural aversion to death. And so, six months after the catastrophe, the majority of Americans, those who had little direct involvement in 9/11, were desperately wanting to put this nightmare behind them, and to recapture life as it was before.

The dramatic media coverage of incidents of alcohol abuse and combativeness in firefighters fueled the public's waning interest in our national heroes. The sensationalism of the stories was more evocative than the notion of educating the public on these common symptoms of post-traumatic stress. Even New Yorkers, whose grief and trauma had been more intense and prolonged than the rest of the country, were showing less tolerance for signs of prolonged distress and mourning. So no one seemed to mind, or even notice, that the men of the FDNY were closing in on themselves. Inside the firehouses, the men wandered in a comforting solitude among each other.

The news then took a sharp turn away from the firemen and the psychological toll on the city. The dread of financial disaster, in particular for the city, became the cultural preoccupation. The headlines of The Daily News, one of the city's major newspapers, reflected the increasing focus on restoring economic stability: 'Poll finds many took financial hit' (The Daily News, 3/10/02), '9/11 jobless in debt trap, credit card bills soar as work hunt grows bleak' (The Daily News, 3/31/02). The first major research report of the psychological effects of the catastrophe on New Yorkers was also made public, and statistically verified the extent and seriousness of citywide post-traumatic stress. According to the report, the normally highly stressed population of New York was suffering a degree of anxiety that 'more than doubled as a result of September 11th' (The Daily News, 3/28/02). All this depressing news made people feel the need to find something positive to focus on.

Thus began the talk of 're-building'. The public imagination became piqued by proposals of re-building bigger and better than the fallen Trade Center towers. Architectural competition for design of the memorial and the whole site was undertaken. Our American commitment to not forgetting was now outweighed by our even stronger urge to feel the country as once again endowed with life and power. This meant turning away from painful reminders of what had happened, the FDNY. Firemen were the symbol of American heroism, but heroism in the face of defeat.

In those first months after 9/11 the firemen had been held up as the anointed heroes of the day, as mythological figures who symbolized our collective trauma. We longed to touch them, to brush them as they had brushed death, to feel their strength in our shared helplessness and grief. Throughout the fall and winter the world found comfort watching these men on their television screens in the morbid and largely futile process of digging, shoveling, raking and sifting, searching for body parts, pieces of clothing, any evidence of life at Ground Zero. The firemen were featured in news specials, calendar pin-ups, photographic exhibits. Trinkets with the FDNY logo, toy firemen and fire trucks, T-shirts proclaiming 'Never Forget' were mass produced and on sale all over the city. The FDNY was the face of 9/11.

In witnessing their dedication and persistence in the rescue and recovery operation those first days of September, we endowed these men with the heroic possibility of redeeming the nation's wounds and grief. The physical separation of the men from the rest of the world made it all the easier to pour our own pain into these men, and then to project onto them from a distance the feelings we had that we didn't want to directly feel ourselves. Projection, putting one's own feelings on another is one of more basic defences, a psychological mechanism the mind resorts to when it is so strained more effective ways of coping are not available.

But now firefighters were losing their hero glow. Their steadfast refusal to stop in the recovery operation, their dignity and persistence in light of the circumstances – the massive loss, the limited success of the recovery effort and the continued terrorist threat – was reminding us that America had been brought down by the unseen enemy of terrorism. They were coming to be as much a symbol of our weakness and failure as of our strength. And the reports of firemen's less than stellar behavioural problems didn't help sustain their image of heroic fortitude. The very same men whom we had so desperately wanted to connect with were slowly becoming less appealing to the country and the world beyond. Fewer visitors were stopping by the firehouse and the media seemed less and less interested in covering New York's Bravest in the daily news. To what extent this was callousness, moral failure or self-centreed insularity of a country with a penchant for slogans over long term solutions it's hard to say. But it certainly reflected the short attention span and our cultural aversion to prolonged states of mourning in our feel good society.

For their part, the firemen were relieved to be out of the public spotlight. The men were becoming increasingly alienated from the public. Adding insult to injury, not only did they feel used in their hero position, they started to feel that even their trauma, so hard for them to accept, was getting co-opted by many individuals and sectors of society laying claim to their own 9/11 trauma. This helped unburden them of their obligation to uphold the idealized image of moral supremacy and emotional invincibility as national heroes. Feeling freer to do what they needed to do for themselves, they closed ranks and withdrew from the outside world so that they could mourn in privacy. As for their fellow Americans, even fellow New Yorkers, we were content to corral these trauma carriers away. It was as if their pain was still contagious, that it might trigger memories and emotions that we were aggressively pushing away now.

But for anyone entering a New York City firehouse, entertaining any teasing fantasy of moving past things was out of the question. The fact that the catastrophe of months earlier was continuing to wreak havoc on these men was undeniably obvious. In addition, the men themselves were resolute in resisting the silent but steady pressure from the outside world to let go of their grief and morbid preoccupations. The outside world could no longer bear seeing and hearing the grief and pain they were trying so hard to get past in themselves. Try as they might to oblige other people's need to avoid showing pain, those gripped in grief are simply incapable of putting it away. The anger of unrelenting and unrecognized grief will refuse accommodation. Do not pass go. Do not collect $200. There's no way to win this game without giving death its due.

There was no escape for the men of the FDNY. Even so, they too had to go on. After all, fireboxes were still being pulled, alarms set off by fire and flood. Apartments were on fire from faulty electrical plugs and heaters, children playing with matches, careless cigarettes. Trash cans were set on fire by pranksters and incautious pedestrians. People were always calling 911 for car accidents, heart attacks and other medical emergencies. Just emerging from the dull numbness of their own trauma, the men wanted to be left alone to do their job. The men made fun of the pamphlet the department put out, entitled 'The New Normal', which summarized and normalized the many physical and emotional symptoms of trauma and grief. Poking fun, they began to talk about 'the new abnormal'.

One day one of the men rolled down the red garage door, the door which to that moment had been kept open 24/7 to the public since the morning of September 11th. No one said anything. The public's months' old makeshift memorials were left outside on the sidewalk. A boundary between the public and the private life of the firehouse was reinstated. Totally bereft, the only thing the men really felt they had left to believe in was each other and their ability to merely keep going. That's the way it was at the FDNY a half a year after September 11th.

* * *

The Homeland Security system of lights signaling the level of terrorism risk was starting to get on the men's nerves, even affecting their reaction to the alarm bells. On a yellow day they were calmer, but on red light days everyone was on edge in jittery anticipation of what those alarm bells could mean. The very same bells that used to excitedly awaken the men's anticipatory preparedness had now become Pavlovian triggers for feelings they were not accustomed to as firefighters – fear and helplessness. The loss of control over the Trade Center situation with its massive loss of life had severely undermined the men's confidence in their professional judgment and competence.

In hindsight it might be hard to believe but before 9/11 no one, including the government, military or the fire department, had seriously considered, much less prepared for jumbo jets being used as bombs and breaching the presumed impenetrable barriers of American soil. Nor had anyone, until moments before the collapse, imagined that the World Trade Center could be taken down. Despite the earlier terrorist attacks against America abroad – the USS Cole bombing in Yemen only the year before and the US Embassies in Kenya and Tanzania in 1998, despite the terrorist bombing of the Alfred Murrah Federal Office Building in Oklahoma City in 1995, where 168 people, including 19 children were killed, despite the fact that the World Trade Center itself had been the target of a previous bombing attack in 1993. Despite all this evidence to the contrary, we believed we were safe.

It is a well documented fact in trauma psychology that the more powerless a person feels, the less control an individual has during a traumatic event, the greater the risk is for the person to develop post-traumatic stress disorder (PTSD), major depression or an anxiety disorder. Standing helplessly on the sidelines at the disaster site as the buildings came down in a matter of a few minutes' time, knowing their brothers and civilians were doomed inside, was exactly the kind of experience that had the potential for making a fireman vulnerable to PTSD. Without conscious intent, the men instinctively coped by converting feelings of powerlessness into activity, and helplessness into anger. Anger is an organizing emotion which can make a person feel less vulnerable and out of control than incapacitating anxiety.

They put energy into things they could do something about – helping the widows and the children of the lost men. They found it much harder to deal with things they had little control over. Their anxiety about future attacks was expressed in frustration and anger about preparedness, in particular what they felt was the inadequate effort to redress the severe shortage in man power and proper equipment. Most painful to them was the continued failure to replace the outmoded radio system – the very same system that was in place back in the 1993 bombing, and that was believed to be attributable to the death of at least 121 firefighters at the Trade Center in the North Tower.

The men's anger possessed an incongruousness that captured the essence of their contradictory nature. One minute they were simmering with vaguely threatening 'don't look at me' expressions, the next minute they were blushing shyly and exuding a manly boyishness. Certain guys adopted a clever cynicism, expressed in comments like, 'Sure today we're heroes, but soon enough believe me, you know we'll be back to being zeroes…. They'll honk when we block the streets and complain that we don't work hard enough for our big pensions.' With this kind of cutting humour they were also subtly letting me know I wasn't a true insider and I knew nothing of their history with New York City. They were conveying, as people trapped in raging grief and traumatic stress can do, that no one could possibly fully understand what they were going through.

As a hybrid inside/outsider or outside/insider (I was never sure which dominated), I became a place marker, a repository, not only for their grief but also now for the surge in pain laced anger that neither they nor I could fully manage. The unrelenting 'bitching' began to demoralize some men, while others seemed to still get some relief in venting this bottomless pit of resentment to someone from the outside willing to listen.

* * *

My fellow clinicians in other firehouses and I formed our own Group for support. We shared war stories, and confided in each other about the problems we were confronting. We shared our dismay over the melee of mixed emotions that we thought had been relegated to the forgotten past of our early years in the field, feelings that were now peaking and dipping in a roller coaster of tumultuous confusion. One minute we felt helpless and disconnected from the men, the next we were almost intoxicatingly identified with them. We confessed how much our confidence and emotional reserves were flagging, even as we reasoned that these feelings were partially a counter-transference mirroring of the men's feelings. We acknowledged feeling intense anxiety and dread that would unexpectedly alternate with equally intense feelings of relief and a paradoxically gratifying but grounded sadness. We expressed all these things then voiced questions we'd each been asking ourselves and having to bear alone. Like – How long will I be able to do this? Will I ever feel sure of myself in this work?

I listened to the experiences other women clinicians were having. Some were finding that the men were more open because they were a woman, while in other firehouses the men were clearly antagonistic to the presence of a woman and defensively protective of their all male culture. One thing was common to all the firehouses. The firemen were consciously and unconsciously reacting to the personal vulnerabilities of their counsellor. In some cases it seemed like they were deliberately pushing the buttons of their therapist as a way to deflect attention from their own problems, literally transferring their own anger and frustration onto the therapist and into the therapeutic situation. This displacement of feelings is a common form of transference. And each of my fellow clinicians was having his her own counter-transference issue to work through. We laughed a lot, cried a little, and reminded ourselves and each other that personal growth comes with personal upheaval, as the saying goes, 'no pain no gain'.

In our discombobulated state, we firehouse clinicians sometimes couldn't resist the temptation of defensively falling back on psychological platitudes and the familiarity of diagnostic labels to explain what was going on with the men, ourselves, and the therapy. Psychoanalytic interpretations became our life rafts. The labels I heard floating around ran the gamut from 'unresolved grief' to 'oedipal disappointment', but mostly we relied on the au courant terms of 'Trauma' and 'PTSD'. We did this even as we talked about the negative impact of labeling, especially for the firemen. A massive public health campaign following the disaster was changing the country's attitudes about mental health, almost making trauma seem like it was an expression of patriotic involvement in the country's historic tragedy, but for first responders 'trauma' and 'mental illness' still signified illness, lack of competency, professional failure.

As psychologists we were susceptible to doing what the people around us were doing, attributing the various physical symptoms the men were complaining about to psychological sources. The fact that trauma, anxiety and depression manifest in physical symptoms – headaches, fatigue, gastro-intestinal, respiratory problems to name but a few – made it all that more difficult to make accurate assessments of what was going on. Though the lingering corrosive odour in the vicinity of Ground Zero raised flags about the air quality, in our collective need to deny the grim possibility of what might lay ahead, people bought into the official position of the Environmental Protective Agency – the air was safe. Eventually the damage to health from exposure to Ground Zero would be indisputable as more and more workers and local residents began to show signs of long term health problems. They were primarily appearing in chronic respiratory conditions, gastro-intestinal problems and blood diseases, mostly manageable. But as time wore on, some individuals developed cancer and other terminal illness. At this point in time, none of us really spoke about the risks to physical health. Unconsciously we were probably thinking it wouldn't do any good worrying about getting sick. The damage was done.

In the sometimes crushing atmosphere of the post-disaster firehouse world we therapists defensively clung to psychological diagnoses and interpretations,, much as the world outside was holding onto the idea of the hero and our collective trauma. In our peer support group we kept promising to do better, to help each other find ways to stay emotionally engaged without falling into clinical labels or cultural stereotypes in relation to the firemen. Grabbing onto theory was our way of finding our footing in unfamiliar territory. It was also a way to combat the feelings that the disaster brought up for us. We were searching for answers to unanswerable questions about the healing of trauma, massive grief, and the existential questions that unexpected death of any sort, and mass murder especially, raise about human nature and life. I was aware of this and yet I watched myself periodically fall into the comfort of theory alongside them. It didn't feel right, and worse yet, it made me realize I had no one to turn to but the men themselves.

* * *

There was a certain solace I found in seeing the men sitting around the kitchen table with their typical affectation of masculine nonchalance or patiently occupied with making coffee, polishing the equipment, sweeping, and other firehouse tasks while they were waiting for me. For hours, days, months they'd gone to memorials, funerals. Sitting with these men as they waited for remains to be recovered, for much needed department wide changes in policy and procedures, for the lung disease to take hold, for the promised new equipment, for the chance to retire, I became aware of my own struggle with forbearance. As we sat together waiting for the bell to rescue us from ourselves, their fortitude helped me discover a storehouse of patience I didn't know I had.

My father did wait for me. He waited for the four or five hours it took to drive one hundred miles over a two-lane highway from Key West back up the coast to my parents whom I had left safe and sound less than forty-eight hours earlier. My father waited for his son to get a flight from Boston that had a stopover in Philadelphia but got him to Florida before it was too late. With my husband, mother and brother by my side, I sat with my father and waited for him to die in the intensive care unit of the local hospital. The machine life of the cardiac care unit was abuzz with the pulse of others in wait. Nurses waiting for the relief shift, families waiting for the moment or the miracle, patients at death's door waiting for what we cannot know. Surrounded by flashing signals and numbers, IV lines, and heart monitors, my father lay panting. He had no last words, no last look into my eyes, no final squeezing of my hand in response to my stroking his face, smoothing his brow, and holding his hand in just the way he had wordlessly, seamlessly, shown me throughout my life. No one knew what to do, how to decide. It was just the kind of thing we had always depended on him for. We just waited. Could he hear me? When would be the right time to give the okay? For it was only a matter of giving the cardiac ICU nurse the nod. She had the routine down pat. There was no bell that tolled at the moment. Only one long digital monotone bleep.

Before 9/11 I believed in that much tossed around term 'denial'. Within the first hour of being at St Vincent's, that term, along with other psychologically and psychoanalytically facile concepts, went out the window. These families who trailed into the hospitals for hours then days looking for their 'missing', those firefighters raking and fisting through the ruins, at first desperately, then methodically, carefully, never giving up, were not 'denying reality' or 'refusing to accept death'. Those people who would not and could not, say 'My loved one is dead' did so out of a loyalty based in primal attachment body to body. A hat, a shoe as evidence of being alive or dead sometimes will not do. Treating technology as the new god of life and death, we rely on sonograms, heart and brain monitors, DNA to affirm life, pronounce death, identify parenthood, solve crimes.

The remains of two of the lost men from the firehouse had still not been positively identified. They guys 'knew' they weren't coming back but they differed among themselves about when to begin the task of commemorating their death and knew the final decision was up the families. I'd spent much of my life trying to make sense of life and death. My father couldn't wait any longer for me to figure it all out. I had to call the moment and pray I did the right thing. When do you let go of hope that there's a chance for the missing to return or for the 'dead' to come back to life? No one has the corner on truth – when life begins and when it ends.

We love a person for their mind, heart and their soul but we come to know and embrace one another as embodied beings. While love lives on long beyond the corporal existence of our loved one, it forms, develops and is sustained through our physical existence. To proclaim a person as dead without a body can feel like a betrayal and abandonment of that person. The primal need to 'have a body' is more than 'closure' or 'acceptance', as our psychological gurus would tell us. These terms do little justice to the profound complexity of attachment. The men were needing to find a path that honours the dead yet makes way for the living. In firehouses, as in every family, people die, people come and go. And the life of the firehouse continues. Regardless of how anyone feels.

In this strange period of time, with life as we knew it taken from us, and the future full of uncertainty, we clung to the present. For me, this meant continuing the formality of ringing the bell to the unlocked door of the firehouse every time I went there. Having a bell to ring, a hand to hold bracketed the past and future with the present moment. Anything not to hear the absoluteness of the monotone sound or sight of the straight line on the heart monitor in my mind.

April

I thought the guys and I had a good thing going. The glow of positive transference and counter-transference was sustaining us through darkness. In a kind of Peter Pan fantasy they were ignoring evidence of my limitations that might take away from their faith in my healing powers and I was enjoying being the Wendy-like big sister who's taken the lost boys under my wing. But time and transference don't stand still. And of course every Peter Pan story has its version of a Captain Hook. Ours was in the form of Robbie, one of the oldest guys in the house, if not chronologically, psychologically.

Among the firefighters, Robbie Taylor, along with Bobby Walsh, William and Phil, had spent more than a dozen years in the firehouse. This meant Taylor knew the guys and the house policies and politics longer than the others. And that he had a history with each of the lost men that went further back than almost any of the others, which carried a lot of clout in the house. Until 9/11 Bobby Walsh had been the official house leader for many years. He was in charge of running things and led the house meetings. These meetings were held in private and restricted to men in the firefighter rank. In these monthly meetings decisions large and small of firehouse life were made and any conflicts among the men resolved without involving the officers. With Bobby Walsh gone that left Taylor, Phil and William as the naturals to take his position. William was preoccupied with his own problems. Phil liked leading in a more informal big brother way. That left Robbie Taylor, who was more than ready to fill this leadership role.

Taylor, like William, tended to avoided Group and when he did show up he typically hung by the kitchen door and didn't contribute to the discussion. I knew that as a key figure in the house I had to make a connection with him. Whenever I tried to engage him in a conversation, Taylor said he had something to do and quickly walked toward the staircase leading to the sleeping and officers quarters upstairs, which was off limits to visitors, and was the one part of the firehouse I had never seen.

One day as I was wrapping up a group meeting, I felt his razor sharp gaze on me from the doorway. I turned to see him leaning against the wall, hand on his chin with a wry half smile. I smiled at him. He turned away, refusing to look me in the eye. I walked up to him, assuming an attitude of no nonsense pragmatism and put out my hand, 'Glad to finally have a chance to meet you, I've heard so much about you.' He took my hand in his with an unyielding grip, and in that split second of eye contact we shared an unspoken mutual recognition of something yet to be fleshed out. Without a word Taylor released my hand, and walked out of the kitchen towards that frustratingly alluring second floor. It felt like I'd been playing by the rules of one game but he had switched to another game altogether.

Two weeks later I spied Taylor stealthily making his way toward the second floor. I went right up to him. 'Hey, Taylor, wait up, I need to ask you something.' With begrudging awkwardness, he muttered something I couldn't make out, then turned on his heels and nodded for me to follow him in the direction of the stairway. He took a seat at the landing halfway up, as though it was the obvious thing to do. I sat down a few steps below. I was avoiding presumptuous authority or intimacy by sitting above or too close. So a step below was where I found myself, and where I got stuck as time went on.

He got right to his point. 'Look, I'll tell you straight out, we don't need this here. I take care of the guys here, but if that's the way it is, well...these groups . . . They're not . . . I know the guys, I know what . . .' not completing a sentence. I smiled in an understanding way, trying to hide my rising frustration with his obstinate negativity and refusal to say what he was really thinking. We sat in silence for a moment or two.

'I'm trying to get this place in order.'

'You think it's disruptive,' I offered, hoping to gain his confidence that we're not adversaries, that I'm on his side in trying to do what's best for the guys. I kept thinking about the warning and advice we were given when we started the program, that we had to get the key man in the house on our side because all it would take was one man to ruin it for us. I persisted, 'I'm not committed to running groups. It was a way for the men to get to know me and me to get to know them. But I'm open to your suggestions. Tell me how I can help you and the men, who you think is in trouble, who I should I reach out to.'

'I'm going to tell you again, *I* know what my guys need', the 'I' cutting with the precision and force of a master knife thrower that leaves no evidence of its intent or impact. '*You* meet with me when you come and I'll tell you what's going on'. I was so relieved that he was willing to talk with me that I agreed to his presumptuous and bossy proposition.

Thus began our private 'meetings' on the stairway going upstairs. As soon as I arrived at the firehouse, before I could hang around with the guys downstairs, if Taylor was on duty I had to follow him to the stairwell as the guys hanging around watched in silence. Each time we sat there he talked about which men were out on sick leave, who was at counselling, who was taking time off, as if he was the expert on their mental status. A concept I had my doubts about but did not challenge.

I was growing more and more uncomfortable with this developing ritual. I began to question my having agreed to go into the stairwell in the first place. I'd thought that once I got Taylor's confidence, I'd be able to shift into a more open way of connecting. But it was feeling like Taylor had somehow managed to have taken control of the firehouse and my relationship with the men, and now with him! He was pushing hard against the boundaries of the therapy structure, the framework of our therapy on the run that had never been formally articulated but understood and fully accepted by the guys, in which the men gave each other a wide berth when one of them was talking privately with me, but we always remained in the public areas of the firehouse. The men knew my private office minutes away from the firehouse was available when needed. But Taylor was demanding I make private time with him a top priority during my visits. I wasn't sure how the men felt about this, especially the odd tete-a-tete meetings in the stairwell.

The therapy structure, with its formal boundaries and defined roles may seem arbitrary or unnecessarily rigid, but it serves as a crucial safeguard against patient exploitation and a protective function for the therapist. In looking back, I should have known that once a certain line is crossed, things can and too often do go awry. But the firehouse program was no ordinary therapy situation, and these first months after September 11th were no ordinary times. If I had recognized how deep and disavowed Taylor's needs were, I might have done things differently. But hindsight is always twenty-twenty.

One day, as per our new ritual, Taylor was right by the watch entrance when I arrived. He gave me the nod; we walked silently toward the institutional concrete stairway, me several steps behind him. He took his seat on his spot at the landing, and I took mine, a few steps below. In an effort at an end run around Taylor's tendency to control the conversation and our relationship, I started things. 'It must be hard for you, having to take care of everybody, running the house meetings, dealing with all the different stuff that comes up now, trying to help the widows and their kids, all the people wanting to come and do stuff, the media hype. And you've got your own family too. What about you in all this?' Surprising us both, his cold grief and tough guy demeanour gave way and he haltingly replied, 'Between here and doing the tours down at the site (Ground Zero) I don't remember when I had a day off. My wife's real annoyed with me. She says I lose my temper with my kids.' I tried to normalize things for him. 'I know a lot of guys' families are having a hard time.' He barked 'Call me at home,' then abruptly stood up and turned to go upstairs, where I couldn't follow him. This gave me some hope he was warming up to me and that he might help get other men more involved with counselling. So I agreed and called him at home.

We talked once, twice. I gave him referrals for family members. I convinced him to take some time off. 'Call me,' he kept insisting, under the guise of keeping me in the loop of what was going on. I wasn't comfortable with this arrangement but I didn't feel I could say no, or even raise the issue of what he wanted from these calls. It wasn't the use of the phone for therapy that was feeling creepy; between session phone contact and phone sessions are an accepted part of standard practice these days. It was his controlling me, his challenging my authority, and artfully getting between me and the men. In these calls he rarely talked about problems in the firehouse. He refused my suggestion that he come to my office and he never really opened up in these phone calls.

But I could tell these calls were touching certain needs aside from his need for control. It felt like he just wanted to hear my voice, how much was for comfort he couldn't own up to, or how much was for sheer assertion of control I wasn't sure. But it was clear that he wanted to feel that I was there in some special way, a way that seemed more secretive than confidential, since it was obvious that he never mentioned our calls to anyone.

Taylor's possessiveness of me made me feel uneasy and concerned about slipping into an unwitting complicity with a longing he was keeping secret from the world and himself. Taylor was never willing to talk about his grief over losing so many of his brothers. But he did take the two week R & R medical leave offered as a post-disaster de-stressor as a number of men did in this period.

When he was out on leave, things seemed to relax around the firehouse. I told the men we weren't going to run the groups for a while. I went and hung out, to 'see how everybody's doing', and inevitably ended up in what you'd call a heart to heart, fireman style. Or we had informal group discussions that started out talking about things like skiing then sometimes turned serious. I felt like the guys and I had finally found our groove, and that I'd really become the house doctor as the program had been envisioned. Like an old fashioned family doctor who comes by for lunch and a chat, who was available and could be counted on when needed.

Then one day, a few weeks after Taylor returned to work, when I arrived at my scheduled time, both rigs were just coming back from a call. As the truck was backing into the garage I waved hello but none of the men waved back. I didn't think anything of it but then I noticed that after they disembarked from the rigs no one was talking to me. A few nodded hello, then dispersed to parts unknown. For a while I just stood there alone not quite able to figure out what was going on or what to do. I thought something might have gone wrong on the call. I went into the kitchen and began fixing myself some tea. I asked the guy preparing lunch what was going on. Trying to be matter-of-fact as well, he explained, 'Some of the guys don't like the groups, and Taylor, well, we had a house meeting last week, and he said . . . something about counselling, ah . . .' I told him we'd not been doing the groups. He went on, 'I don't know exactly, I just heard rumours, I wasn't working that day,' then apologetically but guardedly added, 'Sorry Doc, house rules, I can't say. Everything in house meetings – strictly confidential. Don't mind Taylor, that's just how he is. He loves this house.' I thought that was going to be the end of it.

But the next week I got the same bum's rush when I arrived; the rigs were in but the guys scattered as soon as they saw me. I approached one of the men who had been openly supportive of my presence in the house. He reiterated what I was told the week before, 'It's Taylor. He told the guys at change of tour, "I told Goren we don't want counselling here. Anybody who's got a problem with that better come talk to me." That's what he said Doc. And you know he's the senior man in the house now. Things have changed around here. You know that, Doc.'

Then I turned to the officer in charge. He was noncommittal, 'Honestly, Doc, I don't know what to say.' I knew that the officers depend on the leaders within the rank and file to handle personnel problems, intervening only when things get seriously out of hand. It was clear no one was about to directly challenge Robbie Taylor. Confused, frustrated and wounded I backed off. I didn't go to the house for several weeks.

I went to see one of the captains at the Counselling Services Unit. 'I know Taylor, he's a tough guy,' he told me. He was sympathetic. He reminded me how each firehouse, like every family, is unique with its own idiosyncratic personality and set of rules, spoken and unspoken, and that my house was one of those firehouses where the firemen themselves pretty much ran the show. He said he'd spoken to several officers and firefighters from my house. 'People seem to like you well enough,' he reassured me. He then went on to say that he'd heard there'd been conflict brewing in the firehouse before 9/11, battles for control not uncommon to firehouse life, and that these had apparently escalated since. This was an indirect reference I thought to tensions surrounding the aggressive way Taylor was trying to replace Bobby Walsh, who had been the undisputed leader of the men in the firefighter ranks. Apparently I and 'counselling' had become the battleground for this internecine warfare, and an easy target for misplaced anger and grief.

'Do you want to be reassigned to another firehouse?'

'No.'

We agreed that I should give it another few months. Upset but unwilling to give up, as I rose to leave, I asked, 'Any suggestions or thoughts you care to impart?'

'Good Luck.'

I did not tell the captain at the Counselling Unit what had happened the last time I had a private talk in the stairway with Robbie Taylor, that this tightly-wound man had suddenly broken down sobbing, his body shaking, his trembling hands attempting to cover his face in shame. I did not tell him that once Taylor let go of his brittle armour, we both abandoned the chess game we'd been playing, which allowed me to finally be his therapist. I moved up a step and put my arm on his shoulder. This guarded man with an imposing build and manner then crumpled onto me. We sat that way for a while, not talking. I patted him gently as he shook with dry, soundless tears, his head on my shoulder.

No one wanted to rock the boat. Shutting me out became the focus of the longing to restore life as it was before September 11th, and the chance to exercise some form of control over their environment, however minimal it was in relation to what they had undergone and were still feeling about their situation. My presence was a symbol of a psychological conflict that was forming between those clinging to the pre-9/11 'Keep It In The House' firehouse tradition and those who believed we're living in the 'New Normal', that things had irrevocably changed and that they were going to have to change with the changing times. All brought to a head by senior FF Robbie Taylor.

The battle between those who wanted counselling in the firehouse and those who wanted it out was being waged in polite silence. I continued my weekly visits until one day when I called to say I was on my way and was told, 'Today's not a good day.' Days later I was given the okay, but with little enthusiasm. When I managed to push my way in, the guys were pleasant but diffident. A few said things like 'Guys aren't really going to talk about anything serious here at the house, around each other.' There were exceptions, officers like Lt. Darby and Sal, and guys like Phil, Pauli and Sean, who had been the most open to counselling all along. They made a point of expressing their appreciation for my presence and efforts to help, but clearly felt they had to maintain allegiance to Taylor and whoever in his crew wanted me out.

It got to the point that when they knew it was my time to be in the firehouse they weren't even there. The man on watch had the unfortunate task of having to come up with some vague excuse as to why they had mysteriously disappeared at the very same time as they expected me there. Some days I waited for them to return, other days I just left, depending on my mood, which is to say just how much of a glutton for punishment or optimistically resilient I felt on that particular day.

I can't remember how long I continued in this way. Probably it was only a matter of weeks but it felt like an eternity. Eventually I came to the conclusion that I had made a grave error in my therapeutic intervention with Robbie Taylor, one that might prove fatal for my work in the firehouse.

* * *

I was learning my lesson the hard way about the fine art of taking the analytic couch into the streets of New York City. I knew I was down, and I wasn't sure if I had it in me to get back in the game or how to do it. Suffice to say I was angry and hurt, but mostly I felt like I was momentarily one down in an ongoing fight. I told people that I wasn't giving up, that I just needed a break, but I really didn't have a plan. I retreated to the practised comfort of my 18 x 20 foot office twenty-three storeys in the air, and soothed my wounded pride by focusing on my patients and the few firemen who had begun therapy with me. One of them, Jack Smith was from another firehouse that had also lost a lot of men, and was still acutely traumatized by having escaped the collapsing towers by the skin of his teeth. Despite evidence to the contrary, constantly forgetting or confusing the day or time of our sessions (even when he'd put the appointment card on the visor of his car window or I'd call to remind him) Smitty was taking to therapy like a hand to a glove. He was frequently canceling at the last moment because he was kept overtime or had to do an extra tour of duty or had to take his kid somewhere or just plain forgot, but then came in a few days later. I understood this as trauma based instability. Smitty explained it as 'This is why I need help.' Despite the fact that Smitty was constantly asking for make up sessions and extra time between sessions, which I gave him, flying in the face of general principles of proper therapeutic technique – despite all these therapeutic glitches and abnormalities – Smitty was, as far as I was concerned, a model patient.

Though not yet able to reflect or articulate what was going on for him, he eagerly responded with 'Yeah, yeah I guess that's right' to the way I put into words the strange thing called traumatic stress reaction that had overtaken him. Unlike some of his fellow firefighters, Smitty's self-esteem appeared untouched by letting others help him. He made no bones about it, he was depending on me to function as a personal storage facility for his shaky memory, to help him remember what he needed to, and to remember for him those things he had to block out. Smitty depended on me to guide him in every aspect of his life, on every decision he had to make, from the most mundane to the most crucial, like what he should tell his daughter's teacher, or whether he should break up with his girlfriend. He relied on me to be there for him as he struggled with the pain of leaving behind the person he'd been married to for fifteen years. And with the existential burden of his apparent destiny to be a survivor. Because, as Smitty put it,

'September 11th wasn't the first time, Doc. There was that other time on the job, but I'll tell you about that some other time. And then there was the time I got into a thing with a guy who tried to cut me off. I can't remember who threw the first punch, but the next thing I remember is some lady a couple of inches from my face with a mask on, you know like the kind in a hospital or emergency room, telling me 'You know Mr. Smith, you're lucky, you almost died from that stab wound.' Everything about Smitty, as for most firemen, was about being able to deal with death and danger. It took a long time for him, like for so many of the other men, to accept the idea that it wasn't weakness of character but the extremity of the conditions at the Trade Center and the sheer numbers of people lost, that took him down. He kept saying that he had gotten out physically unscathed. It was hard for him to believe that his complaints – the flashbacks, mental confusion and memory problems – were from his exposure to trauma.

Old fashioned individual therapy in the intimate safety of my office twenty-three storeys above the fray – this I knew like the back of my hand. Working so closely with Smitty and other firemen who came for individual therapy helped me gain some perspective on how hurt and confused the guys from my firehouse were, and why they hadn't been able to come to my defence with Taylor. It was good for me to have some relief from the pressure of being the firehouse therapist.

By this point Lt. Darby had become a regular of sorts, wandering into my office for periodic 'check ups'. Neither of us brought up what was going on in the firehouse. He was there to address his own personal issues. He had a pattern of making an appointment, cancelling it, then making it in a few weeks later and focusing on issues of concern with his family and friends, like when it seemed to him that people were acting like they'd forgotten about what happened or problems other guys were having that he didn't know how to handle as their officer. Often beginning with a series of shaggy dog stories he always settled down, eventually getting to himself. The only way he could describe what he was going through was to say 'I just don't feel like myself.' This was often followed by a thinly-camouflaged anxious query, 'Is that normal, is that the normal post trauma stuff you been talking about?' I reassured him that *he* wasn't crazy. I said what I truly believe, that *what happened* was crazy, and that when the world goes crazy it's normal to feel crazy. That trauma, what he was experiencing, was a normal reaction to an abnormal event and situation. To which he typically quipped, 'So why do they keep calling it *post*? When will it ever be post?'

Darby almost always made sure to express concern for me with what became his stock line, 'Enough of me. Hey, Doc, how are you doing with all this?' He'd look up from under his baseball-capped visor as he sat with arms crossed and interrupt our discussion and ask, 'You taking care of yourself, Doc?' While I understood this to reflect his discomfort about being 'a patient' and 'in therapy' it was also clear that he was genuinely concerned about me and didn't want to burden me with his problems. For Darby's sense of self and manhood was so much about being protective of women and the rescuer of anyone in need. He'd confess, 'This feels like an indulgence. Not that I don't want to come. I really like coming, but the kids and the wife, and the men. You know how it is.'

There's a delicate tango of giving and receiving between a female therapist and male patient that's rarely acknowledged and is often best left unanalyzed. It entails the subtle ways a man affirms and cares for a woman, and a woman for a man, while maintaining appropriate conduct for their respective roles. I was partaking of the powerful physicality and protectiveness of these men, while they were taking in my comforting reassurance while playfully treating me like a mother or older sister who looks out for them. For a middle-aged woman therapist whose sexuality is wrapped up in a maternal professional expertise, the older woman younger man scenario allows for a muted sexual interplay through which once-threatening oedipal desires can be enjoyed by both with impunity. The younger male feels taken care of and appreciated for his youthful sexual prowess, while the older woman is appreciated for the sexual comfort and knowledge that comes with her age. All this can be comfortably enjoyed when there's absolute trust and assurance of never acting upon any of these feelings. I never talked about these dynamics with the men. Some things, particularly in the matters between men and women, are better left alone, unspoken, untouched, and untarnished.

* * *

Between my weekly sessions with Smitty and other firemen, the comings and goings of Darby, my other patients, including former patients with a trauma history who had returned to therapy as a result of the disaster, September 11th was with me every day. Everyone in my practice needed to talk about how 9/11 reverberated with their own lives. For some the crisis brought a certain clarity about life, loosening the hold obsessive worries and conflicts had on them, enabling them to re-define priorities, and to engage life in a more positive way, with a more active sense of purpose, than before the disaster. It was a stressful but extraordinarily enriching time to be a psychotherapist. Nonetheless, I couldn't get the guys from the firehouse out of my mind.

One day I was returning from a run and suddenly took note of something I'd seen a hundred times but somehow not registered before, my Red Cross apron rolled up in a ball at the bottom of the hamper. Inside the pocket was the small scrap of paper I found on my way home from volunteering at Ground Zero in September. Unrolling the apron released the reeking odour of the site's poison, taking me in a flash right back there, seeing, smelling, hearing everything as it happened in a way I'd not thought about for some time. I looked at the paper in my hand. My tattered scrap was merely one of thousands of pieces of paper that rained down like confetti on the morning of September 11th in mockery of all the celebratory parades marched here from City Hall down through Wall Street over the city's history. Within a matter of days the paper that coated these streets, even blowing over to Brooklyn, was swept away, taking with it the sacred traces of human life contained in the toxic dust and ash.

Paper is a powerful imprint symbolizing so much of our cultural currency and values. Money, identity, proof of possession, a measure of a day's work, a statement of a person's worth – all printed on paper. The terrorists chose the World Trade Center as a symbol of the western way of life. To me that cascade of tattered paper was a call not for revenge or retribution as the war mongers proclaimed, but for us to stop and question how much our way of life revolves around commodity and consumption. Those fallen papers had been handed from one person to another, some of whom made it out alive. My one little piece of paper did not necessarily carry great import, but like each person involved with it, to me it was unique and an important part of the whole.

I turned that mysterious piece of paper over, studying it for clues as to its identity and history, and imagining that it might even have been a prayer card. I made it into my 9/11 talisman, an amulet that tied me to the dead and that I could look to for the strength to go on with this work. I briefly entertained the idea of saving the apron, then thought it best to not preserve this contaminated piece of history. I sealed it tightly in a Glad garbage bag and dropped it down the incinerator shoot. But the tiny piece of cardboard I kept as the remains of human life that I had been able to recover. I saw it as a relic of life before 9/11, representing our naïve grandiosity among other things, but I also believed it may have had religious origins and possessed spiritual potential. I put it in the pocket of my favourite old pair of jeans for safe keeping. I had endowed it with an irrational totemic power and used it the way Darby used his rabbit's foot, as a good luck charm for my returning to the firehouse, and to give me faith in myself and the men.

* * *

This time I made it all the way all the way up the stairs to the second floor of the firehouse. I was sitting on one side of a broad metal desk, across from tall, gaunt and chillingly stern Lt. Ross in the private officers quarters. On September 11th, Lt. Ross had been the officer in charge with the men who barely made it out of the tower lobby alive. I anxiously fidgeted with the stuffing that was poking through holes in the broad arms of the thick cushioned leather chair from the fifties while he sat with calm cool demeanour, waiting for me to explain why I had asked for this meeting. The room was darkened by blackout shades and outfitted in grey green military. What was I thinking to have asked for a meeting with another weird uptight guy? With Robbie Taylor on his campaign to keep me out of the house, I needed an officer as an ally. I had to win him over, but wasn't sure he was going to give me a chance.

'So what do you think, Doc? How are the guys doin?' A deft opening salvo, giving him an impressive but annoying advantage. I could feel myself shrinking further down into the seat. My mind began racing and I glanced around me, noticing the cot against the wall, with its tightly tucked in hospital corners and army blanket. What the hell was I doing here? I don't belong with these para-military types. I'm an anti-authoritarian, anti-establishment leftover from the sixties. He's polite but I can tell he thinks I'm just one more softie liberal, some rich New York do-gooder with fancy shrink ideas, and Jewish to boot!

Doing my best to ignore my own rising anxiety and the specious tone of his question, I retorted, 'That's what I was planning to ask you,' and hoped he wouldn't detect my own ingenuousness. We covertly agreed to politely ignore the other's transparent falseness.

Just then Ross jumped up and came around to my side of the desk and asked me to get up. I complied with some trepidation. He then moved the dried out leather chair in a gentlemanly fashion so that it directly faced him, then suavely scooted back around the desk and sat back down. The unadorned room, which a minute ago felt bleak and vaguely threatening was now feeling impressive in its simplicity. I smiled in deference to his gesture of masculine gentility. Then without meeting eye to eye, from our respective seats, we danced together in a confusing mixture of distrust and recognition of each other as man and woman from different worlds sensing we shared something beyond our blatant differences.

Ross told me then what he honestly thought. 'I think the guys are OK, frankly. Don't cha think guys are taking advantage? I think it's a lot of hullabaloo, if you ask me, this taking time off.

Ya just deal with it.' Since the guys had intimated that Ross never talked about the events of the 11th, I wasn't surprised by his insistent stoicism. Though his pain came through in his flattened voice, stooped shoulders and the dull look on his face. As far as Ross was concerned, only physical problems with known physical causes were real. From his point of view, there hadn't been very many serious physical injuries sustained on 9/11. With a few horrific exceptions, those on the scene that day were either dead or alive. The idea that there might be serious health consequences for survivors was still only a matter of speculation. Without established medical causes to validate the men's complaints, Ross was doggedly refusing to grant legitimacy to any psychological post-traumatic stress reactions.

I took his tendency to minimize the men's trauma and to flatly deny his own as his own way of coping as a survivor. He went on, 'But Doc, really, if you think they need it, the time off, and the counselling and all this stuff, tell me. Heck, what do I know?' in what I came to recognize as his characteristic self-effacing scepticism. Unlike Lt. Darby or Sal, Ross rarely fraternized with the guys. He was the kind of officer who maintained the distance of the crusty older authority, but he clearly wanted to do the right thing for the men. I knew that I needed to tread lightly so as to not disturb the stability he maintained through denial and a certain emotional distance. I was about to say something about the different degrees of post-traumatic stress reactions when he raised his slumping body up from the chair, leaned towards me and looking me straight in the eye and asked 'You got kids?' Something had allowed Ross to let go of his self-imposed aloneness and take what for him must have been a huge leap to try to connect with me.

That's how it started. I told him about my kids, which high schools, colleges they'd attended. He said he had two boys; I told him I had two girls. We laughed, cautiously, trying to cover our amazement at discovering the similarities neither of us expected. Our kids had gone to the top public high schools in the city. His older son was just accepted into Harvard; my older daughter was just about to graduate from that same venerable institution. I was surprised to learn how well read and thoughtful he was. He was surprised to learn that I had grown up in working class Boston. Neither of us acted like our surprise was apparent to the other. We spoke of our children's achievements with humility, both of us secretly thrilled as only a parent can be at being surpassed by one's progeny.

'My older son's a good kid. My younger son too, but my wife and I don't agree here. She spoils him. He stays in his room all the time, I don't know what he does in there all the time, just playing music real loud.' When I said something about his son reacting to 9/11 Ross stiffened, 'My son, he's angry all the time, but I don't think it has anything to do with this.' Then I asked where his older son was on September 11th. This led Ross to once again jump out of his seat, this time going into his locker and taking out a folded 8 x 11 piece of paper. Unfolding it slowly, his long fingers pointed to the writing. I asked him to read it.

'"Dear Dad, Just want to tell you I know I don't act it, but I'm proud of you and proud to be the son a fireman. Love, Jim".' His voice quivered ever so slightly. He looked like he was about to say something, then thought better of it. Then in his methodical manner, Ross silently refolded the note, carefully placed it on the shelf above his civilian jacket and pair of shoes, and closed the locker.

My relationship with Ross, like that I formed with a few of the other firemen I became close with, was based on the elemental sense of instinctively knowing what makes each other tick, cementing a bond which rendered insignificance to our superficial differences. Ross's hair was kept as tightly cropped as mine flopped about in curly disobedience. He acted like the introvert, and I the extrovert, but we both had the carriage of sexual aliveness of those past their prime which allows for an unthreatening freedom of expression. But our link was more than the old story of the irrepressible person being drawn to someone seemingly more 'in control' and the inhibited person being drawn to someone who seems less repressed.

Both of us had come of age in the sixties. In those years I believed myself to be a subversive, rejecting anything patently establishment like the military, and gravitated to the intellectual world of academia. Ross, on the other hand, had rejected the anti-establishment liberalism of those 'soft' sixties types who avoided the draft. He served in Vietnam, only later going to college. Though he had the 'blue collar' job and I the 'white collar' profession, I estimated that between his job in the FDNY and his sideline construction business Ross was making as much if not more money than I was. He had the benefits and restrictions of working in a civil service organization while I had the freedom and insecurity of self-employment. Both of us knew that life could have easily turned out diffcrently. I might have ended up teaching in a high school like his wife and he might have been a manager in a corporation like my husband.

Several weeks later I was sitting alone in the 'kitchen' watching the television. A few guys had walked in, said hello, then quickly slipped away. I felt like a kid being ignored by everybody in the school yard and wasn't sure how much longer I could stay there with the tepid reception I was getting. Just then Lieutenant Ross made a rare appearance and sat down right beside me. The two of us sat looking towards the ever-on blaring TV. The local newsman first reported on a child's death by a stray bullet, then on a twenty year old 'nice young man' according to neighbours interviewed, who had murdered his parents while they were sleeping. When the Lieutenant shook his head and remarked in his unflappable fashion, 'Life's hard,' I heard myself blurt out in mock comedic shtick, 'Tell me about it.' I couldn't believe that I had momentarily forsaken my professional demeanour to say something so silly.

Ross's only reaction was to embark on a scornful refrain, 'Everybody's a victim.' Ross clearly had zero tolerance for society turning life's tragedies into pop culture fodder. We shared our smoldering sense of alienation from the disaster turned Trauma Tourism cropping up all over the city, especially the commercialization of Ground Zero. He started going on about how revolting it was how many people were 'claiming' to have been traumatized, 'as if they were really there in the towers.' His quiet rant bore not even the slightest hint that he was one of those people who were 'really' in those towers and who managed to escape. I knew not to bring this up with him, and shifted the conversation by asking him what he thinks enables a firefighter to be able to go into burning buildings that people instinctively want to escape. Smiling, he answered, 'the pension'.

And then, despite my worries over losing credibility with this man and the rest of the men by exposing my flawed self in all its neurotic glory, I proceeded to catalogue for him my various woes – as wife, mother, and therapist. He had caught me at a moment when I was just about ready to call it quits. What did I have to lose at this point? With the guys and my personal life in its own post 9/11 turmoil, my runner's spirit and knack for creative intervention was flagging.

I wish I could say that my openness was a preconceived strategy to model how to be an authority figure without having to pretend to be the rock of Gibraltar. But that wasn't how it was. My seeming professional abandon was more like, once I'd admitted to being real, there was no going back. There was only thinking about why I was there, to help the men in their pain.

After that day in the kitchen with Lieutenant Ross, things changed between us, and between me and the other men. I stopped trying to be The Psychologist. I started making my visits on days I knew Taylor wasn't on duty. I resumed my routine. First I sat down in house watch and tried to get something going there. Next I made my way back toward the kitchen area, sat down and if I couldn't get anyone to strike up a conversation with me, I picked up a newspaper and casually leafed through it until a guy came in, and then tried to engage him. While the more reticent and suspicious guys were happy to have an excuse to still avoid me, most of the guys were simply ill at ease and didn't know how to handle the situation. Some guys acted like nothing had happened, and resumed their welcoming friendliness. I wondered whether they had even heard the news about Taylor trying to banish me from the house. But knowing how news spreads around the firehouse, I doubted that this was the case. Ross befriending me in front of his men turned out to be the crucial support I needed to wear down the strain that had developed between me and the guys. No one brought up the subject of Group or Taylor and his pronouncements about not needing counselling in the house.

We resumed talking about the weather, the apparatus, the runs they'd gone on, food and families. And what felt most strange to me but in my gut felt like the right thing to do, talking a little bit about myself – the ultimate sin for a psychoanalyst. I wish I could say clinical theory had led me in this direction. But my actions at the time, like many in life, were partly driven out of desperation. We were trapped in a stalemate. If something didn't happen I would have been marginalized to irrelevance or forced out of the firehouse, as was the fate of a number of other clinicians in their firehouses.

Modern psychoanalysis considers the notion of the ideal therapist as the silent all knowing doctor an outdated model based on debunked images of male authority. Nonetheless, analysts today still believe that when it comes to the matter of a therapist disclosing personal information, discretion is the better part of valor. In other words, less is more, and in the overriding importance of the therapist making every effort to not impose her own issues and needs on the therapy.

But there comes a time in certain therapeutic situations when getting real is the only way to break through an impasse. I wasn't sure it would work and thought it might even backfire and further alienate the men from me. But I also knew that many of the men were straight up sorts who respected honesty and directness, and hoped they might appreciate that I was prepared to practice what I preach. If I was asking them to be open and real about their lives and struggles, then I should be prepared to do the same.

So once I'd opened the door to my personal life with Ross without losing credibility as a therapist, there was no stopping me with the rest of the men. When a man asked how I was doing,

I told him – things like my mother's sick, my kids are OK. Life's fine, life sucks. And they started telling things like the wife and I are having some trouble. My mother's sick too. My kid's got a problem. How am I going to afford the mortgage? What we saw down there, Doc, it's nothing you can imagine. My response: I know, I was there.

The men started talking more freely to me again. They had decided, most likely without consciously thinking it through, that being asked to take Robbie Taylor's side at their own expense wasn't fair. They started inviting me to lunch again. 'Gonna eat with us today, Doc?' 'I didn't put any money in the kitty.' 'Don't worry, Doc, there's always enough.' 'Sure. Why not?' 'You're little, you don't eat much!' 'Yeah you know I'm a vegetarian, so I won't touch all that meat you guys eat.' We were back on track.

* * *

I spread the word around that instead of Group, I wanted to meet privately 'just once' with each of the men, hoping this might be a way to reach the men who were most in trouble but hadn't talked to me. The guys jumped at the opportunity to turn the study room into an office, joking that they were going to hang up a sign outside the door, 'The Doctor is In'. Located just to the side of the trucks and equipment, centrally located between the front area open to the public and the rear kitchen area, this tiny windowless room did double duty as a storage area and as the only place in the firehouse where a man could be alone. Where a closed door meant no one would open it, at least before knocking. A refrigerator, cases of beverages, mounting boxes of donations and two chairs took up what little space there was next to a linoleum desktop shelf. 'Our hero' thank you notes and pictures from schoolchildren were pinned to the shelves on the few free spots on the wall. A computer, instructional books and manuals, stray Playboy and firefighting magazines, and the latest information packet from the Counselling Service Unit lay on the desk. In the dimly lit tight quarters of this study room the men told me their stories. Stories like the one Mouse told me.

We had started out with the safest subject, kids, and how tough it was for them to cope with what had happened. He told me his son had given him a book Chicken Soup for the American Soul, saying 'I guess he thinks about it.' And then this short skinny man who wears his nickname with aplomb began the guys' now familiar refrain 'It's just not the same any more.' To which I responded with my now familiar response, some bland reassurance to him and myself that he is not alone, and that I can help. To my surprise, Mouse suddenly became agitated. Standing up he said 'They're leaving in droves,' as he went over to the stack of books on the shelf and pulled out a large black ledger. He opened it on the desk, then ran his finger up and down page after page, showing me the long list of the men who have already retired since September 11th and those about to retire. He pushed it toward me and asked rhetorically, 'Who's going to be left when the dust settles?' Triumphant in defeat, he put the ledger down, and with a sarcasm I'd never heard from him before he said, 'They don't care. They just don't want law suits.' Darkness came over his face. 'You know, I've seen things . . .

'One time I went in and found a civilian, his arms were like this.' He demonstrated, contorting his arms to show someone clawing his way in smoke choking darkness. He paused. 'But nothing like this. I wasn't prepared for this.' He began talking about what he witnessed on the plaza of the Trade Center that morning. Steeling myself to absorb what he clearly needed to get out, I just tried to maintain eye contact. Mouse went on, 'One lady, a beam went straight through the body, but it's funny . . .' That word stopped him. I understood that his saying 'funny' was a way of taking some distance and giving us a brief respite from the unbearable horror of what he'd just said, and what I then realized he had to say next, '. . . the way her arms were reaching straight out. The thing was, her arms were outstretched perfect. Perfect red polish on her finger nails, not a scratch, just perfect. That's how I knew it was a woman.'

My mind was fighting to take in the gruesome images tumbling out of his mouth. Was it the horror or the desire to remember that was blocking my mind? He was needing to voice the things in his head in order to dislodge them from the hold they had taken on his brain and to make sense of it all. Was I so concerned about my function as a therapeutic listener that it was interfering with my being able to stay present and listen? Between the momentary madness in his eyes, my dread and compulsion to block out what he would say next, I felt myself pulling back to the point where I felt like I was an outside observer trying to record what was happening. But once Mouse had gotten this out, his tension was visibly lessened. Still holding me in the grip of his desperate need to maintain eye contact, he continued in the face of my misgivings.

It took all my mental strength to register the words coming out of Mouse's mouth and to stay emotionally connected with myself and Mouse. The gruesomeness of the images was enough in itself to make anyone recoil. The wild confused look on the face of this normally mild mannered man told me that he was as unprepared as I was for the torturous memories spilling out. Neither of us had anticipated that the safety of the tiny private office and the invitation to talk would release the floodgates of all the tragedy and trauma he had been so intimately involved in. It was crucial at this moment for me to make sure Mouse did not become re-traumatized in telling his story. For this I had to absorb, take some of his pain and memory into myself, but not to the point of becoming vicariously traumatized and losing my own grounding, which would have not have helped either of us. At the time I felt guilty, as though I had let Mouse down. After the fact I realized that my moving outside myself was a reflexive protective measure to gain some emotional distance to prevent both of us from going too far. Then I managed to calm myself down. Mouse sensed this, and with his own instinctive mechanisms to protect himself and others, he took a breath, and finally sat back down. He left re-living and re-playing the other horrors he saw for another time, and wrapped up things by telling me the rest of the story in the more packaged way I'm sure he had told it many times before.

'We kept looking, we had to look for our guys. Even the guys like Sean and William who were part of the group that made it out, they didn't want to go home till they found the others. But then Thursday night (9/13/01) the commander down there saw my face I guess and said, 'Go home'. It was then I knew. All seven of our missing guys were dead. They'd already recovered the bodies of the guys from the engine, with the rig . . . buried. It was me that found Thomasini. Later.'

Every trauma therapist knows that in telling one's story there's a fine line between catharsis and re-vivifying the trauma itself. Which is one reason why survivors are often so reluctant to talk about their traumatic experience. While the survivor struggles to manage his emotional state in recalling and confronting what he went through, it's a delicate balancing act for the therapeutic listener struggling to manage her own feelings in receiving the trauma survivor's story. Neither Mouse nor I could handle more at that moment. Or more precisely without it becoming more like traumatic flashbacks than therapeutic recovery of disturbing memories. We had to trust in the natural process of healing, and have faith that the human need to transform trauma into meaningful memory would continue at its own pace.

* * *

The war in Afghanistan was flagging and no longer serving to re-inflate the battered ego and shaken psyche of America. No longer consumed with grief, people were feeling a generalized anxiety that they were channeling into xenophobia and narcissistic paranoia. Communities around the country, regardless of their geographic location, size or strategic importance, were preparing themselves to be the next target of attack. With xenophobic panic and misplaced patriotic zeal, some questioned whether their Muslim and Arab neighbours were terrorists or terrorist supporters. Counter-terrorism operations and war games gave people something to do, and provided a concrete place to put all their feelings.

Here in New York, things were changing as well. Spring was finally lifting our spirits. I felt the frozen ground softening beneath my feet as I ran, and didn't mind when I tracked mud into the house from my running shoes. Despite our well heeled grittiness and cynical stubbornness, despite ourselves, we New Yorkers were ready to move on. Even the firemen, trying to be resistant to spring's seduction, almost despite themselves, were changing.

* * *

One day as I was heading back to the kitchen to set out a bunch of copies of articles on post 9/11 health problems, I nearly bumped into one of the younger firefighters. Like other younger guys, especially those relatively new to this firehouse, Pauli had diligently attended all group meetings. But knowing he was low on the totem pole, he tended to be deferential and was usually too intimidated to talk in Group. Pauli must have popped out from behind the engine to seize the chance to talk with me. With a self-conscious effort at nonchalance that I recognized in my self around the firehouse, Pauli blurted out, 'Hey, Doc, do you have a minute?'

I checked to make sure no one was near us, then set my pile of papers down on the ground and put my foot up on the bumper as though I was setting to hang out. I tried to make him comfortable by mirroring his casual demeanour. I asked how his baby was doing. Pauli smiled from ear to ear and then proudly announced that he was expecting another baby. He pulled out a photograph of the latest sonogram, and grinning from ear to ear he announced 'This one's a girl!' Due so close to September 11th. Neither of us mentioned the significance of the due date, though I was sure it wasn't lost on Pauli, for whom this next child was to be an unspoken commemoration of 9/11.

Crossing his arms across his broad chest, shifting his stance from one foot to another, Pauli then asked with a worried look, 'Doc, I just got a quick question for you, I know you guys like dreams and stuff. What does it mean when you keep dreaming the same thing over and over, like you're at a fire, you're standing at the door, you know there's somebody inside and you're thinking, I don't want to go in?'

'It means, Pauli, that you're about to have a baby.'

Unsatisfied with my comment, he added, 'But this isn't my first. It's my job to go in. The civilians and the guys, everybody counts on it.' I tried to reassure him that dreams are our way of solving problems in our sleep. I also said it was normal to feel hesitant now about going into fires given what happened, and that it would go away over time. I did not add the rest of what I was thinking, 'assuming there's not another attack.' I suggested he take one of Counselling Unit's mental health pamphlets and read it at home. I tried to put him at ease, 'Don't worry, you'll do the right thing.' Even as I knew I had absolutely no idea exactly what 'the right thing' actually was. What would be the right thing for him, with another baby on the way, for me, for anybody, to do when the next catastrophe strikes?

Shortly after my conversation with Pauli another guy announced a pregnancy. And then another. Some of these '9/11 babies', as they were called, had been conceived purposefully, as an answer to the existential crisis wrought by the disaster, others were the accidental consequence of the terrified and grief stricken seeking comfort in each other's arms. Perhaps it was purely base animal instincts at work, the ethological pull to regenerate. Or imagination longing to magically fill the hole left in the wake of loss. Whatever was behind the increased birth rate in the year after 9/11, the anticipation of new life was improving the atmosphere in the firehouse.

The many ways grief finds expression can't be easily fit into clean cut 'stages' such as packaged by devotees of Kubler Ross or spoon fed us in self-help books. Neat theories of grief leading seamlessly from denial to anger, depression, resignation and finally acceptance, are fine as ideas. But grief and trauma, all significant human experience, refuse medical, psychological or even spiritual categorization. Loss leads with its own baffling peculiarity. In real life, for those who mourn, certain things repudiate meaning; certain things can never be forgotten, some things never forgiven. Even so, it was becoming clear that the rage and despair, the self-recrimination that had held sway over the men's psyches was starting to lose its hold. There was a glimpse of a future to live for, to work for, a reason to put themselves in harm's way for. Life and the sensation of aliveness was returning to the firehouse.

* * *

One afternoon the guys were preparing for one of the house's famous spaghetti and meat ball dinners. Phil was holding forth at the stove. I jumped up onto the metal table counter next to the spaghetti boxes and joined in the conversation as we waited for the water to boil. Anthony opened the frig and pulled out an institutional-size jar of peanut butter, which he spread thickly on a cracker he'd found by scrounging around the boxes of Entenmanns snacks piled by the window. 'Can't you wait?' Phil scolded, sounding more like a fuss budget older sister than a big brother. Anthony's only response was to shrug his shoulders like a kid as if to say 'I have no self control,' and to proceed to shovel another mouthful down. One of the other older guys wistfully chimed in, 'At your age I could eat like that too. No more.' In support of his buddy, Pauli, my man of many dreams, took some unidentifiable leftovers out of the refrigerator and offered me some. I joined in with the ribbing, 'No thanks, Pauli. Hey, Anthony I have to ask you. Do you consider this a snack or a pre-dinner meal?' To which he quipped, 'My fifteen meals a day.' The guacamole then came out, which naturally required opening a bag of taco chips. The talk moved on to diets, calories, exercise, each guy making determinations as to how many pounds another guy needed to lose. I piped in, 'I thought only women talk like this!'

Sal stepped into the middle of the circle, pulled the belt-less waist of his pants out Charlie Chaplin style and boasted, 'Look how much weight I've lost!' We nodded, impressed. Unable to contain himself, Lt. Sal confessed, 'Nah, these were from when I first came on the job nine years ago. I forgot my stuff today. I found 'em in my locker.' Irrepressible, he added, 'But I'm only five pounds heavier than I was then.' To which another guy retorted, 'Oh, that explains it,' laughing as he pointed to Sal's hairy legs exposed above the white uniform socks. The dapper dresser I imagined Sal to be was now playing the clown. Phil added, 'I thought you were too cool to wear them that short.'

Sal responded, 'Seriously, I got to lose weight. I got to get in shape. I'm getting married.' To which someone said, 'We'll believe it when we see it.' He went on, 'I gotta knock her up quick. I'm already too old.' To which I quipped, 'Are you kidding? How old are you?' He answered, 'Forty-eight.' I was shocked. The fact that Sal was as dangerously close in age to me blew the illusion I'd been enjoying of an innocuous flirtation between a mother and her grown son. But before I had time to fully register this news, they were on to the next topic, the reasoning behind marriage. The consensus they came to was 'Kids'.

The conversation then turned into a riff on the techniques and technology of reproduction. The younger single guys drifted away. Enjoying the chance to play with me and take centre stage again, Sal asked 'So Doc, do you think I can sue the city? I haven't been able to have sex since this whole thing.' Unprepared for the rapid-fire banter of the house, I took his question at face value and began to talk about the effect of medication on sexual functioning. Laughing, he quickly stopped me, 'I was just kidding!' sparing me from further exposure of my gullibility. All of a sudden Sal changed his tone and the tenor of the room by saying how he still 'gets that feeling' when the terror alert is raised, which makes him wonder if it'll ever go away. All I could manage on the spot was an ever-ready therapist cliché, 'It may never go away, but people do different things.' Unsatisfied with my psychobabble or wanting to protect me from further embarrassment, Sal returned us to the safer, favourite subject – sex, and its latest corollary topic, pregnancy and births. Sal said he was worried about his sperm count because of his age and stress. His buddies tried to help him out saying things like 'I heard you gotta do it every other day,' and 'No, it's as many times as you can, I think.' Sal explained, 'That's why I'm taking those horse pills.' Another guy shook his head, 'No, they got tests now you can take. They can even to tell you when to do it, like to have a boy or a girl.' Anthony advised Sal, 'You know what you should do, don't you?' To which Sal replied, 'Yeah, yeah, I know about the don't-wear-underwear.' Then Pauli brought in the big guns, 'I was told at Columbia where a lot of firemen have gone for that fertility stuff . . . it's the gear.' Then the idea of going out sick when 'trying' came up, followed by the suggestion that greying pubic hairs were a telltale sign of aging infertility. Then Mouse added that it's just 'silly superstition' to think masturbation lowers a guy's fertility, because, he pointed out, the amount of semen is not related to the amount of sperm. Finally one of the guys turned to me, and chimed in, 'Hey, Doc, I been telling my wife she's got to do it cause you said it's good to relieve stress. She doesn't believe me. I told her you're a sex therapist. She says she's gotta talk to you!'

* * *

I saw a group of guys hanging around the house watch. As the official place for vetting visitors, taking telephone calls, and receiving dispatches about the location and nature of the alarms, the cubby size semi-private room at the front of the apparatus floor was a natural place for the guys to talk shop and for casual talk to turn more serious.

They were into one of their pet gripes – the inadequate radio system. I noticed that Danny, the probie survivor, was among them.

Danny had been out on medical leave in my first months in the firehouse and so had not attended any of the group meetings. I knew that between his age, inexperience, and the circumstances that led to his survival on September 11th, Danny had added challenges to a strong post-trauma adjustment and recovery. He'd only graduated from the academy a few weeks before September 11th and in the confusion of that morning Danny ended up with the ladder instead of the engine company, but in the many odd twists of fate that day, he and the group he was with all survived while the probie he'd switched places with died along with the all the guys in the company he was supposed to have been with.

You could see the dark shadow that the spectre of his uncanny survival, and the feeling of 'it could have been' or 'it should have been' me cast on this young man's whole being. I could tell the guys were cutting him more slack than they gave the other probies, not giving him a hard time about the distance he kept since he returned to work. They didn't tease him about his not participating much in the social side of things. Even Taylor spared him the treatment he gave the other new guys. But shoptalk, especially an animated discussion of the radio system must have been too hard for him to resist.

This was a chance for me to informally connect with him. He was tentatively standing by the doorway, with a golf club in hand. The guys were complaining that the administration of the fire department wasn't doing enough to pressure the city to replace the failed radio system. I went to sit on the bench and saw what I can only describe as a gizmo, some kind of instrument in the category of 'tools', so near and dear to men's hearts and imaginations, and so beyond my female comprehension. With the graceless hand of the mechanically unimaginative I picked up this black box with a set of dials and a wrapping of several layers of grey duct tape. Holding the Rube Goldberg device at arm's length, I asked with a tool novice's incredulity, 'What *is* this?!'

Anthony grabbed it out of my hand, pointed it out into the garage area, and then began a detailed demonstration of what I surmised was some type of smoke detector that Phil had retrofitted with duct tape to make it completely fireproof. Someone talked about how they'd just used the detector last week on Canal Street. The guys then went on relaying various details of this and other runs, assuming that I understood what they told me. Having a limited capacity to digest such technical matters, I nodded in appreciation of their inventiveness and professionalism.

Just then Lt. Darby sauntered in and squeezed in beside me on the bench. The shoptalk went on to the flood in a high rise apartment building earlier that week. I could feel the mood shifting. One guy started pacing in place. The man on watch pivoted his chair around to focus on Danny, who started tentatively swinging his golf club. I was thinking that maybe it was the moment to get up and leave. Darby kept chatting but must have also sensed things were winding down. He popped up off the bench and said, 'Hey, Doc, before you leave, can you wait a minute? I got something I . . .' and walked out of the watch without finishing his sentence. He was back in a flash, with his arm outstretched toward me and his fist closed around something. 'Open it!' he laughed. In his palm was one of the silver bracelets that I'd come to know as the signature of this firehouse. I could fmattinally make out the inscription. In simple black, 9-11-01. Darby smiled, then added with a rare touch of awkwardness, 'You're one of us now, Doc. You should have this.' I was finally an official member of the firehouse.

May
It turned out to be only a matter of months between the time that Lt. Holland arrived in the firehouse and when he 'transferred out', as I was told matter-of-factly one day when I mentioned I hadn't seen him in a while. This was the first of many 'Outs' I was to hear over the next several months. I took it as an inherent part of firehouse life. I was getting a feel for the kind of family this firehouse was, the kind of place where people moved in and out. It made me see that I wasn't the only one unsure about their place here. For instance, I knew that the guys who came on board after 9/11 felt like they'd missed out on the most important thing that had ever happened here. I gathered from the men's attitude about Holland's leaving that he had never become fully integrated into the firehouse. But there was something foreboding about the

'outs' I was hearing. There was a tone of 'things will never be the same again' that reminded me of Sal's medical leave and the long list Mouse had shown me of men who had transferred out or retired and the even longer list of those waiting to leave.

With so many men gone or getting ready to go, I doubted anyone gave much thought to Lt. Holland's abrupt departure. Everyone knew Steve Holland and Bobby Walsh had been friends, but did they connect the dots? With the pulse of the firehouse beginning to return to its pre-disaster pace, the men were getting back into the routines of their pre-9/11 work day: cleaning the equipment and responding to alarms for the things they were used to and trained to handle – mattresses on fire, boilers blowing, trash cans and cars bursting into flames, accidental and deliberate overdoses, real or feared heart attacks and the like. Keeping busy kept their minds off thinking about the voices and shadows that beset this haunted house.

I assumed that Holland's transfer had been at his own request. I wondered how much he'd talked with the guys about Bobby Walsh, and whether they'd thought much the lengths he must have gone for a re-assignment to this firehouse. Had he ever been able to share with them what he had revealed to me that day then never mentioned after, 'I knew I couldn't take his place or anything. It wasn't that. I just thought I'd do it for Bobby'?

When I asked around, no one acted like they knew what happened, why he left so shortly after arriving, or where he'd been transferred to. A few of the men expressed regret that the house was losing a senior officer with so much experience on the job and who clearly had had leadership potential. But no one referred to the connection of Holland with Bobby Walsh. Maybe that was the point, certain things were not to be spoken of. Sacred or shameful, there was silence in the chatter that filled the spaces in the firehouse, a silence so thick not only with shared grief but with mutual renunciation of things that couldn't be understood or accepted.

It must have been painful for Holland that the men weren't ready to talk about Bobby Walsh. But I doubted that a man with as steady and dutiful nature as Holland would have allowed that to control his actions. I was pretty sure that what must have prevented him from being able to stick it out in the firehouse was that he couldn't bear the unremitting awareness of Bobby being there and not being there. Whatever redemption, solace or forgiveness he had hoped to find here had not been met. Wherever Steve Holland was now, I was sure he would eventually discover what people of action sooner or later realize, that changing the scene or 'doing a geographic' can't solve every problem or guarantee curing the ailing spirit. Lt. Steve Holland was, like any other survivor of massive catastrophe, a plagued man.

* * *

Because the men had to maintain constant readiness for action during their tour of duty, in-house counselling could at best be therapy-lite. It couldn't have the usual pacing of the 45 minute 'hour' where a person knew he had the time to warm up, let go of life preserving armour, then plunge into the difficult things and then have time to prepare for going back out into the world. In-house counselling could relieve some of the tensions interfering with optimal functioning, identify issues they could explore further when off duty, and introduce them to therapy.

Working more intensively with firemen like Smitty in individual therapy gave me insight into what the men in the firehouse were going through in their private lives. What I saw happening with Smitty one week in my office would be evident with someone in the firehouse the next week. I was seeing the impact 9/11 had not only on the firemen themselves, but the disruptions it caused in family life, especially the strain it put on marriages and children. I became an eye witness to watching trauma unfold over time, and work its way psychologically from one generation to the next.

It was an ongoing challenge for me to figure out what was going on with Smitty at any particular moment in time – how to separate out what was the result of his charming but frustrating

Puck-like personality, what was due to his past or current trauma, and what was attributable to his rapidly and frequently changing life circumstances. Smitty was only recently separated. He was without a settled home, suddenly in a new relationship with a woman who seemed to be at least as good as he was at instilling confusion in others, still working down at Ground Zero and spending a lot of time as a family liaison helping out the grief stricken parents of one of the dead men from his firehouse.

Like so many firemen in this period, Smitty was vulnerable to falling into the arms of a woman willing to help him forget. Firehouses around the city were magnets for all sorts of young and attractive female do good-ers, making it hard for some of the men, even those of strongest moral fiber, to resist lustful abandonment as a momentary respite from the unrelenting dull pain within and surrounding them. These 'sniffers', as the guys called them, were drawn to firemen like moths to a flame, all looking for respite from pain just like everyone in the city was after 9/11, and with a fantasy of rescuing and of being rescued. The woman Smitty was involved with came from a very different background and seemed to harbour hopes for marriage in the future. Smitty was in no shape to consider a serious relationship, but he genuinely cared for her and in his desire to better understand her and improve the relationship he brought her to session a few times, just as he occasionally brought his daughter in.

One day, Smitty surprised me and arrived for our appointment pretty much on time, only five minutes late. We were spared having to talk about his lateness for a change and had enough time to talk about all the things on his agenda. Smitty gracefully slid his six foot, two hundred pound frame into the small leather chair a few feet from me. Matching Smitty's movements in the unconscious attunement that develops between therapist and patient, I adjusted myself in the therapist Eames chair in which my five foot, one hundred pound body had been roaming for decades. Dressed in shorts and loosely laced sneakers Smitty looked more like an overgrown school boy in that typically adolescent combination of inability and refusal to tie things together. He began giving me an update, as he did each session, on his physical symptoms. That week he'd had a headache that lasted for several days. In subsequent years he developed back pain, then had one injury after another – shoulder, knee, the kind of self inflicted 'accidents' that careless guilty men suffer, physical pain expressing what his mind and spirit could not articulate.

I noticed he didn't mention the numbness that confused and bothered him from the beginning of our work. The only emotional state he was aware of and could formulate was the sensation of lacking feeling, what we identified as numbness, one of the most pronounced and common symptoms of trauma. Perhaps he was growing inured to the feeling of not feeling. His numbness was accompanied by a general apathy that left him indifferent to his surroundings, whether it was his seedy temporary apartment or the firehouse where he'd find reasons to go, like to do his laundry, when he didn't know what else to do. Like many of the men in my firehouse Smitty didn't feel comfortable anywhere. Like them, he couldn't be alone and couldn't easily put what he was experiencing into words. Being so off balance, like some of the guys in my firehouse, he felt less out of place in the firehouse than elsewhere. And though, unlike Smitty, most of the other firemen were managing to hold their marriages together under the strain of the catastrophe and its aftermath, Smitty was by no means the only fireman whose marriage was brought down by 9/11. Smitty was getting so accustomed to being disturbed and his life in disarray, he was starting to accept it as what the Fire Department called 'the new normal'.

Smitty then went on to discuss something in his daughter's conduct at school that worried him and that he wanted to 'check out' with me. Smitty was trying his best to keep his routine going with his daughter. Unlike other subjects, when it came to his daughter his thinking was intact, his feelings strong and his behaviour usually on target. His unwavering commitment and determination to be with her as much as possible and to take care of her gave me a hint of what Smitty's pre-traumatized capacities must have been like, and what the other firemen were trying to manage in their own families. No matter how bad he was feeling, whenever he was off duty, he showed up every morning to drive her to school, and waited outside at the end of the school day. And when he was working he often managed to finagle things to get off early just to be there when she got out of school to take her out for a snack. He took her to breakfast, he took her to soccer practice, to Central Park to roller blade. He brought her to our sessions, implored the school to help her, tried to get her into her own counselling. On her school vacation he arranged his time off to take her on a ski outing. Being on the road with Meghan, they could escape and forget, be together like old times.

His daughter had been shaken to the core, not only by the divorce but by the catastrophe, as most children in New York City were, especially those who lived in the area or whose parents were directly involved. Meghan refused to talk about what happened to her father in the towers, and in a childlike defensiveness tried to act as though it had little effect on her, even flat out denying that her father had been there one day when I tried to talk with her about it. I took this as a signal that the topic hit too close to home. The idea of her father being in danger was too threatening to contemplate. The trauma of her parents' divorce was as much as she could handle at the time. While many New York City children had increased anxiety and other stress reactions in the period following the disaster, the effects of 9/11 on kids like Meghan only became manifest years later.

After talking about maybe bringing her in for a family meeting, Smitty raised the subject of what was going on at work. Being a scrapper, Smitty found himself in the middle of the firefighters' fight to bring about changes in the system that they felt were crucial to prevent another 9/11. We were nearing the end of the hour, and Smitty raised the question of whether he should get involved with the firefighters' union. 'One of the guys told me I should become a union rep. What do you think?' I thought Smitty might be needing some encouragement to assume more responsibility in his work. So I gently suggested that being union rep might just be the thing that could help him feel effective and in charge of his life once again.

Smitty was quick to shoot this down, pointing out that becoming a union rep would require taking the test for officer being given very soon. I pressed the idea again but I was met with, 'I don't know, I don't know . . . Studying, I can't study, it's never been my thing, I don't know'. It was then clear to me that Smitty certainly had the brains, but might not have the ambition or the psychological balance right now to put in the kind of effort, mental concentration and self discipline that's required to study for the gruelling officer exam.

He went on, 'I've been studying a little, when I'm at the firehouse, but not like some of the guys.' I asked him whether he just didn't feel like he could think straight enough now to take on the challenge. He repeated his catch-all phrase 'Oh, I don't know,' and added that he'd never been much of a student. Clearly Smitty was ambivalent; he wasn't enthusiastic but he wasn't entirely opposed to going for the promotion. I kept pushing it, trying to get him to take himself more seriously. In my mind it seemed appropriate for his age and stage of career. When I heard myself again pointing out that it might be 'just the thing' he needed, I realized I was getting caught up in a counter-transference reaction. I was ignoring the reality of where Smitty was and unconsciously pushing my own values and hopes onto him. Thankfully, Jack Smith is the kind of person who's relatively immune to being pushed into something he isn't comfortable doing. He instinctively knows his limits. Smitty wasn't being resistant out of stubbornness or fearfulness. In his indirect but adamant way Smitty was letting me know that he accepted himself. Like a lot of his fellow firefighters, he was a very good fireman, but being an officer wasn't in his blood. It was true he wasn't in a psychological state to focus on studying. But more to the point, he didn't want that kind of responsibility. With a 'Maybe next time,' he put an end to that topic.

In his charmingly obstinate way, Smitty glided back to the previous topic of relationships. He said his girlfriend was complaining that they didn't talk enough. With a hint of irritation creeping through his veneer of vagueness and confusion he kept repeating, 'What does she want'? He was perhaps unconsciously asking this question about me as well. We only had a few more minutes left. I was thinking about what I might offer to neatly wrap things up when Smitty tossed a whole new subject into the therapeutic air. 'One more thing, Doc, I forgot to tell you. The guys are talking about a protest or something. They're closing Ground Zero. Can you believe it?'

That was the first I heard about the protest. I knew the guys in my house were upset about the possibility of shutting down the recovery operation but I didn't know the plan was definite. The firemen and other recovery workers were continuing to volunteer their time at Ground Zero, thoroughly committed to the process of the rhythmic raking and sifting for remains, waiting and hoping beyond hope to find some tiny piece of human life that would allow for a proper burial, a funeral with a body.

I sensed Smitty was waiting for me to say something, but I wasn't sure what he was really looking for. So I simply said what I believed, that the whole idea of 'moving on' was premature, that I thought money was driving the push to begin rebuilding so soon, and superseding our moral obligation to the families still waiting for recovery of their loved one's remains. It was impossible to gauge what Smitty thought about what I said. We were running five minutes 'over' by now. Smitty put an end to the session and to his protest of the closing of Ground Zero. 'Some of the guys from the house are going on a golf outing that day, one of those ones somebody donated. I think I'll go play some golf.'

* * *

'1.6 million tons of material from the collapse of the World Trade Center have been dismantled . . . That fire-spitting, hellish mound—crushed concrete and scorched metal and body parts – reduced . . . to a few piles on a bedrock-bottomed pit . . . Some mutter that the firefighters are moving too slow, but there is no overtime being paid . . . the rebuilding phase, will begin . . .'

The New York Times, May 3, 2002

* * *

The recovery operation at Ground Zero did end. This marked another breach between the firehouse and the world at large. There were not only economic forces behind the push to begin construction of a new Trade Center. The recovery operation had come to represent American failure and defeat. As a society with little patience for prolonged states of vulnerability, and with a cultural identity of determination and invincibility, the country was motivated to charge forward and to recapture its sense of strength through building. And to be liberated from the moral imperative of constantly remembering. Without any official announcement the name of site was downgraded from Ground Zero to ground zero. Despite the pleas of the thousands of children, widows and others who lost loved ones, despite the organized protests of firefighters willing to put their own health at risk to continue the recovery effort, and the fact that there were over a hundred people still classified as missing. Despite the moral controversy of prioritizing New York's economic recovery over responsibility to continue to recover any fragments of human life still buried at the site. Despite it all, Ground Zero was closed down less than nine months after September 11th.

But the minds and hearts of those inside the firehouses of New York City beat to their own drum. While they were beginning to feel a faint sense of the future in anticipation of the births of their own 9/11 babies, this wasn't enough to erase the unrelenting sorrow and loss that is the hallmark of traumatic grief, the course of which won't be dictated by external pressures. Mourning is at once uniquely individual, communal, and universal. The firemen, like all those who have lost loved ones or who have undergone a disaster of this nature, were moving along, but at a pace that put them at alienating odds with the world outside their grief. They took the closing of Ground Zero as another failed mission. Their inability to stop the closing of Ground Zero re-invoked the feelings of impotence and futility over the Trade Center they were just beginning to overcome. Once again they were racked with self-doubt and guilt about not being able to fulfill their responsibility. Rescuing lives is, after all, the heart and soul of firefighting.

* * *

'How long is too long to search for a finger?'
New York Times (5/3/02)

* * *

June
The closing of Ground Zero brought home a truth the firemen had no choice but to accept. It was time for them to move to a different psychological place. Fewer people were coming around to gawk or to give, and the men were no longer complaining about feeling objectified and commodified by the public. For better and for worse, they'd finally been left alone. It deepened the bonds between those most intimately involved with 9/11.

One day when I arrived at the firehouse the men were eating. Their lunch had been interrupted by a false alarm and now they were eating cold hamburgers and French fries. Lt. Darby was there, but out of uniform, obviously off duty, and regaling his captive audience with one of his shaggy dog stories. I realized I hadn't seen him around for several weeks, maybe even a month. The guys were comfortably bored being entertained while they ate and listened to the TV in the background. No one took notice of my arrival. I tried to make my way into the conversation by making a wise crack to Darby about how slim he'd gotten since I last saw him. 'Oh you say that to all the guys,' he joked, in feigned feminine delight. Once again he'd broken the ice for me. Emboldened, I went on, 'What's the secret to your success?' Just then the bell rang again, calling for both the ladder and engine. Boom – in less than sixty seconds, everyone was up and out, leaving the half eaten burgers and soon to be soggy fries on the table, and Darby and me by ourselves. He disappeared into the inner kitchen and in a flash was back with aluminium foil which he proceeded to tear into sizes he instinctively knew would fit exactly around each plate, explaining 'It'll keep better'. Despite the fact that this had been the second aborted effort to finish lunch, Darby was determined to have lunch for anyone who was still hungry on their return. I joined him in the tender task of covering the half a dozen or so plates left on the table, and putting the perishables back into the refrigerator.

Darby suggested we go into my 'office'. This seemed strange to me since no one else was in the firehouse at the moment, but I went along. Darby clearly had something on his mind. 'We'll leave the door open,' he made sure to add, 'so we can hear if anyone calls or comes by,' and, I was sure, so as to not raise any eyebrows when the men did come back. I was impressed at the deftness with which Darby seemed to think of everything, all the while looking like he was just a high-energy, easy-going kind of guy tooling around.

We sat in my dimly-lit makeshift office for the better part of the next hour, talking philosophically about the nature of luck and the difference between religion and spirituality. At first mesmerized by those tattooed arms of his dancing in the air, I didn't notice how dangerously low, almost to the nail bed, his fingernails had been bitten down. Then I realized that his thick hands were looking wan, and his biceps almost wasted. Had I been so seduced by Darby's irrepressible warmth and amiability that I failed to recognize the seriousness of his post-traumatic anxiety? Trying to calm myself I remembered that he once told me he had a lifetime habit of biting his nails.

As I tried to gather myself, Darby went on to tell me that he'd been away for a month on reserve duty. It was something he'd always liked but this year he said 'I just wasn't feeling right.' He'd even told his commanding officer he wasn't himself. The officer had been sympathetic, even describing his own difficulties after Vietnam, but told Darby the best thing to do was get right back into the cockpit of the fighter copter and fly. Darby completed his reserve duty, but he said he never got back into it the way he'd always done.

At this point both companies were back in the firehouse. Darby gave the door a smooth shove with a wave of his arm to close it. It was clear that he had something more he needed to talk about but instead he started telling me one of his shaggy dog stories. We were periodically interrupted by someone opening the door, apologizing with embarrassment on seeing Darby and I together, then backing out and gently closing the door behind him. I wasn't sure if or when Darby was going to get to what was really on his mind. I'd come to trust that imbedded in the nervous chatter of Darby's presentation, were the hints of his underlying concerns, conflicts and fears, and that if I could sustain enough patience I would be rewarded with something that cuts to the quick and touches the soul. At times he'd refer back to something we'd discussed in our infrequent meetings in my private office. But my patience was wearing thin. All I could think about was hoping Darby would get to the point already.

Uncannily sensing my anxious inattentiveness, he explained, 'I'm just a bit off today because I've got the big test tomorrow,' meaning the medical test of lung functioning. Because lung disease is an occupational hazard of firefighting, medical testing of lung functioning is routinely administered. But because the risk of lung problems was exacerbated by the prolonged exposure at Ground Zero, the men were being monitored more closely. So I assumed it was routine and his physical problems the result of chronic stress. His anxiety, always so palpable to me, was increasing now. His speech became more pressured and then he coughed what I told myself was probably just nerves. Or was it?

Darby was trying his best to maintain a nonchalant chattiness, but then he blurted out, 'I've probably done my last tour.' He broke into a spasm of coughing. That's when I faced it, but still, even then, I didn't want to believe it was true. Patrick Darby was sick.

I shouldn't have been stunned by the fact that Darby was among the first to show signs of the debilitating respiratory disease that would later take down scores of other workers from Ground Zero. He had been one of the leaders of the rescue operation and spent a great deal of time in the recovery effort. I'd heard from the firehouse grapevine that Darby was having some vague medical problems, but I didn't want it to be true. Maybe it would turn out to be just chronic asthma that Darby could live with for the rest of his life. Though the asthma he was diagnosed with was definitely putting an end to his days as a fireman and pilot, it might not kill him. With the spectre of life threatening cancers and other diseases from intense and prolonged exposure to the toxic environment at the disaster site, I was trying to convince myself that Darby's asthma might be non-progressive and was likely exacerbated by post-traumatic stress. But it wasn't really helping. My stomach was so thick, my thinking so unclear, I couldn't ask Darby any details or to find words to express my concern. Both of us upset, neither of us could find a way to talk about it. And because the body speaks when the mind cannot, I sat mesmerized by Darby, my eyes glued to those brightly drawn arms and dancing hands of his talking to me.

Unable to linger in this painful reality Darby digressed into a tangent about another officer in the house, who he described as acting in such an angry obnoxious way that the men under his command had complained to him. The implicit comparison of himself with the other lieutenant seemed intended to be both a metaphor for his own state and reassurance that he wasn't as 'bad off' as the other officer. Darby shook his head in a disquieted amazement, telling me that since I was the house clinician, he thought I should know that the other officer 'really needs help'. I didn't say what I was thinking, that he was the one who 'really needs help', something more than erratically dropping in for spot check therapy as he'd been doing.

Then Darby switched gears and started waxing nostalgic about when I first came to the firehouse. 'I'll never forget that first day, Doc. I just made some joke about Viagra and then you go and say straight out, "well, yeah, sometimes sex is affected", and jeez, here I was thinking about you like a sister or something,' he trailed off. He said that he'd gone home that day and told his wife how they brought a sex therapist into the firehouse. I was moved by his wanting to share memories of the last year, but I was preoccupied with figuring out how to get him to see that he needed to come for therapy more regularly now. His drop-in approach to our meetings was clearly not what was called for given his current medical and psychological condition. Just then he dropped what felt like a non-sequitur, 'To tell you the truth, I've started seeing a counsellor.' Not 'another' counsellor, just 'a counsellor', but with a confessional tone that confused me.

I was taken aback, to say the least, by this news, but I was also relieved to learn that he was actually doing regular therapy. Though in all honesty I was a bit disappointed he wasn't seeing me, I understood that he might have found it awkward to work too closely with me given that I was at the firehouse. He quickly reassured me that his counsellor was located near his house by way of explaining his choice. Wanting to put him at ease I told him I thought it was great. 'Really?!' he yelped as though flabbergasted. I was clearly still missing something. 'To tell ya the truth, I slinked when I saw you come in today, and thought you knew. It felt like I was cheating and here you go and say "great".' I laughed.

Finally relieved, he shrugged his shoulders, shook his head and laughed too, then resumed talking. I reached over to his hand which was gripping the arm of the chair, and wrapped mine over his. We sat there like that for a moment, defining without words the end of the session and smiles that conveyed how much we valued our relationship. I had some work to do on my own. I had to come to terms with the inevitability that some of these men

I had grown so fond of would get sick. There are moments in a relationship when there really isn't anything to say that will make a difference. That's when we have to remember that when words fail, the body can talk.

September

During the summer, the dread I experienced when I first started at the firehouse was coming back in anticipation of my visits. With so many of the guys on vacation and being away a lot myself the frequency of my visits to the firehouse had dropped off. Having had a taste of the lighter side of life on my vacation at the end of August, I wasn't looking forward to returning to the place my mind associated with tragedy. For the first time I was feeling an avoidant impulse similar to what I saw others feeling months ago, wanting to avoid being with those so manifestly suffering, especially in anticipation of the upcoming first anniversary.

The beginning of September had always held poignancy for me. The sadness of marking the end of summer's leisurely pace and the excited anticipation of what lie ahead. But since last year, September's sweet sadness will forever be eclipsed by the sights and sounds of planes crashing, buildings on fire, collapsing into a cloud of smoke visible for twenty miles away, the screams and moans emitting from faces of horror, people jumping to their death.

That first week of September came and went, and I didn't make it over to the firehouse. My early self-doubt re-surfaced. I questioned the usefulness of the program, my impact on the men, and the men's impact on me. But I couldn't fool myself. This was defensive resistance, the kind of rationalization that people use to justify avoiding uncomfortable situations and people in pain. I knew the only way to work through my fear was to get back up on the horse.

So to prepare myself for my first visit back I decided a quickie personal manicure with my second cup of coffee might just give me that little extra something to get me in the right frame of mind. Applying a second coat of nail strengthener for added protection for what lay ahead, I thought about a colleague asking me a few days earlier how 'my' firemen were doing, and how I made a lame excuse for why I hadn't been to the firehouse in some weeks. It made me guiltily aware of the fact that I'd managed to block them out of my consciousness for a time. I splashed on a last sheer topcoat, though I knew full well that my post vacation gleam wasn't going to last.

* * *

On the days leading up to the first anniversary the firehouse was alive with activity in a way I hadn't seen before. The men were in high gear sprucing up the house, painting, putting up a donated memorial, cooking, cooking, planning for the families, and greeting the renewed number of visitors bringing consolation and food. Local television was once again broadcasting almost constant World Trade Center coverage, returning the firemen to the media spotlight. By the evening of September 10th, with the preparations completed, the men were left with nothing to do but wait, alone with their own thoughts, and together with the muffled sounds of the TV and their brothers moving about.

I knew it was going to be a difficult evening for the men. No one had even given me the 'don't bother Doc' line when I suggested that I come by after I was done at my office. A man pretty new to the firehouse whom I didn't know was on watch, but he seemed to know who I was. He nodded hello and turned back to the tiny TV on the desk featuring 'Report from Ground Zero', with the intentness of a student. The fire captain on the program was describing his experience of the minutes before and immediately following the tower collapsing. The young man was clearly feeling like a fish out of water being in the firehouse that night, and unsure whether to feel relieved or excluded by not having been involved in the biggest thing that had ever happened to the FDNY. The 'Report from Ground Zero' gave him something to focus on and was likely helping him feel more a part of what happened. I let him be.

I walked back to the kitchen where a small group was gathered. They were watching a TV special on the football rivalry between New York City police and firemen. Someone pointed to the couch and I took a seat right in the middle, not unlike that night I watched the football game with them many months' ago. The camera spanned our team on the bench, moving past Lt. Holland who had come and gone from the firehouse, and then onto Anthony who wasn't there that night. No one brought up Lt. Holland's name.

Someone grabbed the remote and started flipping through the channels, stopping at the 'Report from Ground Zero'. Together we just sat quietly watching the television tell us the story of what had happened on September 11th in New York, as though it had happened to other people, as though there was a coherent whole, one real story to tell.

* * *

It was the first anniversary, September 11, 2002. The taint of visceral trauma was faint, and order had been restored to the city of New York. A massive memorial service was to be held at Ground Zero for the families. Each firehouse also organized its own thing. My house was planning to hold its own memorial service at the neighbourhood Roman Catholic Church where they had held the initial memorial service for the seven lost men. It was to be followed by a luncheon at the firehouse. One or two of the families wanted to attend the Ground Zero ceremony first, so the family liaisons were going to escort them back to the firehouse afterward in the chauffeured limousines provided by the department for the occasion. Everyone was hoping the timing would work out, but we all knew it wouldn't. And it didn't. For if September 11th taught us anything, it was that timing and chance can make all the difference in the world.

I cancelled all my appointments until late afternoon. As soon as I woke up, I put on the TV. Local and national television stations were covering the service. At 9.59 when the first tower went down a year ago, they began the first of what has since become the official 9/11 anniversary ritual at the site, calling out the names of each and every person who died at the World Trade Center on September 11th. Once more it was a list of names, that year it was 2819. The number would rise over the next years as more bodies were positively identified. Nearly 10% were foreign nationals, and of those the majority were from the United Kingdom.

I just had to go out for a short run before confronting the rest of the day. It felt bizarre, almost wrong, to jog on this day of all days. But that's what runners do when we don't know what else to do, when nothing seemingly more appropriate for the occasion will work. It's not a matter of running away, of running to or from something. As any runner will tell you, once you've logged in so many miles on so many days in so many seasons of your life, running becomes your way of dealing with things, what you have to do, in good times and bad, and in the indefinable times. That's what makes a runner. Being the kind of person who has to hit the pavement, who needs to hear the sound of her own breathing and her feet thumping, to feel the sun shining, the rain dripping, and the wind blowing, when you can't make sense of anything and can't seem to get yourself together. And so, I double laced my Saucony's, stashed my keys in the key pocket of my running pants, and feeling that it would be disrespectful to turn off the televised ceremony, I left it on in my empty apartment and closed the door behind me.

The air outside was fresh. The unforgettable smell from that fateful day was long gone. But on stepping outdoors that morning, somehow I was surprised that there was no smell. It was as if I was expecting it to magically return because it was September 11th – because it was early in the morning, with the same sunlight, with the same warm feeling of transition in the air, no longer hot and humid but not yet brisk with autumn, just as it was a year ago today. I fully understood the irrationality of my thinking, but it didn't stop me from feeling the way I did, that the smell was strangely missing.

It was a smell of fire unlike any other I have known. There was no mistaking that smell for the fire from a winter fireplace, from burning autumn leaves, a forest fire, or even any of the more unnatural smells of electrical or chemical fires known to city life. This was the unforgettable and unforgiveable smell of unspeakable origin – jet fuel burning with metal and mankind. It first arose from the mound in the midst of wailing for the unimaginable disintegration of humans in a matter of minutes. Had we inhaled their burning bodies, and with it their terrified last cries, their hopes and dreams? As time went on that smell dimmed only to quixotically return when the wind changed direction for months after September 11th. Eventually we couldn't exactly recall the smell but we knew it resided somewhere still inside us, along with some part of those three thousand souls that were now a part of us.

Looking back, I can see how my preoccupation with the smell, like my focus on the paper falling from the Trade Center, was my mind working to make sense of the events of 9/11. It was my way of trying to integrate the past into the present, ensure its place in my memory, so that I could permit myself to move forward. Smell, that most primal and lasting form of memory, along with touch, trauma, indeed all of life's most elemental experiences, resides in the body. Internalized through the senses, implanted in the most primitive recesses of the brain, then encoded in the viscera, such knowledge and memory obeys laws beyond control of the conscious mind. And yet, as any psychoanalyst can tell you, it is often the reclaiming of our most buried sensory and visceral memories that makes for profound and lifelong change. As Freud first taught us, healing is the freeing of oneself from unwittingly reliving and repeating the past by making the unconscious conscious. Memory unconsciously re-lived then consciously re-worked gives us agency, the power to learn from the past, make sense of the present and change the course of the future. Rituals, whether they're jogging, therapy or memorial commemorations, are essentially forms of channeling and transforming pain into something with evocative beauty and life affirming potential.

It is by weaving the fragments of memory into coherence that history – personal and societal – is shaped.

I jogged over to the Brooklyn Heights Promenade with its world famous view of lower Manhattan and the Statue of Liberty. There was a fresh collection of flowers poking through the fence, pointing in the direction where the Trade Center had been. Glass candles flickered below. Thankfully for once no one was trying to capture on camera the now famous empty spot in the skyline. A number of my neighbours were already amassed, their usually harried faces softened into a shared silent contemplation. My jogger's presence also seemed wrong, and so I made my way over towards Cadman Park, at the base of the Brooklyn Bridge, passing some construction workers struggling to unfurl an American flag in the gusty September breeze. I ran past two workers who were removing election machines from the local synagogue where the primaries had been held the day before. How odd, this steady marking of time that the calendar provides. A year ago, the primary elections, which are always held on the first Tuesday after Labor Day, had fallen on the 11th, and had saved the lives of thousands of people by making them late for work at the Trade Center. I passed the Red Cross building, which for months had shuttled the relief workers back and forth across the bridge to the site. Without emergency equipment surrounding it, the building was returned to its quiet obsolescent invisibility, lost in its location adjacent to the Brooklyn Bridge. A low flying military plane broke the peaceful stillness.

I ran onto my time-worn dirt trail at Cadman Park because that is the place where I like to go to think, to hear my footfall slapping the ground as I plodded along, listening to my labored breath in anticipation of the moment when my feet and spirit will be freed, when thoughts will stop pursuing me, and I would eventually bask in the wind wisping across my face. And I can look up to the clouds in the blue line of sky between the trees, and know the world and I are one.

That morning as I hit my third mile, flashes of lucid memory and thought came to me for the briefest of moments. What happened to the family who lived near the Trade Center whom I counselled, on the insistence of my supervisor, that the air was safe enough to return home? I thought of Steve Holland, how he had appeared out of nowhere in the firehouse and then just as suddenly disappeared. The guys from firehouse came to my mind. What will happen to them, to me? Filled with questions for which there were no answers, I kept my steady pace, bathing in the warmth of the early September sun and feeling the breeze softly wafting every which way, making no sense, picking no direction. As though it too couldn't decide whether to go forward or back, to remember or to forget.

* * *

What is it about seeing a man cry? When a woman cries, things are as we expect them to be, and the world remains as is. But when a man cries, for a brief moment time stands still, and the world changes.

The memorial service took place in the church a block away from the firehouse. The civilians sat on the left side and the men from the Fire Department with their families on the right. Unsure of my place at a memorial service for men I had never laid eyes on, and feeling a bit awkward in a Roman Catholic Church, I took a seat in the back corner between the firemen and civilians. All the men from the firehouse were standing in solidarity, side by side, in full dress uniform, including hat and white gloves, with their wives and children intertwined among them, their babies in their arms, surrounding the widows and their families. The ten men on duty were in full gear in the back pews so that if an alarm came, which it did half way into the service, they could leave the church without disturbing anyone. Even on this day the firefighters bespoke a reassuring warmth and strength, their countenance still conveying 'We are here to help you'.

I held the hymnal tightly. I felt a certain detachment, the disconnected sensation of knowing that this horror had truly occurred but not being able to feel it. I took the priest's words in, and though they were in Latin, the rhythm was so similar to the Hebrew I was used to I lost myself in its comforting musicality. For a moment I questioned whether it was wrong for a Jew to sing Catholic hymns, but quickly regained what in my heart of hearts I have always believed. A prayer is a prayer.

I looked for my men. There they were – Pauli the dreamer, Phil the chef cum knots teacher, Anthony the football player, Robbie Taylor my nemesis. And the survivors – Danny the probie, William the firehouse hero, Lt. Ross, and Sean, the survivor from whom I first heard the details of their narrow escape from the towers. I saw Lt. Sal then noticed Darby; he gave me a slight nod and then looked down. I had never seen the men so serious. Over the course of the hour long service, I saw one or two of the men wiping a stray tear, particularly as the priest spoke briefly about each of the seven men individually. Though the guys defy gender stereotype with their comfort in the domestic arts, they are very much men, and we still live in a world that does not give men the freedom to cry.

And then there is the fact that for man or woman, as for these widows, parents, and fellow firefighters in the Brotherhood, there is some anguish – immeasurable sorrow and profound loss – that is beyond tears.

* * *

Back at the firehouse a few blocks away, the ritual sounds of returning to life after funerals and memorials surrounded us over lunch. Folding tables were set in a semi-circle around the apparatus floor. Bowls of chips and plates of cookies were laid on them to keep the breeze coming through the open garage door from lifting the white paper tablecloths right off the tables. The study room, my makeshift office, was the serving area with aluminum trays piled with chicken, pasta, and salad, and replaced as soon as they were emptied. The families that had gone to Ground Zero were stuck in traffic and not yet arrived.

I introduced myself to the widows who were clinging to each other and to the other wives, many of whom were holding babies in their arms and tending to children too young or too shy to wander around on their own. After filling my plate, I found an empty seat, and sat down by myself, across from a chief from downtown whom I'd never seen before. Lt. Ross came and sat down next to me. 'This here's the Doc, I help her out,' he laughed as he introduced me to the chief. When I asked Ross if his family was here, he said he leaves them out of these events whenever possible. We chatted, I ate, and then the tall lanky lieutenant who balked at all 'this hogwash' rose to continue his rounds as ex-officio leader of the firehouse.

The table talk somehow returned to where it had been a year ago. Words and images that had gone underground for many months resurfaced: 'crushed', 'falling bodies', remains', 'last words', and more than anything else 'body parts'. Words that had lain dormant in our post-9/11 unconscious, waiting in the wings for their cue to float back into the room like dancing shadows. On the periphery of the conversation it seemed that everywhere I turned, I could hear, amidst the banter, things like 'picking up body parts with forklifts to save money', as the pie was passed around the table.

'Body parts' – these unfamiliar words that were voiced in hushed furtive tones and had such a crushing impact a year ago were all too familiar now and could be spoken freely now. Thanks to media saturation, the passage of time and our human capacity for detachment, these words had taken on a mind numbing feeling, almost like a sanitized factoid. No one seemed to think our new lingo, the 'raking' and 'sifting' for 'body parts' was bizarre. How impressive is the human mind! Together we distanced ourselves from touching the truth behind these words, from feeling the thousands of persons of all ages who spoke eighty languages who got up that morning and left for work to never return. Is it inherent to human nature to not sustain full appreciation of death and mortality? Are we destined to never fully grasp the reality that one minute we are, and the next we cease to exist, or the cruelty humans are capable of inflicting on each other? The best we can do is to lasso these difficult to comprehend realities into words that provide a necessary psychological distance from what they represent. Words like DNA, DNR, murder, evil, that can be voiced with barely a flinch or a flutter.

Sitting at the luncheon table in the firehouse a year after 9/11 and listening to the conversations around me was surreal, as though I was in a movie. I longingly tried to imagine a Disney theme into it, where tragedy magically ends in laughter and triumph. But the scene felt more Fellini-esque where the brave faces around me were cracked apart by momentary blazes of pain then quickly covered over into a mask of steadiness. For we depend on believing there is coherence and wholeness to the world, even as we fear we are no more than many disparate individuals, our existence no more than a sum of body parts.

I had to leave the table and the 'body parts' conversation. I walked over to an unfamiliar man in his thirties who I noticed had been standing alone by the garage entrance. He introduced himself as a brother of one of the men who had died. With a deconstructivist's eye I looked at his eyes, his nose, and the rest of his face, trying to fit it to the features I remembered from the wall photo of his brother. I used to study those portraits, trying to glean knowledge from those photographs about those seven dead men whom I had never met and were rarely spoken of but who defined this firehouse now.

Assuming I was an official of the firehouse, he asked me whether it would be all right to bring a friend of his over to the firehouse sometime so that he could show him where his brother had worked. As he uttered these last words, he lost his composure and began to weep. The face before me suddenly appeared to break down into separate Picasso-esque planes – his eyes, nose, cheeks held together by tears. I could barely get out the words 'Of course'.

The faces of the firemen who had cried with me over the year flashed before my eyes. An officer from a nearby firehouse who had come to see me for a consultation right after working a fire where there had been fatalities. The incident had triggered an unleashing of the sorrow and pain that he'd been stoically containing in his effort to remain a strong leader in his firehouse which had lost eleven men. I was overtaken by recalling the vision of his head dropping into his hands, the sound of his quivering voice, and the sight of him crying as he described discovering a body charred beyond recognition.

And the broad face of a covering officer whom I'd never met before and never saw after, breaking up before me like so many pieces of a jigsaw puzzle, as he told me his story. Before I knew it, this man with a fullback's neck and shoulders and licensable weapons for hands began to cry with an implacable lack of self-consciousness. Shrugging his tears off with 'Oh, I cry every day now,' he let me take his hand, lead him to a chair, where we sat holding hands, strangers in a strange land.

* * *

I have only one memory of my father crying – when he heard the news of his aunt's sudden death. The image of his stepping backwards, almost as if he were going to fall, the involuntary guttural sound that came out of him is burnt into my psyche. And how I, at ten years old, stood there frozen, unable to say or do anything, watching my father cry. My father had overcome his own series of traumas in childhood alone – poverty, physical disability, the loss of his father and a brother. But he was the kind of man, like the firemen, who carried his inconsolable sadness in silence, revealed only in a certain heaviness to his countenance. When a man whose life is caring for others in that quiet but definitive, not to be taken note of way, there is no other place for sadness to go but inside. And I too knew the feeling of longing for tears that refuse to come, that leave you to dream and laugh in the silence of unseen sorrow.

* * *

Tears are that uniquely human form of expression, not only of sadness and grief, but of relief, anger, frustration, pain, any and all of the subtle feelings that are part of our birthright as humans, even happiness. There are people who cry without shedding a tear, people who tear up at movies and parades but can't cry with or for the important people in their life. There are genuine tears and crocodile tears designed for effect. To some tears feel self-affirming as a powerful release of emotions, while for others tears feel like a self-diminishing statement of vulnerability or weakness. It would make a nice story to tell you that once the men could cry, things would change for them. That they wouldn't be so angry, they wouldn't feel so helpless, and they would be able to 'move on' in accordance to the world's timetable.

But people, even heroes, aren't made to order, and change doesn't happen in a cookie-cutter fashion. And the story of each man in the FDNY was singular and unfinished, separate chapters at best an artificial construction. A year later, we only knew that September 11th ended Lt. Patrick Darby's military and firefighting career, shattered FF Jack Smith's carefree daredevil spirit, and left Steve Holland, along with the rest of the men of the FDNY haunted by the loss of their brothers, a sense of failure and a changed world view. Only the unfolding of time would reveal the full toll this tragedy would take on their lives.

December

It was Christmas and that meant another firehouse gathering. My makeshift office was once again converted to the serving room for the aluminum trays of food kept warm over Bunsen burners and a large cooler filled with ice and cans of soda. Once again the guys were re-stocking the cooler and the empty tins with fresh lasagna, chicken, and potatoes. This time both rigs were in their place in the garage and the food was set up in the kitchen. The kitchen table was covered in a red paper tablecloth and adorned with baskets of fruit and piles of Christmas cookies. Children of all ages were everywhere – the younger ones were running around, the teenagers standing around self-consciously, and the babies being passed around. The gloom and sorrow of a few months' earlier was gone. Finally the faces around me in the firehouse were all smiles. It was Christmas.

I saw a man whose badge identified him as captain sitting alone. I went over and introduced myself. He responded with 'Great to meet you, Captain Shaw here, acting captain, hoping to get the slot,' meaning the position just vacated by the ladder captain who was just promoted out of the firehouse. I could tell by the way he smiled at me that he'd heard about me, and I thought he seemed pleased to finally meet me in person. We chatted about the party, and I commented on how nice it was to see people being happy for a change. Still smiling, he looked down to his plate of chicken fricassee, then said something I was totally un-prepared for. 'Time to wind down, Huh?' An 'order', perhaps one of his first in his new post as captain, politely posed in the form of a gentlemanly officer asking a question. Taken aback, I didn't say anything, and left him to his chicken fricassee.

I saw the other captain, Harris, saunter into the room. He had only come into the firehouse a few months ago, having been assigned to the unenviable post of replacing the beloved leader of the house, Captain McNeil, who died at the Trade Center. Chewing on a cigar, the captain took a spot in the middle of the kitchen and announced to no one in particular, 'Darby's out,' giving the 'OUT' a satisfied flourish, as if he was the umpire calling the end of the game. Perhaps proclaiming an end to 9/11 or asserting his leadership. Either way, people weren't about to let him ruin the festivities. No one said a word. After all, it was a party, it was Christmas, a time finally to celebrate.

But it was true. And now it was official. Darby's respiratory functioning had finally given out. And Holland was out, long gone from the firehouse. Even my nemesis, Robbie Taylor, that curmudgeonly senior man who had tried so intently to take control of the firehouse and push me out, had filed for a transfer out of Manhattan, and was on his way out as well. Rumour also had it that Lt. Sal, still out on medical leave for his knee injury, might never come back. So many of the guys were gone or going, and yet I, the inside outsider always on the verge of being kicked out, was still there.

With so many of the men 'out' how will the firehouse go on? Out with the broken bones, burns, respiratory conditions and various injuries that have always been an occupational hazard of firefighting, that only increased exponentially and with a new twist since 9/11. Few men were even bothering to keep up with the periodic lung testing since no one seemed to have definitive answers on either the causes or possible cures for 'the Trade Center cough' that one man after another was beginning to develop. It seemed like fewer and fewer of the original post-9/11 crew with whom I worked and sweated through their post-traumatic stress, medical leaves, mental and physical crises and recoveries, were still in the firehouse. One after another had retired or transferred – out! But I had come to learn that a firehouse, regardless of its leadership, regardless of any one person, moves on its own sluggish but dependable rhythm, with a destiny of its own. In a firehouse the whole exceeds the sum of its parts

And on this particular day, there were happy children everywhere around me waiting for Santa. I wasn't about to let either of the captains' comments rain on my parade. I left the kitchen and returned to the apparatus room where kids were climbing all over the trucks, sitting in the driver's seat, hanging over the sides and some even sitting on top of the truck. Others were sliding down the gold pole specially polished for the occasion. Joining them I discovered it wasn't that easy to climb the ladder on the back of the truck. As I sat on the top of the truck, my hands full of pretzels I held one of the toddlers until he began to cry at which point I passed him back down to his dad.

Suddenly a bell clanged, the bell I had never even noticed in all the time I'd been coming here. The bell, like the pole, was a relic from the early days of the firehouse that's only used at the Christmas party to call all believers outside the firehouse because, yes, Santa was going to land any time now, on the roof of the firehouse. After passing the other babies down and waiting for all the kids to lower themselves down, I made my embarrassingly graceless way down the ladder, and rushed out to join them in the middle of the street. Everyone was looking up. Santa was standing on the roof waiting to come down the truck ladder. We started clapping, and Santa in appreciation, first slapped his big padded belly then picked up a huge black plastic trash bag and slung it over his shoulders.

Down Santa was airlifted by the hook and ladder to the sidewalk below, Ho Ho Ho-ing to the children all the way. Once he landed down on the ground, with a big grin, he told the kids to follow him back into the firehouse. All the believers in Santa walked back in after him. For the moment we were all believers. The men had turned a corner. The acutely traumatized and grief stricken men whom I was introduced to a few weeks after last Christmas could now celebrate being alive. In the natural time line of mourning and resilience from trauma, they were, a year later, pretty much back to being the selves they were before 9/11. They were and would remain, as we all were and will forever be, the same and yet fundamentally different.

The kids gathered on a circle on the floor, with the adults surrounding them. I didn't have the vaguest idea who was playing Santa. He pulled one marvel after another out of the bag, each one specifically earmarked for a particular child. The whole scheme had been worked out to the last detail by Santa's helpers so that each child got one toy that had been put on his or her list for Santa that year.

Congratulating Santa on his infectious mirth and the success of his disguise I confessed I had no idea of his true identity. Laughing, Santa pulled down the elastic band that held his white tufted beard in place. It was Phil, the chef aka knot instructor. 'This was a lot harder to do last year!' he exclaimed and then sighed, in aching recognition of the sadness of the past and the joy of the present moment. With a parting nod, he picked up his bag of toys and walked out with the determination of Santa with hours to go before he sleeps.

January 2003

While most large scale traumas tend to follow a similar psychological trajectory – shock, denial, grief, anger, acceptance followed sometimes by growth – a community's response to a natural disaster is altogether different than to a man made catastrophe, particularly one purposefully inflicted by humans on their fellow men. Even careless human error, like a nuclear accident, rarely erodes one's basic belief in life and the social fabric of a community the way mass murder does. We are overwhelmed but awestruck at the divine or earthly power of floods, fires, epidemics. However shocked, traumatized, and grief stricken we are, we go on, doing what we can to restore our pre-existing belief systems. Mass murder, the calculated infliction of suffering, strikes at the very foundations of a society, tearing away faith in humanity, and leaving an existential void and inescapable sense of vulnerability in its wake.

Much of America had papered over their grief, becoming preoccupied with the faceless 'war against terrorism', and building a head of steam for going to war in Iraq. The pain of the FDNY, like all who suffered most directly from the terrorist attack, wasn't going to be solved by a drive for revenge.

In the battle against helplessness when faced with indifferent reality and wanton evil, we can choose to retreat inward. We can turn our fear outward to aggression, finding and fighting enemies. Or we can focus on re-affirming life, on creation rather than destruction. From time immemorial we have looked to political and religious leaders, philosophers, and more recently to therapists, those 'secular priests' of modern life, to provide the language for describing and explaining the pain of the human condition. We depend on them to help us understand the whys of good and evil, how it can be that terrible things happen to some and not others, and to guide us with pathways for overcoming personal fear and confusion, and for collectively healing our broken spirit. The firemen of the FDNY knew it was time to move forward, but they didn't yet have a clear vision of what that meant for them as a group and an organization, and who among them could lead the way. To steer them in the direction of honouring those who were not spared while living the life they've been granted and sustaining their dedication to helping others.

* * *

Since Christmas I wasn't looking forward to going to the firehouse. I sensed something going on with the men, but I couldn't put my finger on what it might be. I chalked up this reaction to my wanting the holiday spirit to linger into the new year. Finally I arranged a time for a few days later. I called right before leaving my office, as I always do, to make sure the men weren't out on a call. The man on watch told me both companies were in, but he didn't sound too enthusiastic.

By the time I arrived I was feeling hesitant, almost like the way I felt when I first started out there. Before ringing the bell, I peeked through the two small eye level garage windows. Both rigs were in place. I saw the new 'permanent' bronze memorial plaque that was put up at the anniversary dedication, and on the floor below it a few cards and flowers, still in their plastic wrapping, drooping over the top of the vase. Scanning the apparatus room I didn't see any of the men but I spied a pair of black rubber boots right by the truck looking like miniature Beefeater Guards at attention. Each leg of the fireproof pants bib was rumpled with precise care over the boot, at the ready for its wearer to glide effortlessly into them, then don his fireproof jacket, and be ready to go from the moment the clarion call came over the radio.

I rang the bell, as I had each time I arrived for my visit over the last year. No one buzzed or came to the door. I looked through the window again and I still couldn't see anyone. Strange. I rang again. Still no one came. For the third time I looked through the small window, and this time saw William putting up his arms in a joking 'Don't blame me' way. I made a face back at him to the effect of 'Very funny, now please come open the door.' He disappeared. Not knowing what else to do, I just kept ringing the bell. It began to dawn on me that the men were deliberately not answering the door. Could they be hiding from me and hoping that I'd give up and just leave?

Finally someone came to the door and I went in. By that point it was too late for me to retreat with dignity. But this was the moment when it struck me that my work inside the firehouse was coming to an end. The men as a group had come to the point where they didn't want counselling in the firehouse any more. Not wanting me to take it personally, they didn't know how to tell me. In hindsight there had been signs I just wasn't picking up on. But it was all quite clear to me now. I was fundamentally an outsider. After some resistance, they had come to accept me, include me in things, and some of the men fully embraced me. But the bottom line was that I was never going to fight fires or provide emergency medical service, in the physical sense anyway. And therefore I could never be a permanent part of the structure and functioning of this or any firehouse. I had been brought in precisely because I was outside the wounded system. Like an organ transplant, I was essentially foreign to the body of the organization and it had struggled hard to not naturally reject me. But the truth was that for the firehouse to be restored to health and to its identity and integrity of purpose, it had to return to being just a group of firefighters – not people in need of therapy.

As their 9/11 therapist, I had also become a 'trauma trigger'. The very sight of me at this point was setting off a kind of auto-immune reaction. It was a new year and I had become a reminder of feelings and memories they needed to put behind them. Though I can't say I wasn't upset at the idea of leaving, I knew that what the men were doing now was right. They weren't rejecting me. Nor were they using me as a scapegoat to avoid dealing with things. They were just at a point where they were finally ready to put the trauma of 9/11 behind, along with their assignation as survivors, heroes, victims, so that they could resume their life's work and identity – being firemen.

That was not my last official or unofficial visit to the firehouse. But that day was a defining moment for me. That was when I recognized that my job now was to help the men, and myself, find a way to end. As their therapist I had to lead the way to 'termination', as it's euphemistically referred to in the psychoanalytic world. I had to show them they could openly, directly declare they were ready to stop the counselling program. And as for me, I had to come to terms with a few things. I had to face the fact that in the final analysis I was a psychologist, a psychotherapist, maybe even a damn good one some days. But neither I, nor anyone, could bring back the people killed on September 11th or return this firehouse that hadn't suffered a death of one of its own in the fifty years before to what it was before September 11th. I had to leave them be now to grapple on their own with their loss, guilt and memories.

My involvement with this firehouse came to an end but for these men, as for so many people, their 9/11 story had yet to fully unfold. For those inside the tragedy, there wasn't yet, and may never be a tidy story, one with a beginning, middle and end, a narrative that makes sense or captures their truth. For them there was only the before and after. Yet life moves on.

Human resilience is extraordinary. It is a testimony to the natural healing powers of time and the human heart that the men of the FDNY wanted to fully live life again. It was 2003 and up to each one of them, as for each and every one of us, to find his own answers to the penultimate question of life – Is there meaning in it all?

Part III
Therapy
2005

'The day they announce the pit is empty, that the last dust has been swept out, what are *we* going to be left with? Tears and 15,000 body parts, that's what.'
New York Times, 4/16/02

It's 2005, more than three years since the terrorist attacks of September 11th. 9/11 has receded to the background of the collective consciousness, a barely discernible hum that can be awakened in a heartbeat when something unusual disrupts the illusory insulation of our quotidian routines, like when a plane or train crashes, or on the anniversary of that day. The impact of these world altering tragedies is absorbed into the fabric of people's lives, then invisibly woven into the lives of those they touch, thereby steadily and unobtrusively leaving an indelible mark on the entire society and molding its history.

The following pages are annotated personal therapy notes written shortly after the sessions in 2005. I have left the notes largely unchanged to retain the state of mind of that particular period. They are meant to be a window into the therapeutic encounter, to show what actually transpires between therapist and patient, how the therapist as well as the patient evolves psychologically in the course of therapy, and to reveal the individuality of recovery and the uniqueness of each therapy relationship. In sharing our experience, we hope to help you better understand the psychological challenges that you or someone in your life may face. We may not be first responders facing death on a routine basis, or survivors of a major disaster, but as trauma studies have shown, most of us will undergo at least one major trauma in the course of our lives. And no one escapes loss in life. Though firefighters are accustomed to tragedy and trauma, the terrorism and scope of this disaster have affected these men as nothing before had and hopefully ever will in the future. You'll get a feel for the impact of 9/11 on the lives of two officers, Patrick Darby and Steve Holland, and Firefighter Jack Smith. Each of these men, like any trauma survivor, is fundamentally the same person as he was before and yet also vitally changed. They are familiar strangers, to themselves and to those who know and love them. Though they did not physically succumb to death, their spirits are inscribed by an end to life as it was before. Massive catastrophe not only takes people from us, it takes away parts of our own self – robbing us of our former innocence, sense of purpose, and more than anything else, the capacity to be carefree.

Firefighter Jack Smith struggles to retrieve the irrepressible spirit and resilience that was the hallmark of his personality. Lieutenant Patrick Darby wrestles with the challenges of re-location from his lifelong home in New York to Florida which he hopes will ease the asthma that forced his retirement from the FDNY in 2002. Steve Holland continues his battle with grief and trauma as he rises in the ranks of the Fire Department. In the years since September 11th these men have restored a certain normalcy to their lives. Now they labour to regain faith in themselves and the world as they continue to work through their unresolved grief and trauma. On my part, if I'm going to hold their trust in me and therapy, and help them move forward, I have to remain open to experience myself the pain, sorrow, and despair that they live in, while making sure that I do not become defensively hardened, or do not protect myself and become traumatized.

Come inside my office, and learn alongside us about the magic and mystery of psychotherapy.

January 2005

As I approach my office building on a bitter morning, I see Smitty waiting for me on the sidewalk. Outfitted with only a GAP sweatshirt, with his hands in his pockets, he looks like he's dancing, lightly shifting from one foot to the other to keep warm. He greets me with a broad smile. His response to my questioning what he's wearing in this below freezing weather was simply, 'Been doing roofing, you know, on my days off; I need the money.'

In many ways Smitty is once again the fun-loving, affable and rough around the edges guy he always was, but inside he is permanently changed. Over the last three years he's managed to restore a degree of stability to his outer life. He's remarried, with triplets on the way, and is a senior man in his firehouse. His inner life, however, remains starkly bleak and confused, in the grip of trauma. His thinking is often disjointed and scattered like the people, paper, and buildings that day. He is still prone to bursts of horror and fear-driven anger. Like a few weeks ago when he went off on one of the younger guys in his firehouse who was all excited about the equipment that as first responders they were being trained to use in the event of a biological or chemical attack. Smitty became agitated and called the kid a jerk for being into it, yelling, 'We'd last as long as a snowflake in hell' in the event of such an attack.

Jack Smith is the real thing, a genuine tough guy. He might not feel the need to wear a coat in the middle of winter. But he has no compunction about admitting how different he is from how he was before 9/11. He talks freely about not caring or feeling much about anything, except for when he thinks about another terrorist attack. And then he's scared, 'for what will happen to the kids'.

Opening the lid to my piping hot coffee I remember the Christmas gift certificate to Starbucks he'd just given me, and guiltily think I should have bought him a cup. Paying no mind to my stirring the sugar in, Smitty begins the session. 'So I was working on my sister's roof the other day, I'm trying to get it done.' What the hell is he doing up there in the middle of January? Is this his death wish? Is this the return of his pre-9/11 daredevil self or the earlier post-9/11 self-destructive Smitty that I had thought therapy was curing him of? For the longest time after September 11th Smitty was compelled to flirt with danger. This is a complex common post-traumatic reaction. It reflects a physiological and psychological numbness from having witnessed massive suffering, death and destruction, that leaves the person feeling like life doesn't matter. Danger-seeking behaviour can also be acts of desperation in an effort to regain the feeling of aliveness knocked out by trauma, as well as a certain kind of death wish driven by survivor guilt and difficulties coping with the pressures of normal living.

For Smitty, as for many survivors, it is in those moments when he's poised on that roof ledge, racing down the mountain on the edge of his skis, or even being in an actual 'accident', as he was last winter that took him out of work for three months, that he feels fully alive again and able to connect to a desire to live. More than three years after September 11th, Jack Smith is still perched between life and death.

'There I was, I just got up the ladder and was about to put my duff on the roof, and my cell phone goes off. 'It's Mary' (his ex). 'She's drunk and yelling all this stuff, saying I'm going to regret it, sayin' I'll never see my kid again. I hung up on her.' Seconds later Meghan, his daughter, called, asking him to come get her. 'Can I pick her up and take her to her guitar lesson? There I am, trying to get this roofing job done, and Katie's been complaining I don't spend enough time with her, and Mary calling all the time.' 'She's jealous,' I suggest. But this misses the point.

The point being that Smitty is faced with the painful reality that he cannot save his ex-wife or protect his daughter from her mother's problems. The whole situation personifies the self-indictment he never dares say out loud: Why did he not die in those towers? No matter that he was finally able to leave an unhappy marriage that he could not forsake before 9/11. To the tabloids, the heroics of firemen like Smitty now seem cheapened by the directions their lives have taken since 9/11. The news portrayals of the divorces, affairs, drinking and fighting that have scarred their lives subtly put their heroism into question. As though a man could do and go through everything that makes a hero and remain unaffected. As though being dubbed a hero could cure or compensate for it all.

No matter how good things may appear on the surface, Smitty continues to struggle with the pain of feeling relatively little control over his life. His ex has full custody of their child and he's had to move back into the two-story match-box house where he grew up, living in the apartment upstairs from his parents. 'It's temporary,' he says, to reassure himself and me. 'This way I can look out for my parents; they're getting older.'

Just who's looking out for whom may get a little muddy. Smitty in the position of having to borrow money from his parents more often than he'd like to help with the legal fees incurred in his relentless custody battle. All the issues that brought down their marriage in the first place finding their expression in court battles over their daughter. Whatever conflicts persist between them, and however indecisive Smitty is about so many things in his life, he has no doubt about his decision to leave his marriage. As he explained to the state child case-worker, 'I stayed around for the first five years of her life. I'd take her around the house, I tried to make it a game, every morning, finding the empty bottles. I was thinking it was better for a kid to have one parent sober. But then I started to think, what kind of a role model is that? So when she said what she did when I came in the house that day after the Trade Center, that was it. Something snapped in me, I guess.' The case worker naturally questioned him about what his ex-wife could possibly have said to provoke such an extreme response as to walk out of a marriage like that, and on September 11th of all days. He didn't care to repeat to what he flatly related to me when first came to therapy about what made him walk out on his wife, 'She said I shoulda died there.'

Jack Smith's smile is the enigmatic smile of a man neither fully alive nor dead, but destined to survive. Whether he's destined or doomed, Smitty is not sure. Before 9/11 he'd already survived a major fire on the job, and an attack in which he'd been stabbed, beaten unconscious and left for dead. Smitty told me he'd spent the first years of his marriage 'drunk and in a blur', then 'One day I just decided, without AA or any therapist, to stop drinking, and I haven't touched the stuff since.' Jack Smith can rescue others from burning buildings, and he can survive deadly fires, but he can he can't stop his wife from drinking and he cannot spare his own daughter from being part of her mother's self-destructive tendencies.

All he can do is keep his mobile phone on all the time. Even up on the roof. When his daughter calls him and begs 'come get me' all he can do is tell her he'll be there as soon as sets the few tiles where the roof is exposed, then rush over to his ex's house, and wait patiently outside the door as he keeps pressing the re-dial button to call his daughter, and hope she'll answer the phone. And when she doesn't answer, all he can do is to keep leaving messages, 'Come out. I'm here, waiting in the truck.'

Smitty knows he's lucky to be alive and that by all accounts he should feel happy, only he doesn't. After all he is 'El Gato', as his buddies at the firehouse call him, survivor of so many life threatening situations on the job and off. He can't understand why, after recovering from alcoholism, after emerging unscathed, at least on the surface, from his previous brushes with death, and then escaping from the Trade Center within a matter of minutes if not seconds of being crushed in the collapse, he isn't bouncing back now. Wasn't 9/11 just one more brush with death? While he readily admits that the magnitude of 9/11 far exceeded anything he'd been through before, he can't grasp why the extraordinary resilience that is his essence, and that of all good firemen, could be failing him now. He can't accept that this disaster was apparently the final blow, as it was for many others in 9/11 who also had a prior history of trauma, the trauma that took him down. The knowledge that he is not alone in his inability to spring back provides little comfort. It's not that Jack Smith, and others like him with a stable upbringing and solid personal and social resources, have lost their capacity to cope. Survivors often know all too well how to survive. They don't know as well how to live, and how to feel about life.

Obsessed by the twisted faces, the torn and burnt bodies that he had to pass by to save his own life, Smitty is now a haunted man, like so many other survivors of the Trade Center, unable to make sense of why he survived when so many of his buddies and thousands of innocent men and women did not. No matter what he does or where he goes these days, the taunting voice of his ex-wife is a constant reminder of the deeper question that lurks behind everything he does. You may have survived, Smitty, but for what? Leaving him no place to go but to the roof. Where he can see the winter sky, and hammer nails into tar tiles to keep the house from leaking. Only a phone call away. Up on the roof where things look different than at ground level. Where if he had to, he could jump and survive. Or not. A daredevil's challenge, a child's play, a ladder that might just fall in the winter wind and find him beyond reach.

I'm watching the eleven o'clock news. The lead story is that two firefighters have either fallen or leapt to their deaths from the windows of the sixth story apartment building in which they were trapped to avoid being engulfed in flames. In another fire that same day another firefighter died of smoke inhalation while searching for a missing child, making this the largest number of deaths sustained in one day for the FDNY since September 11th. The question on everyone's mind is just why the firefighters, in a place where the fire truck's ladders couldn't reach them, were not equipped with ropes, which had always been part of their standard gear, and could likely have saved their lives. I watch the department's media spokesman attempt at spin control by claiming that carrying ropes was an outdated system that had been dispensed with because it was deemed too cumbersome for an already excessively weighted-down fireman to carry (firemen having about 60 to 100 lbs on them). I wonder if the truth was more that the decision to suspend wearing ropes was based more on saving money, making it one more disastrous result of budgetary constraints, like the inadequate radio communication system which failed on 9/11.

The next day the media is all over it and the public appears shocked. With morale sagging as the war in Iraq drags on, this surely will whet the public's voracious appetite for tragic twists of fate where men lose their own lives in the effort to save others. With recent reports of prisoner abuse in Guantanamo and Abu Ghraib and the rising incidence of major psychological problems in soldiers returning from deployment in Iraq and Afghanistan, it's now the American military's turn to fall from grace as national heroes. People are far more sympathetic to post-traumatic stress in theory than they are about the reality it wreaks on lives, especially when it detracts from the American self-image of strength and invincibility. And so for the moment at least, New York's Bravest have been restored to favoured hero status.

I know the guys from my firehouse must be shaken. I hadn't been to the house in some time but I know that I should try to contact them now. When I screw up my courage and call, I'm taken aback when the man on watch answering the house phone doesn't recognize me. Nor does the officer in charge who I'm passed on to and who blows me off with 'We've been told not to have the public in, what with all the negative press and all . . .' These guys must be new – I'm not 'the public'!

A few hours later I get a call from Smitty. 'I got to see you right away,' he insists with adamancy. So unlike his typically casual brusqueness. The next day I take my seat in my therapist's misnamed 'stress-less' chair and watch him gracefully jerry-rig himself into the chair closest to mine. It's the same chair that he's sat in for the last three years but that is now less easily able to accommodate the weight he's gained. With a chuckle, Smitty glancingly acknowledges his expanding girth, chalking it up to 'stress, I guess.' I wonder about the different functions his weight gain serves: at once it is a protective layer to fortify him for being in the world these days, a guilt-driven form of self-punishment, and a turning inward of the raging grief he cannot articulate. It may even be an unconscious and more socially acceptable way for him to be taken off duty and out of the firing line for another catastrophe. Mentioning any of these issues at this moment would serve no therapeutic purpose, for his weight is at the bottom of his 'to do' list and farther down the road to recovery in my estimation. So I just make an equally jocular comment, saying something vague about the importance of staying fit for health and safety on the job.

Knowing it's going to be hard for him to bring it up, I take the lead and immediately ask about the fire. Smitty shakes his head and with a half smile responds, 'No one'll be blamed. It'll be the same as always.' 'What about the rope?' I ask. 'Yeah,' he mutters, meaning: change the subject.

We are now in an instant replay of September 11th, 2001. Like many survivors of trauma, the incoherence of Smitty's inner life is reflected in his disorganized outer life, which bizarrely mirrors and acts out, without awareness, the chaos of the events that transpired during and after the disaster. Today he appears particularly preoccupied; he cannot formulate a clear thought or feeling in his mind, and so there's no way he can communicate clearly, just as he couldn't think straight that day, just as he was unsure of what had happened or what was going on around him that morning. It's not that he has been reliving the past in the present so much as it is that he remains frozen in the trauma with time collapsed. Today, every day, feels the same as that day three years ago.

Since his dramatic separation from his first wife right after September 11th, Smitty has struggled with the challenges of co-parenting in divorce, caring for aging parents and working overtime at the firehouse as well as at a second job to make ends meet. In fits and starts, like an engine revving up or about to give out, Smitty takes me through the events of his week, telling me about the various people and problems he's had to deal with. But none of this is new. I've heard all this before, the week before, the month before. Why the insistent call now?

Should I ask whether he knows one of the men involved in this accident? Maybe these tragic deaths have triggered a reactivation of memories and symptoms that were beginning to come under control and recede from consciousness. As if reading my mind, and many psychoanalysts believe this happens, that the patient and therapist come to read each other's thoughts and feelings automatically without even knowing they're doing so, Smitty answers my question. After announcing 'Guess it's time to stop,' he hurtles through our time-worn dialogue, 'Heard one got his whole face burnt off, and a second guy's about to go.' Now I understand why Smitty had to come in today. He wanted me to help him not become haunted by two more faces.

* * *

Later on in the week someone comes in for a consultation. He begins by asking if I mind him taking off his shoes off. I encourage him to make himself comfortable. After we exchange a few pleasantries of introduction, he proceeds to explain his reason for coming to see me. 'This has to do with a man I know, uh, knew, and what happened that day. I mean September 11th.' His words shake me to the core. I feel like I'm inside a bubble observing the situation. My body tenses, sights and sounds blur. My mind has to fight the impulse to drift away.

Questioning myself, I wonder why I'm suddenly reacting to talk about 9/11 when I'm dealing with it all the time with so many patients. Has my protective psychic barrier gotten so thick I'm now inured to the catastrophe and rendered me unable to feel adequate empathy for victims? Is this the burnout, or 'compassion fatigue' they talk about in the trauma therapy world? Perhaps so. But I'm pretty sure something else is going on. There's something about this man that I'm unconsciously responding to.

I try to shake myself back to attention. Did I miss, or perhaps he hasn't told me yet, just how he knew this man. From my bubble I hear him explain, 'I'm a rabbi. But he wasn't even in my congregation. He was a friend. From high school.' The rabbi is now telling me how they were talking man-to-man, in a meeting of mobiles, each man glued to his cell phone. The rabbi was on the street in upper Manhattan, no more than two miles, but worlds away from the towers. His friend from high school was trapped on the floor of one of the towers right above or below where the plane had crashed into. I have to fight to stay present yet I am also feeling gripped in a way I can't put my finger on.

A therapist needs to have emotional boundaries which are porous enough for her to experience in her body as well as her mind even the most dark and fragile states of her patient. At the same time she needs to remain intact in her separateness so that her own psychic stability doesn't become threatened. I count on my ability to enter my patient's psyche while feeling solid and able to think clearly. Feeling rather unnerved by this new patient forces me to consider that 9/11 may have had a more deleterious effect on me than I've wanted to admit.

It's true, whenever a plane is flying low in the sky, or when the subway stops inexplicably for moments just too long to seem normal, that hyper-vigilance can re-surface in a flash; that was my and many New Yorkers' experience for some time after September 11th. On occasion my pulse still quickens in these situations. But I've understood these reactions as normal trace effects from the catastrophe that have dissipated over time and that I trust they will eventually disappear, assuming there isn't another attack. Just what is it about this man, his story or our meeting that's getting to me? Suddenly it hits me – the man before me today is talking about 9/11 while sitting in the exact same cross-legged, stocking-feet position as my patient was in at the moment that I spotted the plane flying past my office window at 8.45 on September 11th, causing my building to shake so much that I interrupted her to ask about it. Clearly this must be the trigger for my tension and momentary withdrawal.

Making this connection helps bring me back to the here and now. His desperation is palpable. I encourage him to go on. He tells me that the friend he was talking to in the Tower told him he had already managed to reach someone in his family. Then, with a clear-headed urgency that the rabbi found strangely amazing under the circumstances, it occurred to him to try to reach his old friend because he's a rabbi. The caller needed his advice. He was sure the flames were rapidly engulfing the floor he was on. There was no time for Socratic philosophizing or Talmudic weighing of the pros and cons by which most rabbinic decisions are arrived at.

Haltingly the rabbi in front of me explains, 'He said the heat was unbearable, coming up from the floor . . . Suicide as you know is against Jewish law, but then . . . the circumstances . . .' Mumbling something I cannot make out, he buries his face in his hands.

It is at this moment that I realize I'd become enveloped myself in an invisible blanket since 9/11. It was true, I was connected enough to have pre-consciously registered the profound pain of this man and the burden he he's been carrying. And yes, I know how crucial it is for me as a therapist to maintain enough distance from the patient to prevent myself from becoming so affected I lose my capacity to be effective, or even vicariously traumatized. But I think I may have taken it too far. The shield I'd built up working with survivors may even be getting in my way therapeutically. To help this man and continue trauma therapy with people like Jack Smith, Patrick Darby, and Steve Holland, I must shed this layer of self-insulation.

Letting myself take in his need to unburden himself of the unbearable memory he's been carrying alone, I can feel myself becoming more and more present in the moment. I'm sure that the rabbi has heard his own share of 9/11 stories, and given counselling to many around the spiritual meaning of that life altering day. But here he is, three years later, looking to me to help him understand what transpired between him and his childhood friend, so he won't have to bear the responsibility of remembering alone. Feeling the awesome import of this, I am at a loss for words.

Leaning his head over his lap, pulling at the tip of his socks, he bears on with his story. 'He beseeched me to tell him what to do. Pleading, he asked, 'Please tell me, would it be wrong if I jump? . . . Should I jump or . . .?''

Now I am fully present with him and his friend in the grip of life-ending decisions. I look at the rabbi. His head is shaking in silence. Before I can stop him, and spare him from having to say what I know he's thinking, he quietly cries out, 'I don't know if what I told him was right.'

This session is making me realize how much hurt I, too, carry from that catastrophic day. The rabbi was but one of so many people I worked with in addition to the firefighters whose pain lingers several years after September 11th. His situation is both unique and universal. While his moral dilemma was particular to his life and beliefs, it raises basic questions about life and death that transcend the specific unfolding of events that morning. The capacity to contemplate one's death is our human legacy, what separates us from the rest of the living world. Imagining death is inherent to being human, a way to master our fear of it, and live meaningfully.

On September 11th communication technology turned people around the world into helpless spectators of death. We observed destiny and self-determination play out before our eyes, as one person after another, alone and in pairs holding hands, jumped to their deaths from the windows of the World Trade Center. In those final moments were those individuals graced with 'the white light' of Truth and Understanding? Why does it take such crises as 9/11 for us to fully appreciate the preciousness and briefness of life? I think of how many people seek the pulse and full intensity of aliveness by taking life and death into their own hands, for good and for evil, with a gun, a scalpel, a body-wrap of bombs. And what about those who by career or personal compulsion put themselves in life-threatening situations on a routine basis?

Our relationship to death, whether we feel resigned or accepting of its inevitability, shapes how we live the life we're given. In my experience those most fearful at death seem to be those who have not fully lived. The key to a full life is being able to recognize what's within our power, taking hold of it and letting go of the rest. The rabbi must live with the knowledge of what he chose to tell this man, and what he imagines happened afterward. Smitty will never know what went through the minds of the firefighters who had no ropes, whether they felt that they had taken control of their death by jumping out the window. The survivors of the Trade Center collapse, all of us, must come to terms with choices made and the arbitrariness behind so much of what happens. Life is about capturing a sense of urgency, finding within ourselves the will and potential to live life fully and meaningfully in all its exquisite fragility, horror and beauty. That is what makes the difference between passive and active living and what transforms a victim, bystander or survivor into a hero.

I realize that in deciding to commit myself to working with these 9/11 trauma victims, I'm needing to find renewed courage within myself to really be right there with my patients as they journey through their private hell. It means figuring out when it's best to push through the doubts and fears, theirs and my own, and when it's best to respect fear and let it be. I must take care of myself and them, living and working with them in a way that holds out the hope that there is life past grief, and a world beyond trauma.

February
A few months ago Steve Holland left me a phone message. 'Doc, could you give me a call back when you have the chance? It's Steve Holland, from the Fire Department. I don't know if you remember me. We met a few years ago at the firehouse.' Did I remember him? How could I forget the ruddy red-haired quarterback who had made it his business to get assigned to the firehouse where his lost friend Bobby Walsh had last worked, only to disappear a few months later? He sounded ill at ease but as warmly authoritative as I remembered. First he inquired about the firehouse. Holland then said he was now working out of the Bronx 'closer to home', implying that his decision to leave Manhattan, which a lot of guys did after 9/11, had nothing to do

with wanting to be further away from another potential disaster. Then with the self-conscious humility I remembered well, he slipped in the fact that he'd been promoted to captain shortly after leaving the firehouse and was hoping to go for chief soon. I could feel him hesitating to get to the point of why he was reaching out now.

I took the bull by the horns. 'So, Captain Holland, congratulations! What's up? What can I do for you?' Palpably embarrassed, he explained, 'I was wondering if I could come in with the wife. It's one of those things Doc, you know, like you talked about at the firehouse.' My mind went down the list of topics we had discussed. His stoic demeanour was revealing no clues about what 'one of those things' could be. Suddenly, the light bulb went on, and laughing, I said, 'Oh!' then trying to put him at ease, 'Sure, of course I do sex therapy. Like I told you guys, these things are always affected after what you've been through.' We made an appointment for the next week.

It was clear to me from our very first meeting that Steve's and his wife Stephanie's sexual problems were covers for deeper issues that were not going to be cured by a straightforward course of sex therapy. As serious as Steve's self-diagnosed libido problem was, it was the tip of the iceberg. It turned out that the only reason Steve had finally agreed to come to therapy was because his wife had become suicidally depressed; according to her, because she was so desperately unhappy over their non-existent sexual relationship. While Steve had periodically struggled with erectile dysfunction over the years and was never as interested and uninhibited about sex as his wife, since 9/11 he had been totally unable to perform, or to feel any desire whatsoever. Freely admitting to what he terms his 'deficiencies' in this department, Steve was much more preoccupied and worried about the seriousness of his wife's depression, which was expressed in a general agitation and uncharacteristic non-communicativeness, and had culminated in a barely-restrained impulse to run into oncoming traffic a few weeks earlier.

His wife Stephanie was the 'identified patient' in therapy

terms, the person who is the outward bearer of the disturbance in the couple or family. I knew that Steve's problems, though less obvious to them, were somehow implicated with Stephanie's more transparent difficulties, and that their respective problems were intimately intertwined to the point of strangling the life out of the relationship. 9/11 didn't cause their problems, but it dramatically exacerbated them.

It was going to be impossible to fully parse out the damage of 9/11 from the myriad ways life can wreak havoc on marriage. The marital problems they had before September 11th went into temporary remission during the crisis and the initial period following the disaster. Steve's sexual hang-ups and Stephanie's over-sensitivity to feelings of rejection pre-dated the disaster. As did their dynamic of Stephanie acting the part of being the 'needy' one who's emotionally volatile while her husband played the role of the stoic and capable caretaker. They had unconsciously settled into a pattern which did not allow enough room for Stephanie's strengths and for Steve's vulnerabilities, in and out of the bedroom.

September 11th blew apart this fragile pact. At some point in the aftermath of the catastrophe there was no hiding the fact that Steve was barely keeping it together. During those long months at Ground Zero, Stephanie took 'perfect' care of Steve who moved like a sleepwalker from his double tours of duty back home where he ate Stephanie's freshly-cooked food and then fell asleep on the couch for the few hours left before the whole routine began again. Steve claims 'the only reason I'm still alive at all' is because Stephanie was there. 'Stephanie is my home.' As Stephanie tells it, 'I had to hold myself back, literally grabbing the walls, to keep myself from running after him and telling him not to go back' each morning, as she watched him toss her a half-hearted kiss good-bye in the doorway.

Like generations of firefighters' wives before her, Stephanie was accustomed to the idea of her husband being prepared to sacrifice himself and thereby his family for the well being of other families. But as the months passed after September 11th,

Stephanie's fortitude began to flag and she started to experience pangs of desperation, which she attributed to the heightened threat of the conditions, and which I suggested was perhaps also because the familiar balance of power they had come to rely on had been disrupted. Stephanie's going into a serious clinical depression managed to reinstate the dynamic of Steve being the caretaker and Stephanie being the one in need of care. Though they recognized this dynamic wasn't healthy, it was what they knew. And restoring the familiar was what they felt they needed more than anything in this most unfamiliar of times. The dynamic came to a head in Steve rescuing Stephanie from acting on her suicidal impulse.

With the help of medication and a few months of couples therapy, Stephanie is notably less depressed, even hopeful some days. Steve has come to accept the idea that Stephanie's depression was as much of an expression of their marital problems as it was of her own personal problems, but he still focuses almost exclusively on Stephanie's feelings rather than on his own. It is as if Stephanie is a cipher for all his emotions. He can genuinely empathize with his wife's pain without feeling vulnerable and he can take care of her while appearing to have no needs or emotional struggles of his own.

It is now a few days after Valentine's Day. Stephanie walks into my office and takes the seat at the farthest end of the couch, right next to the alluring window. It is a warning and reminder, assuredly unconscious, to her husband and me that we need to remember the seriousness of her earlier threat to throw herself in front of a bus. Her husband laughs, 'I have to keep my eye on you,' but at the moment none of us are especially worried that Stephanie will try to take a flying leap from that window. Even so, I know they both count on me to be always on top of Stephanie's mental and emotional status. Because I know that the pull of the window for Stephanie, as for any person with suicidal ideation, is directly proportional to the intensity of her desperation, I vigilantly track her emotions from moment to moment. I take care to notice how strongly she hugs the pillows, to detect any minute change in the sound of her voice, or shift in her gaze. When she draws her dark glasses down over her eyes, I understand she is near the limit of what she can handle. Without bringing attention to this fact and risking alienating her, I simply re-direct our discussion to something more tolerable. And I remind myself that for now, at least, Stephanie has chosen to take a different kind of leap: couples therapy.

Steve begins the session saying that Stephanie had purchased a new set of candlesticks, wine glasses and placemats with matching napkins for the occasion. They had decided it would be fun to cook together. Steve explains that everything was fine until Stephanie began to tease him. 'She said, "Eat up. So you'll have energy for later." That was it. The whole night was shot. I was in a panic.' Am I hearing Steve say he actually felt in a panic? Is he parroting therapy language, trying to be a good patient or is he finally admitting that he, too, has feelings? Immediately he reverts to his logical un-emotional self. He looks to his wife then tells me, 'I was convinced she meant it, she really wanted sex. And why wouldn't she?' 'But I was only joking,' she insists in a languid effort at self-defence. Steve retreats into silence.

Once again Steve and Stephanie have done their ritualized therapy dance of demonstrating the severity of their communication problems to me. Stephanie proclaims that she's no longer depressed because 'I've given up any expectations'. I wonder whether this is true. Perhaps that's why she's not shown up several times recently for our weekly scheduled sessions. The marital battle between Steve and Stephanie isn't one of those marital contests of control for the sake of control. That would have meant a far less hopeful prognosis for the viability of their marriage. Despite Steve's expressions of futility and Stephanie's protestations of having 'had enough', the strength of their love and commitment to each other is undeniable. This is a relationship that will make it through the long haul. The question is whether they can stop being miserable and making each other miserable along the way. They both genuinely want to make their partner happy and neither can feel happy as long as the other one isn't.

In their interlocking neuroses they get easily caught up in power struggles. Neither gets pleasure out of controlling the other but in their neurotic dependence on each other, they each try to get the other to accommodate to their own comfort level. Stephanie's self-esteem is far too dependent on her husband and Steve's sense of well-being is far too dependent on his wife's emotional state. Stephanie gets caught up in that all-too-human need to be responded to while Steve is consumed with the need to 'keep things under control'. When feeling threatened by what he perceives as his wife's superior ease and intelligence about emotions, Steve shuts down, setting his wife up to be the one to explode and act out the distress that he has disconnected himself from feeling in adamant stoicism and self-sacrifice. What Steve had unconsciously come to think of as Stephanie's hysteria was no more than her choosing the expression of her pain over the self-denial and repression that Steve retreats even more deeply into when feeling unsafe.

When not in conflict, they agree: Steve is the slow and steady one who brings practicality to the table, while Stephanie brings the passion, each complementing the other, making them feel complete as a couple. Like many couples years into the relationship, they find the traits that originally attracted them to each other are the very things that now drive each other crazy. Steve, uptight in general and especially about sex, fell in love with Stephanie's intensity, especially in the bedroom, but came to feel more and more confused and out of his depth in meeting her demands for intimacy. In turn, Stephanie readily admits to a lifelong struggle managing her emotions and taking control of her life. Initially feeling protected by her husband's take-charge, hyper-rational personality, she came to feel hurt and rejected by his limited emotional expressiveness. A fragile détente of their separate hurts and frustrations became unsustainable after September 11th when Steve became consumed with post-traumatic guilt and grief which made him even more withdrawn and unresponsive.

Stephanie attempts to engage her husband now as she

typically does when Steve withdraws into silence. She turns to face her husband and gives him a big smile, then waits for a response. Steve blurts out, 'I feel nothing. I don't know why. I don't know what's wrong with me, I just feel nothing.' 'Nothing or numb?' I ask, looking for that definitive proof of his trauma. 'No, definitely not numb. That would mean there was a feeling underneath that was being numbed. I mean I don't feel.' Then, as if discovering one feeling he could legitimately claim, with self-disgust, Steve snorts, 'I'm a coward.'

Stephanie and I are aghast. I glance over at Stephanie then look back to Steve. Stephanie immediately comes to the rescue. 'But you're a hero. Look what you do.' He just stares back at her, almost coldly, unbelieving, and ready, I think, to turn his anger outward now, to direct it at her. Unsuspecting, Stephanie goes on, 'because you go to work every day.' He rejoins, 'I thought you said I only go to work to get away from you and that I like being with the guys more than with you,' sarcastically rejecting the idea, himself and Stephanie in one fell swoop.

Seeing his passive aggressive put-down as a defence against more vulnerable feelings, I ignore his comment and pipe in, 'Can you take in what she said? You're her hero.' Before giving him a chance to answer I press forward, 'Can you see it as an expression of love for you, like the Valentine's dinner?' His anger now in defeat, Steve answers, 'Yeah, but I don't know why. What do I do for her? All I do is go to work, put food on the table. I'm grumpy all the time.' Then, as if to punctuate how pathetic he is, and to re-fortify the wall between himself and his wife, he adds defensively, 'I just want to be left alone,' in a way that borders on meanness. Just how is it that at the firehouse, as I remember, Steve can get into the mix with the guys, and come to life when the alarm announces fire and smoke, but when he's in what he calls 'the security of home base', he just wants to be left alone?

The strain between them permeates the room, seeping imperceptibly into me, as is the fate of the truly involved therapist. Stephanie may hold the womanly edge in ease of emotional expressiveness, but her former quarterback husband knows just how to run around his wife's emotional challenges and get that touchdown. Like all couples, Stephanie and Steve have managed to equalize the power in their relationship. Each one knows just when and how to deliver that crucial blow beneath the belt to the other. Having observed them in action in session, I can only imagine how things play out at home, for as open as couples can be in therapy, the best and worst of a couple's life happens in private. In the time since we've begun working together things haven't really changed in the sex department but from what I see and what they say, their overall communication has improved. At least they've succeeded in finding a de-militarized zone when engaged in battle, sometimes even taking that 'time out' we've talked about when things get out of hand.

Stephanie responds to Steve's bitter declaration of aloneness by raising the ante. She brings up an issue that is so painful to Steve he's never been able to raise it himself – having children. 'How can we have children when we don't have sex?' But her question seems to bounce off her husband's self-described 'force field' of impenetrability. Without skipping a beat, he shoots back, 'Because I won't live long enough, that's why.' Okay, so Steve has trumped her, but defeated himself in the bargain. Though Steve, ten years older than Stephanie, will claim he's too old to have a child, age isn't what's really keeping him from going forward with becoming a father. Steve felt robbed of his own youth because when he was twelve, his father deserted the family and his mother told him he had to become 'the man in the house' and take care of his three younger siblings. Steve isn't ready to have a child, and might never be. Being a husband and an officer is as much responsibility as he seems able to handle.

In the isolated cocoon in which they were living when they first came to me, Steve was spending his free time watching strangers on television while his wife sat nearby chatting online with virtual friends. Where would a child fit in? Most importantly, with all his medical knowledge as an EMS officer, acutely aware of the long term risks of being a fireman and now about the long-term health consequences from 9/11, Steve is convinced that he will die young. Having spent his early childhood playing dead to survive his father's unpredictable violent outbursts, Steve coped by being a go-along, get-along kid. He learned to avoid conflict at all costs, and to keep his feelings in cryogenic storage for safe keeping. Only rarely did he give people a chance to get close enough to him to get to know the real Steve. Stephanie was one of the few people he's ever trusted enough to be open with. I suspect Bobby Walsh was another. I wonder how close he'll allow himself to get to me. Since 9/11, Steve says he can't feel anything. It feels more to me that he's half frozen, warmed by the heat of fire and danger.

The next week Steve arrives alone for the couples therapy, claiming 'I wouldn't feel right canceling at the last moment.' I use her absence to press my case for him to consider doing individual therapy. He repeats his mantra, 'I only came here for her. I know I'm damaged goods.' He went on, 'I'm not convinced,' then stopped mid-sentence. I know that beneath his incomplete thought lies a lack of faith in his own ability to change and in other people's ability, mine specifically, to break through his defensive 'force field'. At the moment I'm wondering if he's right; maybe his dogged concreteness is intractable and that I shouldn't push him to come on his own. Sensing something in me, he throws out an unanswerable question that he's asked many times before. 'What's my case? Can you fix it?'

Though I should know better than letting him get to me, I feel as if Steve has 'succeeded' in taking me down with him into feeling the futility which overtakes him at times. Where is my faith in the power of therapy and my relationship with my patient? I can't let his despair get to me. I now see there's no way he could understand how therapy actually works. It's hard enough for therapists to find a language that captures the process of therapy. Including the magic that takes place beneath the rhythm of words exchanged. I can't expect this man, trained in medical science and whose very survival as a firefighter depends on functioning like a finely-tuned machine, to believe in something he cannot see. As 'well defended' and 'resistant', to use therapy-speak, as 'stubborn' and 'difficult' as Steve is in layman's terms, there must a way to get through to him.

I point out that while he may not be thinking about throwing himself in front of buses like Stephanie, his rigid self-control and self-denial are also self-destructive. His long-suppressed emotions have boiled up within him to the point where they are now literally making him sick with various physical ailments. In short, I state with that declarative edge of therapeutic authority, 'you are quietly but most definitely killing yourself.'

'OK, you're scaring me. I admit it,' he confesses, his voice quivering slightly. Immediately I feel regret, and a tinge of guilt. I may have broken through his defences, but I'm ashamed of the way I did it. I lost my therapeutic grounding and ended up reprimanding him and taking my frustrations out on him, not so differently from the way Stephanie reacts to his transparent defensiveness. Freud believed that any break in the analyst's neutrality, no matter how mild or momentary, is to be avoided. Today, the field is much more accepting of the analyst at some point having a strong personal reaction to her patient. Analysts like myself, of the Interpersonal Relational School, believe that these counter-transference reactions can end up being therapeutic. When they are properly analyzed, the therapist can control how she acts with the patient and can utilize her reaction in a disciplined way to move the therapy forward.

My frustration with Steve's hard-headed rigidity gives me a better feeling for what his wife experiences, but it doesn't excuse my over-reacting. I can, however, now see something I've been missing. Steve isn't as resistant to therapy as I've made him out to be. The fact is, he's been coming regularly, whether or not Stephanie is there, and he's deeply involved in the therapy.

No longer hiding behind his wife, and being the real patient that I now see he has become, Steve ploughs on despite my misguided confrontation. He relates an incident that had occurred a few days after the Valentine's Day debacle. One morning he was feeling a re-awakening of his lost sexual interest. Right in the middle of things the telephone rang. They didn't answer it, but a man from the firehouse left a message they could hear. Something about 'a big one', putting an end to their lovemaking. He goes on, 'You know what I said, what I actually said to her?' then sharply, 'I had to turn my back when I said it, but I actually said it. I told her, 'I'm scared'.'

Too quickly, I try to nudge him out of his self-disgust. 'That doesn't mean you're not a hero. That has nothing to do with being a hero. In fact that makes you even more of a hero. You're scared and you still go in.' He replies, 'I was never scared before.' He pauses, and then, haltingly, tries to proceed, 'Ever since. You don't understand. Now I hesitate . . . I don't know.' Able now to remain silent, I let Steve keep going. 'You can't do that. Before, I used to just go in; I never thought about it. You can't think about it – I just went in and did my job. I did what had to be done. It's someone's life.'

For Steve this means being conscious of fear. Gripped in a combination of remorse, pathos and self-pity, he tells me, 'To tell you the truth, it's a terrible thing to say but . . . A civilian, it would be terrible. But I couldn't live . . . I couldn't live if . . . if it was one of my men.' Steve starts to weep. Trying to be with him but to give him leeway to be with himself and his feelings, I sit back and watch him take a handkerchief out of his pocket. Gathering himself, he keeps going, 'What's really crazy is, I'm embarrassed to admit, that I'm waiting for the next one. Isn't that sick?'

'No, you are not crazy.' I tell him that he's not alone in that perversely excited dread of 'the next one'. I explain, 'You need to know . . . to see if you can do it – now that you feel afraid.' The question that looms ever-larger for Steve and his fellow firefighters is whether they'll be able to go into the next 'big one' without hesitation. For any hesitation, they know, can mean the difference between life and death. But what if the next big one involves weapons of mass destruction? Steve heaves a sigh that says he can't do any more today in therapy, and ends the hour, 'I just wish Stephanie were here, to witness this.'

The numbed state of trauma in which Steve and Smitty, like so many other 9/11 survivors, were locked into for so long seems to now be giving way. With the passage of time and enough support from loved ones and their community, people do heal from massive catastrophe. Therapy offers that added ingredient that some survivors find crucial to free themselves from being held hostage to their burden. By trusting someone and giving voice to the pain, self doubt and responsibility of memory, the survivor can face and begin to make sense of what has happened. For Steve to admit feeling 'excited' at the idea of a fire, in fact to admit to having feelings at all, is a breakthrough, not only in his post-9/11 state, but in his lifelong pattern of emotional disconnection and hyper-rational persona. Steve is just beginning to come alive and actually feel his feelings. It will take some time for him to learn how to stay in touch with himself and for him to fully appreciate what part his history played in making him the way he is, and how much 9/11 has affected him.

But I know that with patience and perseverance on both our parts, Steve will get there. Once he can allow himself to face his own grief, he'll be able to forgive himself. For all frozen matter, no matter how 'damaged', will thaw, given time and the right conditions.

March
After more than two years of working together with Firefighter Jack Smith, slogging through good times and bad, unsure where the therapy was going, only knowing that we had to keep going, the therapy is finally feeling different. It's as if we're emerging out of a dark tunnel. The flashbacks, intrusive thoughts and images are still there, but they're less frequent and less disruptive. The fog that marked his post 9/11 life for so long is lifting, and while Smitty never stopped being involved with people, he seems to be more engaged, even enjoying himself again. He's finally able to sleep through the night, and much to his bemusement he's been dreaming up a storm and remembering them in vivid detail. He diligently writes them down on scraps of paper which he hands to me and says, 'Heck, I don't know what they mean. I just dream

'em and tell you.' Looking to his therapist to be the dream catcher and soothsayer who will tell him what they mean.

Disappointed in the short memory New York has for its 9/11 heroes, Smitty refuses to march this year with the Brotherhood in the annual St Patrick's Day parade. We have an appointment set for that afternoon. I decide to take advantage of a free hour and the March melt to go for a quick run. After huffing through the first mile or so I finally hit my stride and am rewarded with that runner's high I'm reluctant to give up. I check my watch. Smitty still has trouble arriving right on time, but I can't be late. I sprint the last few blocks for that last endorphin rush so I can be back in my therapist outfit, notebook and pen in hand, before he gets there.

Smitty begins the session talking about what's going on at the job. He talks about how things just aren't the same at the firehouse, as he often does. When I ask about the new guys he says, 'I guess they're okay', which means they are not his dead buddies and will never be able to replace them. He goes on to say he really doesn't so much mind being one of the oldest guys on the job, but what's getting to him these days is the training they're in for another terrorist attack on New York. Then he says 'It's that', nothing more. Not sure what he's trying to get at I ask 'What?' He repeats, 'It's that', getting more agitated, raises his voice, 'I tell them I'll put a hole in the tyre. I *won't go.*' Meaning walk headlong into another catastrophe, like a potential bio-terrorist attack. His adamancy is not an expression of intent at insubordination. It's the opposite. Smitty's blustery threats are the only way he can convey the dilemma he is in: the dilemma of not feeling psychically up to that challenge and yet knowing that if called to action, he will do his duty and go.

The men of the FDNY have been conscripted into the 'war against terrorism.' Being a soldier of sorts was not what Smitty had had in mind when he signed on to become a firefighter. Now he's on a tirade. 'Preparedness training's a fad. A joke. I'm not crazy. They send us to training, like fifteen minutes of a video

tape! Five, six alarmers are one thing, they're . . .' 'Dangerous,' I
manage to insert in an effort to break through his ranting and help
him calm down. He replies, 'Exciting, yeah. But gas?!'

The word hovers between us. I say nothing. Smitty chalks
off a list of the various chemical and biological weapons they're
being told they should prepare for. Smitty loves his firehouse. It's
been impossible for him to consider doing what other men did
after 9/11, to transfer to a different firehouse, one further away
from downtown Manhattan, less at risk of being in the middle
of another terrorist attack and with fewer sad memories. He's
determined to stick it out right there in the firehouse he's been in
for almost fifteen years. But now, with babies on the way and all
this talk about preparing for another catastrophe, I can tell he's
struggling. Smitty changes the subject. He's got some dreams to
tell me.

'The first one you won't believe this, but I'm in my class A
uniform, in a building or something, maybe on the job. I had
three penises! One of them I had slung over my shoulder . . .'
Smitty laughs, embarrassed, but appreciating the humour of it.
'You mean like an extra piece of equipment?' I ask, thinking
about the added challenges he's facing at work now.

Clearly not wanting this to be too deeply examined, he
responds, 'Yeah, yeah, somethin' like that,' and moves on to
the next dream. 'I'm in a camp setting with some guys from the
firehouse. This kid's there. You know, one of the Curtis kids. He
likened me to his father. He came and showed me a code that was
on his jacket. He asked me for an explanation.' This kid was one
of four boys whose father worked with Smitty and was killed.
Clearly Smitty sees the boy in the dream as looking to him as a
father figure. I interpret Smitty deciphering the 'code' as trying
to help him understand the death of his father. Smitty knows he
can't replace the boy's father but he so desperately needs to do
something for the children of his buddies who died. At the same
time, he has so many things to figure out himself. The most basic
one – the whys of who dies and who survives – is undecipherable
to him.

The next week Smitty dreams of war. A manageable war, the kind that could only be imagined in the fantastical dream life of an 'El Gato' survivor. 'It's somewhere like out west. We're getting a posse out after a group of people. We've surrounded these people. We'd split up. We had rifles, I was aiming. I shot one or two. They went down. I zeroed in on the leader, he wasn't even going down. Other guys went down but we weren't killing them. It turned out they were only bee-bee guns. A guy shot at me but missed and the bullet went into the shaft of a car. I ducked behind a house. This girl was walking by the car. I yelled out to her, 'It's going to blow up.' She got by it okay.'

Smitty may have be able to save the fair maiden in his dreams. He may even dream of fighting where nobody really gets hurt, and where good triumphs over evil, but he knows full well that no matter how much of a superman he strives to be, no matter how much courage and ingenuity he can muster for others, he's up against the impossible in this new kind of war. A week or two later the subject of 'preparedness training' comes up again. He tells me that this time they're being trained to use new equipment especially designed for a chemical attack. Smitty emphatically pronounces, 'I told them. That's it. We're not going. That's all there is to it.' Three-time survivor of death, El Gato knows even he can't dream up a way for us to survive that.

* * *

In therapy, as in a family, it can be hard to tell who's taking care of whom. Steve Holland invited me to attend a satellite conference the department cooked up as part of its bio-terrorism preparedness training, telling me 'You might find it helpful', because it's going to focus on the psychological effects of bio-terrorism on first responders. I know it's crossing the therapy boundary but I figure there must be a good reason why Steve, who tends to be formal if not rigid, is asking me to break out of the rule book and go with him. Even if he's doing it in his typical way, being the one who's offering to help the other person out. I'm not particularly excited at the idea of having to think about weapons of mass destruction being used in another attack on the city, but something tells me I should take Steve up on this unusual invitation.

We agreed he'd pick me up outside my office and drive me over to Headquarters. Around 11.30 I leave my office to grab a quick cup of coffee before our appointed noon meeting time. It doesn't occur to me that the nondescript black car across the street is Steve's until he rolls down the window and honks the horn. Twenty-five minutes early! He's foiled my own 'preparedness' plan for a pick-me-up shot of Starbucks before we met. Time being a matter of relativity, as much a quirk or quark of personality as of physics, Steve greets me with, 'Sorry I wasn't here sooner.'

I sink down into the passenger seat and look around. The large pained man who so awkwardly sits across from me each week is transformed into the Marlboro man behind the wheel. The console of the official car is all bells and whistles. A dispatcher's voice crackles from somewhere unidentifiable in the highly sophisticated radio system.

I inquire whether we have time to stop for coffee. Steve's voice stiffens, and with one hand tightening around the steering wheel, he points with the other to the traffic ahead. Clearly I've thrown a curveball he hadn't planned on. He responds, 'I was thinking maybe if there's time I'd take you on a tour of Headquarters.' I think, if there's time? But I say 'never mind', in cheery effort. What the hell are we going to do all this time we'll now have to kill before this oxymoronic event of psychological preparedness for disaster?

Steve slips a cassette into one of the mysterious slots. 'I listen to the Dead whenever I'm in the car and on a call.' Once the music begins his grip loosens on the steering wheel and I start tapping my feet to the familiar beat. We sit together in the unmoving honking traffic, a man in the old age of youth and a woman in the youth of old age. In our shared but never spoken-of history of being children who had to prematurely assume roles of adult responsibility, humming along with the Dead, on the way to 'prepare' for the unknown.

Steve gets me past security using his pass, and leads me on a guided tour of the brand new headquarters of the Fire Department, introducing me to passers-by by name only, neither of us being particularly interested in explaining or risking betraying the confidentiality of our complicated relationship. A large sign posted outside the door of the room reads, 'Psychological Sequelae of Weapons of Mass Destruction on First Responders.' Once inside, I see no one else is there. Probably only the disaster junkies and people like Steve and myself, with an overdeveloped sense of responsibility and neurotic need to 'hope for the best but prepare for the worst' will be crazy enough to attend a 'conference' on preparing for weapons of mass destruction, or WMD, as I am about to learn they have come to be euphemistically called. The room is set up with several tables facing large televisions equipped with video cameras for audience participation, and a digital timer counting down the minutes before the thing begins.

A thick stapled document lies by each seat, giving the room the deceptively innocuous look of a college exam room before finals. Steve and I stare at the papers in front of us as we wait for the movie version of what we lived through on 9/11. Eventually about a half dozen people join us. One man cynically comments on the sparse attendance: 'People don't want to be reminded.'

They say life imitates art but having a mustached fellow on a TV screen from some place very far away from New York tell New York City's firemen how distressed he was to watch the Trade Center collapse on television from his home in the deep South feels ridiculous and absurd to me. Perhaps it's my anxiety or a streak of competitive cynicism. Maybe this is a re-living of the 'life is a movie only it's not' sensation that I felt on that morning, or maybe it's the sheer surreality of WMD. All I know is that the videoconference feels like it's turning into one of those typical American remakes of reality-into-Disney spectacle. Wondering if Steve is also feeling disturbed, I reach over to touch him on the arm, and whisper 'How you doing?' I'm stung when he barks back in a whisper, 'I didn't ask you to come to take care of me. I thought you might be interested.'

I sit back and listen to the lecture. Some of what I hear I already knew through my years of getting to know these first responders – the danger they face on a daily basis, the demands upon them and their families sets them apart from others, how well they function well under acute and chronic stress, the pride they take in controlling their fear. But then I learn more than I wanted to know about the realities and potentialities of terrorism. The lecturer enumerates the many globe-wide terrorist attacks there have been over recent years: Jakarta, Nairobi, Israel, Tokyo, the 1993 attack on the World Trade Center, Oklahoma City, and 9/11. I learn about what the cult of Aum Shinrikyo was able to inflict on Tokyo, poisoning more than five thousand persons with a frighteningly primitive method of using umbrellas to puncture five sarin-filled plastic bags when the subway doors opened at the station platform. That easy?! I learn about the double bombing attack patterns in Israel, where a second bomb detonates to target those first responders who are on their way to the first bomb site. I learn that a year after the sarin attack in Tokyo, 18.5% of survivors continued to experience significant ocular symptoms as the worst of the physical symptoms and that between 8% and 13% of the survivors continued to experience panic attacks, claustrophobia, flashbacks, impairment in memory and concentration, sleep disturbances and depression. The incidence and nature of symptoms being quite similar to what we had here after 9/11.

I am not surprised to hear him tell us that five years after Oklahoma City, first responders and survivors still need counselling. And that somewhere between 10% and 30% of all first responders will develop acute stress disorder or post-traumatic stress disorder in the course of their routine job career. After delivering this vice grip of facts and statistics, the instructor suggests that 'preparedness training' can somehow mitigate, if not magically inoculate, people from the effects of what is being treated as the inevitable future of continued acts of terrorism, one more than likely, we are told, to involve WMD.

Overwhelmed by the doom-laden blitzkrieg of information,

all I can think to say to Steve on the way to the elevator is, 'Some Mutt and Jeff pair we are.' He replies flatly, 'Well, I am tall,' and I end with, 'And after all, I'm really quite short.' We're quiet on the ride back. Sitting outside my office the two of us, unsure what to say, glance out the front window so as to not have to face each other in such close quarters. Finally Steve speaks. 'It was like looking in the mirror.' He pauses, then continues, 'Not the slides, I'd seen so many like that, but reading those papers, the reactions. It was looking in the mirror.' I'm taken aback by his sudden openness. Before I can respond, he tearfully proceeds, 'I'd never have gone into counselling if Stephanie hadn't forced me. I wonder what would have happened to me.' I'm touched but a bit flustered, now the one struggling for words. Undaunted by my lack of response, Steve continues. 'I have you to thank.'

But immediately he's back to his brusque self. 'I didn't ask you to come today for me.' I wonder if Steve is retreating consciously or unconsciously in reaction to my lack of responsiveness. I make a point of expressing gratitude for being invited to the video-conference. I suggest that he and I understand each other in more ways than can be said, and indirectly try to explain my discomfort by saying that therapists are like firemen, used to being on the giving rather than receiving end of help. Trying to recoup my footing as the therapist, I stumble forward with something inane to the effect of questioning whether he's allowing himself to be helped. As soon as the words are out of my mouth I regret what I've said. I attempt a retraction to repair the mess I'd made with his effort at intimacy and mutuality. 'But the fact is you are letting me help you,' and go on to say something about how our relationship exists on many levels. My voice sounds like it's someone else speaking.

I still don't have my bearings but try to remind myself that this is an inevitable and important part of the therapy process. It now becomes clear to me that Steve's and my separate identities are criss-crossing and blurring into each other, with the different parts of our hidden more vulnerable selves reaching out to each other, even those things we share but have never spoken about.

Steve turns to me in a rare moment of direct eye contact, 'I think I've touched you.' Immediately he turns back and looks out the front window. Also needing to look away I turn to stare out the side window. Did he say he's 'helped' me? No, he said clear as a bell, 'I've touched you.' He's right. This man who claims to be a 'rationalist' with little knowledge about 'feelings' has managed to reach me in a place inside myself that I think I keep well hidden beneath a façade of warmth and openness. And he's done it without ever inappropriately crossing that inviolate boundary that must be maintained between patient and therapist, between man and woman.

Steve and I are more than patient and therapist, more than colleagues or friends who respect each other's professional expertise and authority. Our understanding of the therapy structure and trust that its fundamental rules will be adhered to has allowed the beauty and power of transference and counter-transference to work its magic. It has freed us to go beyond where many patients and therapists do and most relationships ever get to. It has opened Steve to experience me as the sister that he never had, and the parent figure he can trust won't abandon him. And it's opening me to look past his hero image, above and beyond him as the professional firefighting leader I know him to be. It's allowing me to see him in his totality. And to imaginatively experience him as a brother, as the long-imagined son I never had, and as the strong tender father I lost, all at once.

That night I have a dream.

My brother Richie and I are in the water. We are nestled in a quiet cove between high jagged cliffs that look like the rocky New England shoreline where we swam as kids, or where later my young daughters slipped and slid laughing barefoot, and pulled mussels from the craggy rocks and dug for soft shell clams when the tide went out. Beautiful and dreadful, surrounded by the premonitory in the calm bay of the dark sea.

We're treading water. All I can see is his face bobbing on the surface, his curly hair and freckled nose. He's about five, so I'm three. I'm so happy just to be with him there, in that carefree childhood state. Suddenly I'm aware that there is no shore. The water comes right up to the high craggy cliff. How will we get out of the water? I keep my eyes on my brother, watching him, waiting to see how he's going to get out of the water. How will we grab hold of this vertical rock face? I know only one thing. If he makes it, I will.

This dream was clearly precipitated by what just happened with Steve. My brother Richie and I aren't big phone talkers and we haven't gotten together all that much over the years, what with work, children, and all. But in the scheme of things it doesn't matter. We know we've got each other's back, and can count on each other to be there when we need it. Just like how it feels between me and Darby and the guys from my firehouse who I don't see much of any more. No matter how long it's been since we've last seen each other, we pick up right where we left off. They say a firehouse is a family. I now know why. I am bonded to these men as brothers, our fates linked for life.

* * *

April

Air travel, the Federal Aeronautics Administration warns the American public, is expected to reach an all-time high this summer, despite the terrorist attack in Madrid last year, and the long security lines at the airport. Not to mention the tsunami in Asia that recently took tens of thousands of lives, and the terrorist bombings in Israel that have increased over the last several years. But all that feels far away in the city which is abuzz with talk about which plan will win the competition for the re-building of Ground Zero – that is, ground zero. The 9/11 desertion of New York City is a thing of the past. Real estate construction and values are at an all time high. We joggers and bikers have to compete once again with tourists on the small walkway of the Brooklyn Bridge. With the exception of those with loved ones fighting in Iraq and those first responders on the front lines of this invisible war on terrorism, the Big Apple is pretty much back to its pre-9/11 solipsistic self.

* * *

It's springtime and the man before me, Firefighter Jack Smith, should be happy. He's about to have not only one baby but three! Smitty is managing better at home and work. He's dreaming epic tales of vainglorious victory and defeat, usually with one of his firefighting brothers by his side. But he's still periodically felled by breathtaking headaches that have come without warning since 9/11. He still complains of memory problems but he's been remembering where he's supposed to be and getting there on time, including to our sessions. Yet with all the positive changes he's made, one painful thing persists. 'I keep thinking about the guys, the guys in my house. I can't get them out of my mind.' I now have a better understanding of Smitty's PTSD. It wasn't so much the history of multiple traumas on and off the job or his harrowing brush with death on September 11th that determined the extent of his trauma. It was the loss of so many men he worked and played with all at once, men who were as much family to him as his blood relations, that had the most deleterious effect. The depth of his attachments, the importance his relationships play in his life, was the factor that had the most traumatic impact on Smitty. He's stuck psychologically – he can't leave and he can't stay on the job. He's miserable. He doesn't want to leave his remaining brothers on the job. Yet he fears bringing life into an unsafe world, when his job might end up taking him away from them, not for a day or two, or for a week or even a month at a time, but forever.

After giving me the latest pregnancy update, Smitty presents the problem of the day. He has to decide whether or not to have his about-to-be-born babies baptized, and if he does, should it be in the Baptist church which his wife attends or in the Roman Catholic Church where he was baptized and where his mother goes to mass every day? In relating his dilemma, Smitty remembers a dream from earlier in that week that he tells me he's dreamt many times before. He and some of his siblings were in a room playing pool. Something was about to happen. He saw a window, the only clear escape, and the next thing he knew he was climbing onto the window sill, leaving his sisters and brothers standing there.

This dream repeats the theme of other dreams – how to save himself and others. It reinforces my sense that beneath the more obvious worries about having more children lies a deep-seated fear of losing himself in the conflict between addressing his own needs and those of the people he cares for. One of six children himself, Smitty learned early that you're lost in a large family unless you look out for number one. Now, as a grown man living with aging parents who need help, as a husband, father and a fireman, there's little room for 'me first', except in the wish fulfillment hours of sleep.

Smitty's conflicted loyalties are compounded by a crisis in faith and his having 'sworn off' religion after 9/11. He maintains 'I don't believe in anything', but his occasional dreams of supernatural forces suggest otherwise. Unsure of what he believes in any more, he poses the baptism dilemma as a matter of which woman, his wife or his mother, he owes primary allegiance to and should defer to. He seems to be looking to me to be Solomon and decide for him.

I dodge the underlying spiritual and philosophic questions by bringing the discussion to a more therapeutically safe territory, 'relationships'. I ask, 'Do you love her?' leaving him to interpret 'her' however he wants. In turn he responds with similar vagueness, 'I love her as much as I love anybody.' Smitty can't bear hearing himself say these words. Not understanding it reflects his post-traumatic condition, he takes it as a sign of personal failing, an inability to love. He abruptly gets up and begins to pace the room. Saying he's got to 'check on the truck' that's double parked outside the office with the FDNY sticker on the visor, he walks to the window, pokes his head out then playfully sticks out his tongue, trying to catch raindrops as they fall. 'It's got to be good for something,' Smitty says with a quizzical shake of his head, leaving me unsure whether he's referring to his tongue as a rain catcher or his Fire Department sticker as saving him from a parking ticket. He sits back down. His momentary flight of fancy over, he drifts back into glum responsibility. Smitty knows he should be excited, but he isn't. His wife is hurt by his lack of enthusiasm. He tries to make her feel better by saying he's been through it all before. But he knows that's not the whole story. Smitty returns to my ambiguous question about love. 'I told Katie maybe that's why I survived, to have these babies. She got all upset. Well Doc, guess time's about up.' Making it clear, in his inimitable way, that discussion's over.

Whether motivated more to cheer him or myself it's not clear, but at the door, I remind him and myself, 'Next time we meet, the babies will have been born.' Don't get the wrong impression, Jack Smith is no melancholic type. He feels something no one can fully grasp. We can call it survivor guilt, trauma, heck we can call it whatever we want, but it won't change the fact that we cannot entirely understand what it is to be Jack Smith, several-time survivor of trauma and disaster. What it's like for him to live the paradox of feeling restless when in the company of people but unable to be alone, to be plagued by the voices and the faces of those who died that day. He wants to do the right thing, but whose voice does he listen to, the living or the dead? He looks to me to guide him, maybe even to provide a clear answer to questions whose answers have eluded far more wise thinkers than me. I can only try my best to guide him without imposing my own beliefs and values on him so that he can find his own moral compass and choose his own path. 'Happiness', that elusive thing we spend our lives searching for, is no longer something Jack Smith strives for. But one thing that gives purpose to Smitty's life, the one thing that drives him forward, informs every decision and choice he makes, and is guaranteed to bring a smile to his face, is, as he puts it, 'Kids. I love 'em.'

The greatest challenge for me as his therapist, is to remain emotionally present with him through his anguish, to stay connected with him while respecting the powerful aloneness that he exudes and that must be respected. I must resist doing what people feel naturally want to do when they see someone in pain – try to make it go away. This would only increase the loneliness and isolation that is the consequence of what he has witnessed, what he has lost, and what he has survived. It is the truth that Smitty refuses to let anyone take away from him. And that I must accept as Smitty's therapist, even though it can at times leave me feeling utterly alone.

* * *

My contribution to the growing oral history project of 9/11 has been to continue to journal my own thoughts and feelings and the ongoing issues my patients have to contend with. To me, their dreams constitute an excellent snapshot into the inner world of a person and of what's happening in their therapy. However this kind of record hardly comes close to professional standards for record keeping. My official record includes patient information, personal history, the ever-present official diagnosis, and individual session summaries, or 'progress notes' which track the patient's symptoms, mental status, and response to therapeutic interventions session by session. The Record is inevitably a compromise formation between the therapist's obligation to meet the requirements of law, professional regulatory organizations and insurance companies protecting the patient's confidentiality and the privacy of therapy.

Progress Note: April 2005. P.D. (Patrick Darby) Phone contact.

Mood and affect positive. Reported having volunteered at various relief centres last fall in the series of hurricanes hitting South Florida

Work discussion: Laughed when describing himself, 'I'm a soccer dad'. Seems to enjoy coaching and taking care of kids. Reported 'still thinking about' grad school,

getting teaching certificate. Sounds unsure. Needs support
for making career change

Reported family to be adjusting well to move to Florida:
wife found work, P. has reconnected with other firemen
who've moved down there. Needing to find community

Expressed desire to meet when he returns to NY for
visit. Appears to need to maintain contact.

I much prefer my separate private record, the therapist's
'personal notes'. There I can jot down my thoughts and feelings
right after the session, hoping to not lose some of the important
things said and impressions that could easily get lost given
the quixotic nature of emotional memory. I'm not a fan of
standardized ten-session type therapy, and I resist using the new
computerized record systems which mechanically fit people and
interpersonal moments into prescribed boxes of 'symptoms' and
'techniques'. Having come of age long before the digital era, I
crave the experience of bringing my thoughts to life with pen on
paper. So I open my spiral notebook and jot down a few precious
words from our conversation.

Personal Note P.D. April 2005

P. volunteering at the hurricane site – 'The wind, you wouldn't
believe the wind. That was most of the damage, more than the
rain. Strange, Doc. They had us all standing around not doing
much . . . There wasn't much for us to do. Guys, firemen from all
around, there were lots of guys from all over. One guy, he'd been
in the battalion I started in out in Queens, nice guy. Said we'd get
the wives together . . . But there wasn't much for us to do . . .'

In the language of the TV ad for nationwide cellular service,
Darby and I 'reach out and touch' each other, often on the run,
with a patient waiting for me or when he's driving to pick his
kids up from school. Though neither of us ever admits it, there's
something reassuring about hearing the sound of each other's
voice out there, somewhere. I guess for him it's nice to know
there's a therapist who knew him 'when' and who's still there

back in New York holding down the fort. For me, Patrick Darby's humour is infectious, his joie de vivre heartwarming. There's nothing quite like checking my messages in the middle of the day, especially when I'm having one of 'those days' that even therapists have, and hearing, 'Hey, Doc, it's me, Patrick Darby, your favourite fireman. I plan on coming back up through the city soon, Doc.' I just know that one day very soon I'm going to get a surprise call from Darby saying he's actually in Manhattan, asking, 'Hey, Doc, what'd ya' got open? I'm here, just thought I'd give you a try. Are you free?' Whatever's going on, I always find time to see Patrick Darby.

* * *

'You're going to really think I'm crazy now . . .' A humorous therapy opener but rather uncharacteristic for Captain Steve Holland, in or out of the therapy hour. He leaves that sentence dangling and switches to his main concern, and fallback defensive avoidance, talking about his wife, who's recently gone back to school. 'She's got finals next month. This is the most I've ever seen her study, but we'll see, I've seen this before.' Though he says he wants her to be more independent now, I wonder how much Steve's dependency has contributed to Stephanie's repeatedly sabotaging herself. This is her third effort to complete her college education. As important as this issue is, my curiosity is raised by his opening statement about being crazy. So I say, 'I don't think you're crazy. But what were you thinking of?'

'Well, remember I was telling you about having to go to this funeral, the second funeral for this one guy, somebody I worked with for a long time. Bobby Walsh, from the firehouse. I don't know if you remember.' 'Of course I remember,' I casually reply, trying my best to not communicate what I am really thinking. He couldn't possibly think I wouldn't remember who Bobby Walsh was, how important he was to Steve and the whole firehouse. He must be asking whether I remember our last session. Clearly he has no idea of how well I remember the details of our last session. That I was disturbed to the point of having involuntary flashbacks of certain images all week long.

The image of Steve laughing at himself for racing down to Ground Zero when he learned Bobby Walsh's remains had been recovered, as though if he didn't rush there Bobby would be gone. The image of his friend being recovered one bit at a time. First his helmet, then his turn-out gear, then finally a small section of femur, the only body part recovered. All placed as he described it in 'a small bag, a bag so small I could cradle it against my chest.' I'm convinced these images are permanently branded, as such profoundly unsettling experiences can be, onto the most primal memory structures of my brain, the amygdala and hippocampus, never to be forgotten.

It dawns on me that I was trying so hard to block out these images that I wasn't even thinking about how the funeral went. It's as though I too have become haunted by Bobby Walsh. My fellow trauma experts might interpret my strong reaction as some kind of 'vicarious' or 'secondary' trauma, a very real risk for people when working closely with traumatized persons. I prefer to think that I'm just doing my job. That means that as a therapist I must be prepared to go into psychic states that are instinctively shunned, even allowing myself to temporarily lose my mind, trusting in myself and in the therapy process. That means absorbing and temporarily holding the survivor's unbearable and unspeakable pain for him so that he can let go and 'forget' for a while all that he's witnessed and felt morally bound to remember.

At this moment, sharing my personal reactions would only be a burdensome distraction with no possible therapeutic benefit. So I say nothing about remembering all too well the recovery of Bobby Walsh's remains. I don't mention that this meant that there was now a small bit of his body that could be placed in a coffin and he could finally be laid to rest with a proper burial. I don't plan on telling him that I can even imagine Bobby Walsh's spirit emerging from beneath the stairway of the tower where his remains were eventually recovered. Nor do I tell him how 'crazy' I might be for picking up a scrap of paper near the fallen towers a few days after September 11th and imagining that it might have been a prayer card, later even imagining it belonging to someone who didn't make it out alive, like Bobby Walsh. And that I put it into the pocket of my favourite old jeans for safe keeping. In a world where people have taken to blowing themselves and others to bits, who can say for sure who or what's crazy?

I listen to Steve tell me, 'The crazy thing is, I can't get him out of my mind,' meaning Bobby. His phone starts ringing. Checking the ID, he decides to answer, tells the person on the other end of the line he's at the doctor's, hangs up, and picks right up where he left off. 'What I was going to tell you, the strangest thing happened. Somewhere in those first days while we were hauling buckets on the pile. Plastic buckets, can you believe it? Like for plastering and stuff, I don't know where they got them, but it was buckets. We had to be careful, we wanted to rescue whoever we could, whoever might still be alive. There wasn't much time. Maybe I was just tired, because we were there two maybe three days straight, I can't even remember any more, before going home.

'At one point, I know it sounds strange, I was real tired like I said, but everybody was tired, I was having trouble seeing. Someone said 'go sit down', so I did. I swear, I know you're really going to think I'm crazy but I'll tell you anyway. I can't get it out of my mind, it's so strange, crazy really.' Steve shakes his head back and forth. 'I swear I heard Bobby Walsh's voice. That was weird. Your mind plays tricks on you in situations like that. That's what scares me now. You gotta be able to just act, not think. After what happened I don't know how I would do, or should I say, how I will do. I worry about that, not for me but for them, the guys. They look to me, I'm their officer. But Bobby's voice. I swear I heard his voice. You know what I mean?'

'Of course.'

'I just can't get him out of my mind. Maybe I'm feeling guilty because I didn't go to the funeral. I mean the real funeral. I went to that service back then, but I don't think it was a funeral. I don't know what they buried then. I don't know why I didn't go this time. I was thinking that I was definitely going to go. I even told Stephanie I was planning on going, but then that morning it was raining and I put it off, I guess I kind of, I don't know, I just didn't go.' He tears up. I'm struck by what he then adds, 'He was my brother.' Unlike a lot of firemen, Steve has never used that term before in referring to his fellow firefighters. Perhaps he is unconsciously feeling guilty about his biological brother, who's alive but whom Steve hasn't spoken to or heard from in many years.

With therapeutic zeal I raise the subject of his brother and other relatives in his family, a topic which he has assiduously avoided. Steve becomes angry. 'No, it's not the same. My brother is still out there. Yeah, I guess I could call him. I could pick up the phone and call him any time I want. That's the difference.' Instantly he regains his composure. Not wanting to pursue my line of inquiry or let his irritation get the better of him, he assumes the more composed posture of correcting an understandable gaffe on my part. With an emphatic tone, he explains, 'You gotta understand Doc, these guys, they're like family. We work together, we look out for each other. I let him down. It's as simple as that.

'We'd been through a lot together, Bobby and I. We go back a long way. We even got our training together at the Rock. For a while he and his wife, me and Stephanie, we went out together, when we were just starting out. But then you know how things are. They probably wondered why we stopped getting together. They had kids. That was hard for Stephanie. Then their kids were growing up. I don't know, between one thing and another . . .'

I wonder whether Bobby Walsh's widow understood that Steve didn't show up at the funeral because he just wasn't ready to say goodbye or forgive himself.

'It was just too much,' is all I say.

'But his widow called me, she wanted me to go, she asked me to come, and I didn't.' He weeps quietly. 'He was my brother.'

* * *

'You know buddy, I really loved you. And I thought you loved me. Not that we'd say shit like that. We had some good times, you and me, and with the wives. Now, now I just don't know. Not because of that day. Hey, you told me not to go in. Heck, you were right, who would've thought the whole thing woulda blown! But right after, you were so close. I tried to reach you. Whatever, well, that's how it goes. I get it. Remember that time we were working together and we just stood there watching, just a few feet away, watching the floor give way. We knew it was hot. Just dumb luck you and me were standing where we were. Hey, you never know. This time it was my turn, but those guys back that day, hey think of it this way, they were saved from this one.

'Remember that time we were working in Brooklyn together and that jerk, whatever his name was, got himself locked in the toilet, forgot to make sure there were two exits before he closed the door behind him, then started freaking out and we were all standing right outside the door laughing, listening to him beg for help. But then it was you, you felt sorry for the poor bastard, you always were a soft touch, you went in. That's how come I can't understand it. Why you never call her. If it was Stephanie you know I would. Heck, you even got yourself assigned to my firehouse. You did that for me. The funeral, who cares, but can't you give her a call?'

I awaken with a start. Who was that in my dream? I can't remember seeing a person. I could only feel the presence and hear the voice of a man. Could it have been, yes, it must have been Bobby Walsh!? My dream condenses, as dreams often do, many different things and memories, about what's going on with Steve, about stories I heard from the men in my firehouse, and about what Bobby Walsh has come to symbolize for me. I remember guys talking about someone getting hurt when the floor gave way under heat and them laughing about the time a guy got stuck in the toilet during a fire

It's clear to me that I'm problem solving in my sleep, not only for myself but for Steve as well. My dream is making me

conscious of issues that need to be addressed with Steve. Dreams
are less likely today to be assigned prophetic powers, and more
likely to be dismissed as merely epiphenomenal by-products of
neural firing. But even with the scientific scepticism of our time,
people continue to believe that dreams have meaning, that they
are, as Freud put it, the royal road to the unconscious. Dreams
are the stock and trade of psychoanalysts, we shamans of modern
life. People look to us to decipher their unconscious and help
unlock the secrets they're keeping from themselves. This dream
makes me realize that until Steve can forgive himself he won't
be able to move forward in his life. He won't be able to be there
for Bobby Walsh's wife, his own wife or himself. I have to find a
way to help him break out of being so caught up in the vice-grip
of guilty responsibility that he can't give his own pain its due.

My dream is letting me know how much Bobby Walsh means
to me. He's not only one of the lost leaders of my firehouse who
brought Steve Holland to my firehouse and whose remains were
finally recovered. He is a symbol of all firefighters and civilians
whose lives were taken on 9/11 and in the wars that have taken
place as a result. He is the spirit of America. He is not only the
dead friend who haunts Steve Holland, or the creative device of
a writer's imagination. He is everyone's ghost from the past who
lurks in the present trying to show us the way to the future.

May
It's been several weeks now since Steve handed me the transcript
of his interview with the Fire Department's 9/11 investigators
shortly after the disaster. His only comment at the time was
'I'll be interested in hearing what you think.' I set it next to my
notebooks behind my office chair where it's been ever since,
becoming part of the furniture. Steve's asked me a few times
about it. Each time I made some polite but lame excuse for not
having read it and promise I'll get to it soon. Whenever I noticed
it as I went for my notebook I told myself I was going to look at
it later. I knew I was avoiding reading it out of dread of feeling all

those bad feelings again. Unfortunately, understanding doesn't always change behaviour. It was still sitting there.

The fact that Steve wants me to read this now is a clear sign that something has shifted in him. The transcript is about him, not Stephanie, not Bobby Walsh or anyone else in the fire department. He's ready to look at himself as someone who has suffered not only because of what he couldn't do to help others, but as a person who has pain in his own right. We're meeting tomorrow. There's no way I can go into that session without having read it. I reassure myself that there aren't going to be any jolting surprises, nothing that I hadn't already heard from Steve directly. But it's been so long since I listened to Steve tell me his story. Hearing it back then when I was in the thick of the disaster was one thing, having to read about it today is quite another. I brace myself as I pick up the envelope.

'I saw what happened on the television going on. I heard what happened. I saw initially the first one on fire. I got dressed as fast as I could . . . I got down to about the Staten Island Ferry terminal, and I couldn't get any further. Civilians were running everywhere. There was smoke in the air . . . I pulled over there . . . I abandoned my vehicle. I put a mayday on the radio that I was abandoning my vehicle . . . I was heading up South Street . . . on foot . . . (they) picked me up. . . in a suburban . . . stocked with medical supplies . . . when we got to the Brooklyn Battery Tunnel, about at that point on West Street there was a Port Authority cop standing there. They were shouting, 'The tower's going to come down. The tower's coming down. You've got to get out of here.' My thought was I've got to go there. My guys are there. Then boom and the cloud . . .

'Black smoke. Black smoke and people running everywhere. A lot of fire apparatus on both sides of West Street. I didn't see any guys, just apparatus . . . Some stretched lines and things like that . . . I didn't see my guys. This seemed weird to me, all this apparatus but no guys. There were lines stretched on the ground but no guys . . . then boom, a massive explosion. Right in front of

us we saw what looked like a fireball and smoke . . . rolling this way. I said . . . 'we've got to get out of this fucking car.' . . . we bailed out of the suburban. We went underneath it. The thing blew over us. I had my turnout coat on. I put my face in my helmet. The thing blew over us. I felt heat. I felt all kinds of debris and stuff hitting my body. When I opened my eyes, it was pitch-black. I closed my eyes again. I was praying . . . When I opened my eyes a second time it was like skiing in a blizzard. It was just white, a sea of white . . . We got out from under the vehicle. We got back in the vehicle. We jumped over the divider and started driving back down West Street . . . then there was another it sounded like an explosion and heavy white powder, papers, flying everywhere. We sat put there for a few minutes . . . The time line – I don't know when these things actually occurred in real time . . . the whole thing seemed like it happened very quickly from getting no further with the vehicle so let me just pull this car over and bail out, and do what I can do on foot . . .'

I stop reading. All I can think is – this reads like a story from one of my paperback novels. It is a story, but a real-life story. All this actually happened in New York City on a September morning as people were beginning another ordinary day at the office, school, or home.

Steve and his vehicle have survived. But man is not made of concrete and glass, like a building that comes down and can be rebuilt 'bigger and better', like the way they talk about the future construction at the site.

As I come to the end of the transcript, I find myself empathizing with the fire marshal who interviewed him. He too must have been shaken by Steve's story. Because he asked Steve what seems like an extremely strange question. 'How did the vehicle survive when you got out from under the vehicle?' Ever the proper professional despite his own distress, Steve responded with as much precision and accuracy as he could.

'Just covered with soot. It didn't blow out any windows or anything like that . . . So the vehicle survived . . . It was just like

nothing I've ever seen in my life . . . All the apparatus, the fire trucks, everything all blown out, the windows were all blown out . . . Body parts lying on the street, mud, soot, people walking around dazed.' But cars aren't alive. They don't 'survive'; at least not in the way people do. They can be repaired, scrapped, even fired down and remoulded into something new. People aren't made of metal. They absorb the blows of life's crashes in a way that marks them forever.

* * *

'Survivor guilt' was all I offered. A meagre response to another one of his dreams and to the freeze-frame flashback images of the morning of September 11th that he associates the dream to. Sharing a birthday with Sigmund Freud, you'd think I could have come up with something that approximates the kind of transformative interpretation that you read about and see in the movies. I can't believe I fell back on the kind of therapeutic platitude that just came out of my mouth. Thankfully, Smitty doesn't say anything about my comment. He has more important things on his mind, like whether he may have to not only leave the firehouse but leave firefighting altogether. He's been put on light duty again, this time because of problems with his shoulder. The recurring shoulder injury, along with other past injuries, doesn't bode well for his being able to return to active duty. That charming and incorrigible Puck who had balked at his own survival when I first met him is no longer feeling so free to laugh at destiny.

Undaunted by my momentary failure as a therapist with impeccable timing and clinical judgment, Smitty leads us forward. 'Last week when I came in I . . .' He stops mid-sentence, then draws his hand down his arm saying 'Since this morning I've been having this pain down the inside of my arm.' I try to hide the anxiety rising in me. Smitty says 'I think it's from the mask and all,' referring to the typically sixty-pounds and more load of the gear that firefighters carry. Wanting a less frightening alternative than what we're both worried about, he suggests that it might be 'just a nerve' irritated from long term use of the heavy gear and somehow related to his shoulder problem. But with Smitty being thirty or forty pounds heavier than safe for a firefighter, and with one of my closest friends having had emergency triple heart bypass only a week ago, I'm taking no chances. 'You gotta go get it checked out right away,' I say emphatically. 'You're right. It's probably just a nerve in your neck, but you gotta go to the medical unit, it's right near here.' He agrees to go.

Back, knee and shoulder problems are endemic to firefighting. But Smitty seems to have suffered more than his fair share over the last few years. His series of injuries, along with skull-piercing headaches and various other physical pains have become the major way Smitty's psychological pain expresses itself these days. This pattern, 'somatization' in clinical terms, was inevitable for a man without a language for feelings and a great resistance to the idea that he may have to leave firefighting.

I can't help but wonder if Smitty's compromised psychological state has made him more susceptible to getting injured. Could all this physical pain be a form of self-punishment, his unconscious guilt for surviving? But people and their motivations are complicated. So why did I come out with that 'survivor guilt' cliché earlier, and then break out of my therapeutic stance to insist he go to the doctor about the pain running down his arm? It hits me – it was the dream he'd related right before that made him more agitated and worried about the pain in his arm and that made me lose my cool.

'I dreamed one of the babies was only 3 lbs 6 ounces. One was born, the others weren't. We had one baby and she was still pregnant.' When I asked him what he thought about the dream, he frightened us both with his association to it: 'There's never been twins in my family that both lived. And no one's had triplets.'

Understanding now that he's needing reassurance, I tell him that the danger of multiple births was far greater in the days before high tech medicine, and that babies barely a pound now survive. He elaborates on the dream. 'Dave Harris, one of the guys who died, was there. He was my age, but in the dream he was younger than he was in real life. He was making a joke, I remembered he was always telling stories. Maybe it was his son. 'Cause he was my age when he died. In the dream he was like 24. I laughed when I saw his face and then I woke up.'

There's not much I can say to Smitty about the faces of his dead buddies that keep returning. They're haunting him, but they're also keeping him company as they did in life. These faces come to him when he's awake and when asleep, leaving him never free of the sound of their voices and their laughter, of their sad smiles telling him 'It's OK', occasionally with a questioning look, 'Why me and not you?' He doesn't dare ask directly whether he will ever escape these images that overtake him at the strangest times. He doesn't ask because he suspects what the answer is – there is no guarantee that post-traumatic intrusive images and flashbacks totally disappear.

Intuiting that we're near the end of the session, Smitty presses on. 'One more, one more dream I got to tell you. I was pushing a stroller. On one side there was water and on the other side fog. The fog was over the boys in the stroller. The water was at my feet, then started covering them. I couldn't find the sidewalk. It scared me. They were under water. Couldn't find my path to higher ground.' A flicker of overt distress comes over his face. He looks me straight in the eye, waiting for something, an answer to why he would dream such a thing.

I immediately recognize that this dream was one of these rare life-defining dreams that comes at critical times of life. At one level this dream was a straightforward expression of normal parental pre-birth jitters. A father's concerns about being able to protect his children, intensified by post-9/11 conditions. It also alludes to the mental fog that almost destroyed him. But the dream also alludes to deeper spiritual and existential issues. For water, with its life giving and life taking potential, is a universal symbol of Life.

This was not Smitty's first dream about water. In most of his dreams the water is contained, like a swimming pool or lake. The water is manageable, even playful. This is the first time the water in his dreams is threatening and out of control, a sign of how he's feeling about his life. The dream tells us he's battling with the dilemma of continuing as a fireman and putting his own children at risk of losing him. If he chooses to leave firefighting, or he's forced to retire because of a physical or psychological condition, what will Smitty do with his life?

There is so much to say about the daunting challenges of being a parent and a fireman, and more basically about the limits of what is humanly possible. I feel the profound import of this dream, but Smitty is just emerging out of the throes of PTSD. This isn't the time to delve too deeply into things. So 'survivor guilt' is all I manage to muster a second time. Another paltry though clinically correct interpretation by an analyst whose own thinking has also been momentarily fragmented by a flood of emotion.

Shaking his head, Smitty looks up at the ceiling and remarks, rather matter-of-factly, 'Maybe that's why I keep seeing the lady I stepped over to get out, the lady in a red dress with no legs and a charred face. I just saw her in the shower this morning. Maybe that's why I keep seeing her.' At other times he thinks the dress was purple. But whatever colour the dress was, whoever that woman was, and whatever he imagines she felt when she jumped or fell to her death, Smitty is always sure of one thing. This woman wore a dress to work on September 11th.

* * *

Psychoanalytic therapy is a creative intermixing of two personalities and two unconscious minds. It's not for the emotionally squeamish or those looking for a quick fix, a pill or pick-me-up kind of therapy. Nor is it, as some might think, only for self-indulgent highbrows and the intellectually arcane. It's for those who believe in the examined life, in sorting through one's deepest desires, fears, conflicts, and the confusing complexity of important relationships. It's impossible to fully convey all that transpires between patient and therapist and how they come to 'know' each other. In the idiosyncratic imbalance of the therapy situation two people intimately discuss the life of only one – the patient. But psychoanalytic therapy works through a kind of perceptual play of figure and ground, like an Escher drawing with the therapist's life and psyche largely obscured behind the patient in the foreground. A slight shift in perspective reverses the positions and reveals the struggles and longings of the therapist. Generally so focused on thinking about what's going on with my patients and how they are changing, I rarely stop to consider how I myself have changed because of these men. Until I have a dream.

I'm in a large building with an enormous atrium overlooking a large body of water. It looks like the World Financial Center, on the Hudson River, the building whose glass cupola roof was shattered by one of the planes after it had flown straight through the Trade Center. It's a smaller, less bold structure than the great towers. I am with some firemen, Lt. Sal and some other guys from the firehouse. I feel a thrilling aliveness like I haven't felt in many years. For I was 'with' Sal. It wasn't exactly lust, nor did I feel guilt, for there was no sex in the dream. I felt that there had been and that there might be sex, and something more. We're just standing together on the edge of the open walkway looking out in wonderment at the expanse of water.

I laugh when my dream comes back to me later that day. Even in my dreams I can't be unfaithful. Yet I was feeling the passionate fulfilment of sexuality. This is what Freud would call a 'compromise formation'. Clearly to dream of 'being with' a patient is utterly unacceptable, even to my psychoanalytically liberal, child of the sixties, unconscious self. The inviolability of the patient-therapist frame is as deeply ingrained in me as the incest taboo. But Sal is neither my biological brother nor my patient, And he embodies so many of the things I've found so appealing about all the various firemen that I've worked with over these last years, therefore a perfect compromise for my superego.

But this dream runs far deeper than sex. Yes, the 'manifest content' of the dream is about my barely-suppressed sexual longings. But sex is a seductively facile interpretation which can easily obscure other feelings – in this case, intimacy. In the dream Sal and I are standing together sharing in the amazing expanse of water that lay as far as I could see to the horizon. I'm feeling with Sal what I felt with so many of the men in the firehouse, a closeness and feeling of being known and accepted that comes from having gone through something unforgettable together.

Clearly Smitty's dream of water the other day was the spark for my dream. His dream of his babies in the stroller and the rising water was about birth and death, beginnings and endings. In some way so is mine. My year in the firehouse, which was all about death, had to come to an end because it was time for the men to pick up life where it stopped on 9/11. But my connection to Sal and to all the other guys in the firehouse – to Phil the cook and sometime Santa, to guys like Mouse and Pauli, even to my nemesis Robbie Taylor who tried his best to push me out of the house, and most certainly to the survivors, Sean, William the hero, and Lt. Ross who helped me find my way back in – will not end.

Each of the firemen that I have come to know is different from the others but all of them share an unerring commitment to placing utmost value on individual life. This is what endows them with the capacity to put themselves in harm's way for total strangers. I have learned so much with them about what it means to go the distance with people. It is making me a better therapist, person, and hopefully a better citizen of the world.

My dream is also a reminder that involvements with people, chapters of lives, like historic eras and books, inevitably must draw to a close. The final moment of an ending may turn out to seem rather arbitrary, as it did at the moment I chose to have the plug pulled on my dying father. But life goes on. Hence, the sexual feeling of my dream, for the essence of desire and romance is the exquisite intensity of feeling alive in the moment. At its heart this dream is of water, life itself, placid one moment and churned up the next. It can buoy spirits, delight with new vistas and gently carry us to faraway worlds, but it can swallow us up in a flash. Its wondrous frightening power a reminder of our place in the grand scheme. The inexorable flow of the tides is reminiscent of the passage of time and the constancy of change. It gives us faith that endings bring beginnings, and that the past never totally disappears. It makes us who are and brings ever-new possibilities for who we might become.

June
'Just called to tell you Katie gave birth. To two boys and a girl! See you Wednesday.' Having to wait for Smitty as usual, I decide to water my motley collection of Gloria Gaynor 'I will survive' plants. Finally the bell rings. I go to the door to find him deftly holding two babies in car seats while opening the door. His wife is by his side, holding another baby seat, and looking at me questioningly. The triplets have come to session!

'We're on our way to a training,' – Jack Smith shorthand for 'That's why they're here in my session.' It's another one of those damn anti-terrorist training camp exercises that I'm sure will make him feel even less 'prepared' as a first responder in this new breed of warfare. Since the babies are only a week old, they're going with Smitty to the training so he can help his wife, who is understandably a bit overwhelmed as a first-time mother, with triplets no less.

He begins the session in Smitty style, as though it's just the two of us. 'Oh, I had these dreams, you know I even wrote 'em down, I left them on the visor. What with Katie and these guys I forgot to bring them in. Next time.' Smitty sits back into the couch, cradles two of the babies against his body, and heaves a sigh. From all our time together I know this as a signal that he's about to launch into the next subject, probably into one of his many physical ailments. I jump out of my seat and reach for one

of the light bundles, then sit back trying my best to not disturb
the sleeping baby on my lap. I can barely contain myself enough
to sustain some semblance of eye contact with the parents. I'm
soaking up the sensations of holding this newborn. His eyelids
are closed in that firm softness of the just-born, with just a slit of
his blue eyes still moist from the beyond, not quite ready for the
earthly world.

As far as I'm concerned, with this swaddled baby in my arms,
the world can just stop right here, right now. For the moment we
don't have to address the challenges of parenting and marriage that
face Smitty and his wife. We don't have to think about how these
newborns, still perfect in every way, will lose their innocence,
or how what happened to their father will find its way into their
beings. I can just pause and feel this new life and not have to
think about how to help Smitty find a way to overcome the odd
loss of empathy that marks him as a survivor, and to 'prepare' as
a fireman for the next, unimaginably worse catastrophe. These
issues linger silently in the 45-minute air of our session.

I'm suddenly acutely aware of just how much the birth of the
babies is going to change things. It's not only going to be harder
now for him to continue being a fireman, it's going to much harder
for Smitty to come regularly to therapy. And if he retires, he'll
probably want to move away from New York. Psychologically he
may have to. Maybe he'll go live somewhere by the water or up
in the mountains, as his dreams suggest. Far from the memories
and threat of terrorism. I need to prepare for this eventuality. Just
as hot and cold are defined in relation to their opposites, so too
birth has a way of evoking death and endings.

Though the bond between patient and therapist does not sever
with termination, time does have its way with life. Maybe Smitty
will be able to keep in touch and maybe he won't. Maybe there'll
be a moment when he's alone on the road and I will cross his mind.
He might even just give me a call then. But most likely he'll get my
machine. Then again we might just manage to reach other directly.
You never know. I do know that for Smitty to move forward with
his life, he needs to feel free to leave therapy. Therapists have

been known to unconsciously press their patients to keep coming out of their own needs, emotional as well as financial. This is a serious counter-transference danger that therapists must always be on the look out for. I can't let my own feelings for Smitty get in the way of his doing what he needs to do.

But I won't think any more about any of that right now. There's a newborn baby on my lap. I reach inside the soft brushed cotton of the infant swaddling. I wriggle my baby finger into the balled-up five perfect fingers of his infant fist. And I hold his hand in mine.

* * *

I can see right away that Steve is in a bad mood. Months of therapy have loosened Steve's rigidity and emotional constriction, though he still feels like a failure in being unable to express his love for his wife in the way he says she most needs, in the bedroom. Since he's been coming on his own, Steve has gingerly begun to look at his history, trying to understand what made him the kind of person he was before September 11th and to make sense of how that day seemed to irrevocably change him.

Steve's zest for living didn't suddenly disappear on 9/11. His heart had been quietly closing up with the damaging build-up of a series of losses and disappointments long before 9/11. Turned into 'the man of the house' as a child, and with no money for college, he was forced to abandon his dream of becoming a doctor. Instead he joined the army, where he trained in emergency medicine and became a fireman in emergency services when he got out. The person he was in love with before Stephanie died of an accidental overdose.

Images of dead bodies discovered on the job over the decades have been branded onto his psyche. Like the one he recalls today in his black mood. The scorched body of someone who Steve could tell had been still alive only minutes before they reached him. The arms were outstretched and fingers grasping for the door. He takes these memories as recriminating proof of his failure to save people he might have rescued. Even 'worse', however much Steve hates to 'admit it', he says are the images of his brothers fallen in the line of duty that come to his mind today, he explains, because it's the anniversary of the Father's Day fire, when the greatest number of firemen in New York City's history were killed in a single day, that is before September 11th.

He goes on to say that he's been doing overtime as often as he can to save money for the country house he and Stephanie hope to someday own. And that later today he's going to see his mother who lives an hour away, as he does devotedly each week. To sit with her in silence in front of the TV, neither touching the other, not even to embrace hello or good-bye. He says, rightfully, that his mother's physical reserve and general inexpressiveness is a product of her own strict upbringing, but he can't allow himself to feel hurt by it. Though Steve is beginning to see how he has repeated this pattern in his own life, he is far less forgiving of himself than of her or anyone else. No matter how much we analyze the multiple causes of his sexual anxiety and performance difficulties, Steve still can't get past seeing his sexual problems as a statement of his failure as a man. His terror and behaviour on September 11th only served to deepen this conviction. It doesn't matter that everyone else down there reacted the same way as he did. Steve only knows that when he heard that explosion and saw that thundering cloud coming toward him, he was a 'coward' because he ran. For to Steve Holland, a man of few words, it's a person's actions that count. All the things he does for his wife, earning a decent living, cooking and cleaning, sparing no expense or effort to give her whatever she asks for outside the bedroom, are 'sorry substitutes' for his sexual dysfunction.

How simple life would be if we could pin the blame for what ails Steve on either his childhood, being a fireman who's seen too much, or on 9/11 itself, but life's just not that simple. For Steve, as for everyone, personality and history come together to determine the impact of any particular situation. Having the innocence of childhood assumptions of security pulled out from under him as a young boy, Steve came to view the world of people as fundamentally unreliable. He developed what he likes to call

his 'force field' of protective armour, which September 11th
cemented more deeply into his character. Yet, as Steve himself
says these days, at least now he knows that he actually does have
feelings and can sometimes express them. He knows now that 'it
isn't right' to be so mechanical and to treat himself like an object.
He knows better how to question things without being critical or
judgmental. He'll even consider the notion that self-devaluation
can be a form of copping out. But how much change is it fair to
expect or hope for? I can tell Steve wonders in his gut whether
his self-restricting coping mechanisms are so deeply imbedded
that he may never be able to be happy and sexually fulfilled.

He ends our session saying it's his day off, that he's brought
his lounge chair up from the basement, and is going to the beach
for the first time this season before he heads for his mother's. He
loves nothing more than lying in the sun, digging his toes in the
sand and listening to the planes take off from Laguardia and JFK.
With his eyes closed he faces the heavens, looking for Bobby
Walsh and other celestial travellers.

* * *

The phone messages were coming in one after the other. I could
hear the machine picking up, but it's been a morning of five
sessions back to back. I finally have a break. My answering
machine is flashing '7' in digital accusation. I quickly press
'playback'. The first is Smitty cancelling our next session, the
second is a friendly reminder from the dentist to schedule a check
up. The next message begins, 'Hey, Doc, this is Pat Darby. Just
wanted to let you know I'm alive,' followed by a pause, then, 'I'm
not doing so well.' Another pause. My heartbeat quickens. 'Being
that' he continues, then finally, 'Being that I'm surrounded down
here by all these people from Massachusetts!' The last words
pronounced with a clownish imitation of my Boston accent,
and ending with that chuckle of his. I smile to myself and start
to breathe easily again. Patrick was just being Patrick. A long
message ensues. 'I wanted to let you know I'm alive,' repeated

for emphasis, followed by his explaining that he was planning to come back up north when his kids get out of school, 'I was thinking maybe I'd come in and bring the wife.'

Darby's the kind of guy who's on the move, that's his way. He shrugs his shoulders, reaches into his pocket for the keys to his car, motorcycle, or now to his boat, gives his lucky rabbit's foot a tender squeeze, and he takes off. Whether he's soaring on thesug ground, over the water or up in the air, Darby keeps in touch. Though he's left several messages saying he's planning to come see me, I haven't actually seen him since February. I wonder what's going on with him these days.

Could it be that the rabbit's foot he keeps in his pocket for good luck has lost its totemic power? I remember one of our group sessions in the firehouse where the guys were morbidly estimating their odds of survival if the next terrorist attack was another bomb versus some new kind of bio-chemical disaster. Darby had insisted that I give his little piece of fake fur a squeeze 'just cuz you never know.' Maybe calling me works for him the way his rabbit's foot does, to ward off the evil spirits, like the way my mother superstitiously threw salt over her shoulder.

I immediately try his cell phone. Naturally I get I what I usually get on my first try, 'Hey, leave me a message and I'll try and call ya' back!' followed by that distinctive laugh of his. I try his home. The machine has a message recorded by his now pre-teen daughter. I hang up, not wanting to induce suspicion or violate confidentiality. Re-dialing his cell phone, I leave a cheery message that I hope doesn't betray my worry. What does he mean when he says he's 'still alive'? I take it as a veiled reference to the disease that 9/11 has left him with, with the spectre of its progression and the ever-present questions it raises about life. His message reflects the survivor's simultaneous attachment to the dead and the living, that can make it difficult to fully embrace life.

Patrick Darby, with a voice so full of life and humour, with a never-die spirit that reaches out over the air waves, is the epitome of aliveness. I hear Darby, I feel Darby, even though

I rarely see Darby in the flesh. I wonder if this is what those online relationships people put so much stock in these days feel like. To me, there's nothing quite like experiencing the physical presence of another person, of being able to touch and the feel the other. Though I know Patrick Darby will never move back to New York, I refuse to consider that he and I will lose touch. After all, he's always wanting to bring his kids up to see his family. Maybe this time I'll even get to meet 'the wife', the love of his life since college. My spirits are raised. I move through the rest of the messages on the machine but just as I'm about to press the 'delete all' button I stop. I leave the sound of Darby's voice on my machine so I can listen to it tomorrow. Eventually I'll erase it. Though I know he will call again sometime, I don't know when or when I'll see him again.

My relationship with Darby is something different from the usual patient-therapist relationship. We got to know each other under the unusual circumstances of the firehouse right after September 11th. Relationships that develop through a disaster are akin to the unique bonds that form in war. We got to know each other and shared a time when people disappeared from the face of the earth, and when no one was acting quite normal. It's great for me to have a Patrick Darby in my life. Someone who doesn't believe in saying goodbye, a twenty-first century Lone Ranger, the guy who shows up out of nowhere just when you need him only to take off just as fast, leaving you wondering, 'Just who is that masked man?' Someone who calls every once in a while just to let me know he's 'alive'.

July
Progress Note: J.S. (Jack Smith) July 11, 2005

     Overall increase in symptoms, mental status suggests exacerbation of PTSD, set off by second anniversary of 9/11. Less focused on being taken off line for shoulder injury. Increase in other somatic symptoms over last month: pain in neck, shoulder and arms, headaches.

Minimal support from family – Wife preoccupied with her own feelings about 9/11, sister extremely ill. Daughter increased adolescent acting out

Overall memory impaired. Confusion, memory lapses recurring with other PTSD symptoms in pre-anniversary reaction. Affect: volatile. Mood: irritable, continued episodic outbursts. Encouraged S. to communicate his feelings rather than striking out verbally.

Progress – Increasing self-acceptance. Able to say he is a 'survivor' of WTC. Improvement in self-awareness. E.g. Attributed headaches to 'thinking about a month from now'.

Long-term Prognosis – Guarded. Continued difficulty with restoring empathy ('I don't have that'). Exacerbation of cognitive, emotional and behavioural symptoms suggests long term diagnosis of chronic low grade post-traumatic stress disorder.

Treatment Plan – Recommend evaluation for disability. Continue working on acceptance of long term effects of PTSD and traumatic grief on functioning.

On a separate piece of lined paper I jot down some 'personal notes', trying my best to capture what Smitty tells me, evocative things that aren't for the official record like 'I've had it. I want to get away from this.' Talking of moving as far away from 'reminders' as possible. 'Everywhere I go I see faces.' 'She put up pictures of guys from the house, on duty with me the Saturday before. Told me she thought it'd help. She doesn't get it. No one gets it.' Meaning, what it's like to live with PTSD and to have lost so many significant people in his life all at once. Counting on his fingers the men on duty with him that day, Smitty calls out their names one by one. Saying who died, who transferred, and who's left in the firehouse. Laughing nervously, 'They're lookin' at me. Staring at me . . . Like they're sayin', "Why, Why?"'

Smitty can't escape the images of the faces of the men he worked with who died on 9/11. I can't escape the images of the faces of Smitty and Steve pinched in pain. Or the faces of angry men like Robbie Taylor, in unspoken accusation at the world for what happened, at me for not having gone through what they did, and for trying to get them to confront things. Their faces searching my own for clues whether they can trust me, whether I have it in me to do what I pushed them to do – face the hard questions about what really goes on inside.

Smitty is just as caught off guard by the pre-anniversary resurgence of symptoms as he was last year and the year before. This year he is preoccupied with trying to recall the details of how events unfolded on the morning of September 11th. Today Smitty is talking about his interview with the representatives from the 9/11 Commission. All he can remember is that there were guys at a long table, firing a barrage of questions at him that he had no answer for, leaving him to repeatedly respond with 'I don't know. I don't know how I made it out.' His exact words to me the day I met him nearly four years ago.

Needing at this point to piece together the sequence of things, he tells me today,

'I remember going over the bridge. How far do you think the bridge was from the Tower?' Not waiting for an answer, he speculates whether it was a matter of seconds or minutes from when he got out of the Tower and when it came down. Momentarily satisfied, he goes on. 'I was on the other side of the overpass, on the street at the West Side Highway. That's where we must have been when it came down.

'We were running, trying to outrun the black cloud. George was right next to me; I remember that. And I remember the bridge. I'd lost or maybe taken off my gear to run, I can't exactly remember which, but then we fell down, and someone from out of nowhere passed us kerchiefs to cover our faces. I don't know who that was. I got to my feet, pulled George up and we were groping blindly forward, trying to outrun it. Can't remember anything else about what happened next. Just the flying debris, smoke.'

With a twinge of sadness and relief, Smitty finishes, 'That's all

I can remember, can you believe it?' Looking away, he continues, 'Still can't remember to save my life,' and I suppose that's true in both senses of the expression.

Smitty turns to me and simply smiles, reminding both of us, 'My memory's shot. That's the problem. That's why I'm still here, Doc.' Making a permanent record, and getting it right feels crucial. It's the least I can do. So as soon as Smitty leaves, knowing that if I wait too long I'll also be unable to recall the details, I try to get down on paper what I remember Smitty told me, word-for-word.

August

Though no one is really talking about it yet, we're unconsciously registering the fact that the 9/11 anniversary is fast approaching. The slower pace and leisurely atmosphere of the summer awakens the dreamer in us. Dreams are mysterious gifts that reveal forgotten truths from the past, teaching us what we already knew but didn't know we knew, setting the direction for the future. They function like time capsules, capturing the essence of our concerns and what we're feeling at a given moment in time, sending messages from the unconscious to our consciousness, if we listen to them.

Smitty is so eager to tell me this dream he rushes through his health, work and family updates in short order. When I ask about the babies he responds by only saying 'The babies, yeah they're good.' I know his fears for their safety are tempering his excitement at the same time as they are his reason to live. He's intent on getting his 'strange dream' to me.

'*I'm with Mike Mahoney, he was one of the guys . . . that died. We were going somewhere. I don't know what happened, but we missed our plane. I said I think I know where we can hijack a plane. Somehow I don't know how but we got control of a plane. We're on the Brooklyn Queens Expressway, like how I go to come here. It was just him and me. I offered him a free week in my time share in Cancun. Weird, huh. I don't know why. We're on the road, on the highway trying to get the plane up into the air. We're about to take off, I can feel it, but every time we hit a bend in the road we can't get up enough speed or something. We never really feel like criminals or anything. Finally we get up in the air. Then there are other planes flying around. They're trying to force us down. We just keep flying. I said to him, "We'll outlast 'em, these planes."'*

From a psychoanalytic perspective this dream is working on many levels, and reflects how hard Smitty is trying to overcome his trauma. The connections to 9/11 are obvious. In his fantasy Smitty was able to transform reality. He can bring his friend who died in the towers back to life and even send him on a vacation! They turn the tables on the perpetrators by hijacking a plane themselves. Both of them not only escape in his dream, they also take off and fly, successfully evading the enemy in pursuit. On a deeper level, with this dream, Smitty undoes 9/11. He literally reverses misfortune, masterfully overcoming the helplessness and lack of control he felt on September 11th by flying skyward with exhilaration. This connotes a sense of power and spirituality in ascendance. Through his dream, Smitty turns himself from victim to victor, showing his innate resilience, his determination to recover, and his unspoken but strong spiritual faith.

I ask Smitty, 'What was the feeling of the dream?'

Smitty sighs with a smile, 'Freedom!'

* * *

Being the kind of person who finds refuge in concrete reality and in putting logic and order to emotions, Steve is still somewhat leery about dream analysis. With his penchant for the pragmatic and overriding work ethic, he rarely allows himself the luxury of dreaming, whether awake or asleep. Working so diligently in therapy to be a good patient, he's been trying hard to remember his dreams with no success. Finally one day he announces excitedly, he's got a dream!

'*It was a strange dream. Something that's never happened, that just wouldn't happen in real life. I get out of the subway, no it's the elevated train. I'm by myself. I come down the stairs and it's the oddest thing. I can't find my car. I always keep track of my car, but in the dream I can't remember exactly where I parked it. This would never happen in real life. I wander up and down the streets, I go around the block. Still I can't find my car. I'm not lost. It's not that kind of feeling. I know exactly where I am but I just can't find my car.*'

Dreaming of not being able to find one's car is a common dream theme. Along with misplaced keys, backpacks, bags, the personal items of daily life, these dream images typically symbolize a sense of identity. Cars tend to be associated with one's position in life, movement and freedom. Steve has often talked about loving to take off in his car and go for a drive. My first thought is that all the psychological changes Steve has been working to make in his life might be making him feel like he's lost his old familiar self, leaving him with the sense of not quite knowing who he is any more. Especially given how anxiety-provoking change is for someone like him. So I make the interpretation, 'You're feeling confused, unsure who you are any more, and unable to find your way.' Following along, Steve thinks about this idea and free associates, talking about how he doesn't feel like he's in the driver seat of his life. But I can tell something is missing in this interpretation. As does Steve. He persists, 'I just knew it was there somewhere, I just couldn't find it.'

It dawns on me that it wasn't a symbolic loss of his car. Something devastating had in fact happened to his car, as he described in the transcript of the interview with FDNY investigators that he wanted me to read. Sometimes a cigar is just a cigar! This was a dream about 9/11. I now recognize the full import of Steve's car. I remember him pulling up to the curb to pick me up for the terrorism training program. In my mind's eye I visualize him on the morning of September 11th jumping out of his car and crawling under it to avoid being swept up in the rolling cloud of the collapsed tower. This dream isn't so much a symbolic expression of his current state of mind as it is a trace memory of 9/11 that had been encoded in the trauma centre of his brain where it has remained stuck and unprocessed until now. The dream is one way Steve is trying to metabolize and make sense of what he himself went through that day.

Eager to share my realization, I try to explain, 'You said 'In real life that would never happen', meaning you wouldn't lose your car or lose your bearings. But it did! Your dream is trying to help you understand what happened on September 11th. Life at that moment was more like a dream than real.' Steve looks at me blankly. Now I am feeling 9/11 in all its vivid horror and having to will my mind to recall the details he related about what happened when he drove his car to the Trade Center. I understand now why it was so important to Steve that I read the transcript of his post-9/11 report. Steve hasn't been able to talk about the chaos of that morning with any detail or the effect it had on him. His priority has always been on other people. Finally he's permitting himself his own pain and bringing it to us through his dream.

Steve begins to describe what it was like when the towers collapsed. He doesn't mention Bobby Walsh, but he says he had to 'abandon' his vehicle so that he could make it to the buildings on foot to give emergency medical service to civilians. Gently but adamantly I approach these traumatic memories. 'The whole thing actually happened, Steve. It's true, by now it almost feels like it didn't really happen, like it couldn't have really happened. In real life things like that don't happen. Only they did.'

* * *

PART IV
Beyond the Reach of Ladders

Some Years Later

Time can bring perspective on ourselves, others and the things that have happened. It's only with the passing of so many years that I have come to understand and fully appreciate the far reaching ways 9/11 changed me as a person and a professional. Wherever we were on September 11th, whatever personal meaning it has come to carry for each of us as individuals, we all live with the changes in what has come to be known as post-9/11 life.

People come and go in therapy, but a solid therapy relationship endures. My connection with the men from the firehouse lives on, though we see each other only rarely. Jack Smith and Steve Holland still come regularly to therapy, and Patrick Darby makes sure to stay in touch. We don't talk as much about 9/11, but it remains the glue between us. It's the place we are bound to not leave behind in our hearts and minds.

* * *

Patrick Darby swings the door open for my departing patient who's having trouble getting her walker through my waiting room door. He tips his baseball cap and wishes us both a good morning, bringing out a girlish giggle from my elderly patient and dispelling the awkwardness of the situation. I'm struck by the irony that though Darby looks so healthy in contrast to my other patient whose Parkinson's Disease is so blatantly disabling, he too is afflicted with a disease which is permanently altering his life course. He refers to it as 'my asthma', as though it's a friend he's looking out for. Though it's been some years since his prolonged exposure to the toxic air at Ground Zero and his health has generally improved, he is living with the spectre of knowledge that the seriousness of illness has intensified for many recovery workers over time. This could mean a more guarded prognosis.

I remember the day he came to see me when he was first diagnosed like it was today. 'Doc, I feel like I might just have hit the jackpot. They're saying this asthma might just put me out.' He smiled broadly. I couldn't tell if he was putting on one of his typical 'I can handle anything and be a good sport' faces or if he really meant it. He knew full well it would put an end to both his firefighting and flying career. When the time came to leave the firehouse, he talked about how bad he felt 'leaving all the guys right now, with all that happened' and the irony of having the 'good fortune' to be able to retire with a pension so young but having to move to a warmer climate and leave behind all the people in New York that have been his life.

When I said something about the sadness and loss he must be feeling in having to leave the firehouse and his extended family behind I was met with a gentle but definitive correction. 'Doc, I'm a lucky stiff. I'm a working-class guy. I never thought I might be able to retire at 40, and still be able to afford a nice house, and support my family and all.' Patrick Darby convinced me then that he is truly blessed with that rare gift of unwavering optimism which is a highly effective way of coping with adversity and distinguishes the more successful survivors. He brought his instinct to see the glass as half full to the recovery operation at Ground Zero and to dealing with his health condition.

Darby's move to Florida appears to have been advantageous for his mental as well as physical health. He's up in New York and come to see me as part of a cross country road trip he's taking. In that great American tradition of road travel, Darby is roaring around the country on his motorcycle, stopping in firehouses everywhere he goes, chatting it up with the people he meets along the way, gathering stories for his return. On his Harley Davidson, with the air puffing out his jacket, whistling into his helmet, Darby can make it almost anywhere he wants to – even to disaster sites where he volunteers. Now that he's retired, on any given day, Darby can throw his leg over the girl, step on the gas, clutch the handlebars and zoom away. My roaming, on the other hand, remains confined to my leather swivel chair and mind travel over the terrain of 'free associations' and psychological disasters brought to my door.

Unable to sit still for the one hour he's with me, Darby apologizes for interrupting me as he jumps up and goes to the window, explaining he's got to check on his motorcycle. I join him there, sticking my head all the way out the window to get a good view of his Harley parked at the corner in front of the pizza shop. I make the appropriate Oohs and Aahs for his baby. This launches him into the details of his itinerary. We sit back down and finish our session. Before he leaves the office, he walks back to the window for a last glimpse of his cycle from twenty-three storeys in the air.

Peering down Darby shakes his head from side to side and in an offhanded way informs me, 'Doc I don't know about this. You know the ladders, they don't reach up here. They usually go six storeys, the aerial platforms can reach at best 100 feet, that's it. These high rises, they're real problems.' The possibility that I could not be reached in danger, by ladder or by any other means for that matter, had never crossed my mind before. How could I have been so unthinkingly led astray for more than twenty-five years to swallow the NYC coda – the bigger, the higher, the better? In my passion for light and water views I've always been so proud of the picture from my window – south and west in Manhattan all the way to the Hudson River and New Jersey. Up here in one of the tallest buildings in Greenwich Village I have an unobstructed view of the clouds and lightning shows. I can steal glimpses of hovering helicopters and planes on their way in and out of New York. Up here where the air must be thinner because people say they can see things so much more clearly than they can down on the ground. Where from the safety of my stress-less chair I can travel without a seat belt or having to wait in security lines to parts unknown, hour after hour, as people from around the world tell me stories of their lives and of the generations before them. Like all the other city slickers, I'm still addicted to being up as high and seeing as far as I can. The 1993 bombing of the Trade Center didn't do it. Osama hasn't done it – cured us of our love for New York City and its high-rise, high-living life.

* * *

That night I have a dream.

I'm holding a baby in my arms. I put it down on a blanket on the floor. It starts to cry. There's nothing strange about that, but suddenly I realize the body is sheared in half, revealing the insides. I don't want to look but I know I can't not pick it up and hold it. I look into its eyes. I coo and rock it in my arms until it finally stops crying. I find an outfit, a onesie stretchy outfit for infants. I gently close each snap as it lies on a changing table. I ask myself whether I'm trying to hide the missing body or trying to treat it like it's intact. 'Whole' was the word that came to mind in the dream. I carefully set the baby back down on the floor near a TV. We seem content. Suddenly I see water encroaching from all around. I keep myself from panicking by going to make a phone call to get help. When I come back the baby starts to walk, and the outfit has turned into a fur coat. I decide it's not a person, it's an animal, maybe a cat, but it's okay. It looks normal, yet I know it's not. I have this feeling that if I just treat it like it's normal, it will somehow become whole again.

The poignancy of this dream lies in its many layers of meaning, its resonance to my patients, to my own life, and I believe to 9/11 itself. At one level the tenderness I feel for this innocent baby turned damaged creature echoes how I feel about my patients, the care and understanding I have for their wounds and for the primitive feelings and impulses they, like everyone, have. The peculiar human/animal creature with a severed body that I was taking care of reminds me of the severed bodies in Smitty's flashbacks and that many people witnessed at the Trade Center on September 11th. It also reminds me of how Darby's career was cut short by illness sustained from his rescue and recovery work. More abstractly it speaks to how Steve's childhood was prematurely aborted when his father abandoned the family. I know too that the image of those sharply cut, exposed innards represents the raw insides of all my patients who have entrusted me with their care.

At another level, this dream is a gift from my unconscious communicating something in me that I need to pay attention to, for my own sake as well as for my patients. A therapist's credibility and effectiveness lies as much with her humanness as with her humanity, on her willingness to be open and honest, to face her own personal pain and vulnerability to the vagaries of the human condition. For real healing requires real mutuality between therapist and patient. That primitive creature/infant is as much a part of me as it is of those I take care of. My dream is a reminder to my waking self of my own lingering wounds, from 9/11 and from the traumatic loss of my father a few years before. I am both the adult who takes care of others and the baby who needs to be taken care of. Deep inside I am still the little girl whose daddy was abruptly taken from her, who grieved alongside these men. Together we continue to heal.

Soldiers return from the battlefield, policemen, firemen return from scenes of grisly crimes of man and nature. People 'recover' from catastrophes and manage to adjust to a world that requires people to look normal, especially heroes and therapists. Some may even manage to look better than before, however badly or permanently damaged they may be on the inside. The psychological scars from trauma form adhesions deep within the mind and body, attaching themselves to lifelong neurotic patterns, and run far deeper than the promise of the quick-fix things that we look to today – facelifts, TV gurus, twelve-step and ten-session therapies. But through hard work, in the privacy of the intimate analytic therapy relationship, where therapist and patient commingle their separate demons, people do make deep and lasting changes in their lives. This dream, I'm sure, won't be the last of my dreaming about the firemen and 9/11. My dream is a call for me to stay the course with these men and the other people I work with, however long it takes. It renews my faith that together, whether it's across the therapy room or across a firehouse kitchen table, we can discover the invisible ladder that will lead us onward and upward.

This dream also carries a meaning far broader than the pain of my patients' or my own life. For what I believe that dismembered animal hidden within the wrapping of the baby's bunting represents is 9/11 and life itself. Not only does that mutilated body remind me of the beheadings, loss of limbs and many other brutalities of war that have occurred since 9/11, but it symbolizes our collective wounds from 9/11 – our loss of innocence as a society, the cutting off of life as we knew it before. And at the deepest level this dream is about life itself. No matter how well put together we may appear, like that swaddled pseudo-human dream figure, we all end up wounded by life in some way. It is only by reaching out to others, and believing in our common humanness, that individuals and societies heal.

Just in case Darby was right about that ladder not reaching me, a few days later I have the chance to check out my twenty-third storey problem with Steve Holland. By happenstance, when he enters the office he walks over to the window to take in the view, the strange beauty of the pollution-tinted sunset. Trying to be casual, I remark, 'One of the guys said it wasn't too safe up here,' while searching his face for clues of danger. At first unsure of what I was getting at, he eventually gets my drift and replies, 'Oh you mean because the ladders don't reach up here,' as though stating the obvious.

The ladders don't reach the twenty-third floor! How could this be? Unconcerned, Steve goes to sit down and launches into a discursive tour of the department's routine and training for high-rise fires. But I've heard enough. I head back from the window. Not wanting him to detect my unsteadiness, I nod knowingly as I take my seat, and change the subject.

I suddenly realize I had fancied myself a Rapunzel of sorts, happily ensconced in her psychoanalytic tower, imagining a strong fireman would gallantly come to my rescue if needed. It's been so many years since 9/11 that I no longer worry about safety the way I used to. I've resumed living in the pleasant illusion of feeling immune from disaster, in that same false sense of security as my fellow New Yorkers and Americans. Being a therapist is a constant reminder of universal vulnerability, but it can also engender hubris. I'm stunned by the awareness of how strongly I've held onto certain romantic visions and ideas about life, despite all that has happened. I had refused to consider the possibility that my office is on a floor far beyond the reach of a ladder.

The stubborn persistence of my blithe ignorance of this obvious reality for so long is a painful reminder of my own limits as a human being, and has made me take a hard look at what I had unconsciously projected onto the firemen and brought into the therapy. Despite all my efforts otherwise, at the deepest level, I probably idealized and romanticized the firemen as rescuers, at moments looking to them with unrealistic expectations of what is humanly possible. Not so different from what people often do to therapists. Therapists, like firefighters, are fallible human beings. We all long for heroes. My father had always been my hero. I was accustomed to relying on him to guide and protect me, even as a middle-aged woman, and until his death, I secretly harboured the fantasy that he was there on call ready to rescue me.

It's only in hindsight that I've come to see how the terror of 9/11 and the loss of my father drew me to the firemen. The trauma of my father's death re-surfaced with the trauma of 9/11. The pain that I felt enhanced my ability to relate to what the firemen were going through after the disaster. Getting to know these men, who reminded me of my father in so many ways, made the memories of my father and his death come alive. They deepened my understanding and appreciation of my father as a man, and in the long run helped me move beyond my secret longings for a hero.

The last time I saw my father, it was a few years before September 11th, on one of those perfectly warm and sunny days in Florida when it's still drearily cold up north. My dad was glistening in suntan lotion and paternal pride at having his daughter on the lounge chair beside him at the condo pool in the midday sun as only true sun worshippers like us love to do. Like most New Englanders, my father always lived, worked and played by the water. So, despite the fact that he had never learned to swim, when he retired from his lifelong career at the Fish Pier in Boston Harbor and moved to Florida, he bought a place which faced a man-made lake with fountain and artificial ducks in the middle.

My father wasn't exactly what you'd call the talkative type. Much of the time it was hard to know what he was thinking or if he was even paying attention. But he was the kind of person who would come up with a spontaneous profundity to open an intimate conversation when you least expected it – on a morning walk, going to the store for milk, on a Sunday drive for ice cream, or standing at the doorway while we were sitting around the table. Outside the radar of my mother who tended to hold centre stage with her ongoing analysis of people and commentary on the foibles of human nature. My father tried his best to find a private moment to share what he'd learned about life and believed I should know.

That day could have been one of those times. Earlier that morning we'd done our respective laps around the artificial lake. He walked briskly and I jogged slowly, in rhythmic coordination with each other, both of us plugged into our headsets, going in opposite directions, nodding as we passed each other, enjoying being together while we're doing what we each love and usually do alone. We completed our morning exercise with our ritual trip to the pool. I was about to leave for a short side trip to Key West before returning on my way back up to New York.

We lay in the comfort of our sun-worshipping silence. From behind my dark glasses I stole glances at my father as he took in the intense Florida sun. A large star of David, bordering on gauche, hung from a gold chain on his chest. Disturbed, I quickly turned back to my book, hoping he wouldn't notice. It wasn't his tendency to excess that bothered me; by then I found it all the more endearing. It was the sight of how white the thick hair on his chest and arms had become that got to me. My dad cleared his throat. Feeling my attention on him he said something. Something casual, maybe even trivial, exactly what I can't for the life of me recall. I can distinctly remember the sight and sound of his belly heaving one of his Rorschach type sighs, the kind that had always left me wondering what he was thinking. But no matter how hard I try, I cannot recapture those words, his last spoken to me.

I glanced at my watch and realized if I didn't leave the pool right away I'd be late. I jumped up, grabbed my towel, and just as I went to hug and kiss him good-bye I felt the eyes of all the old folks around the pool turning to look at us. The idea of embracing my dad being on display for these strangers irritated me. So despite everything my dad had taught me about showing love, despite the fact that my first memory is of my father's outstretched arms reaching for me and despite the fact that I'd been sitting on his lap with my arms draped around him only hours before, I refused to hug or kiss him good-bye. Rather, I self-consciously called out with a casual air and broad smile as I hurried toward the gate, 'See ya' Dad. Don't forget, I'll be back in three days.' He lifted his head, smiled briefly in my direction, then lay back down, closed his eyes, returning to his sun soporific reverie.

Less than thirty-six hours later I was picking up my messages right at 5 p.m., as I always do when I'm away. The message I'd dreaded my whole life came in the voice of my sister-in-law, 'Sorry to leave this on your machine. But please, call us as soon as you can.'

Only a few days earlier my father groaned the refrain I'd heard all my life. We'd all come to pay no mind to it, treating it as part of the chorus of our particular family melodrama when my dad's frustration with my mother got to a certain point – 'Irene, you're gonna kill me.' But Dad, I was coming back in three days.

We never made it past the cardiac intensive care unit. I stared at my father lying on his back with his eyes closed, his body no longer glistening in the sun. He was cool to the touch, almost cold under bright artificial lights. I watched and listened to his laboured breathing, then his panting. This time we weren't out walking together. We weren't talking. We were waiting for him to die.

I stared at the line on the heart monitor whose sole function was to mark the pace of life ending. I held his hand and smoothed his brow, just as he had taught me. I kissed his forehead. He did not respond. I prayed. One moment I prayed for death to rush in, the next for death to take its time. Then I just prayed. Before the night was over my father was dead. By the late afternoon of that very same day, in accordance with Jewish law, I accompanied my father on his final flight, Delta 407, from Florida back up north to Boston, where his funeral was to be held. He was in steerage while my mother and I sat beside each other in coach, with my brother in the seat right in front of me.

Why did I not take the time to say something important to him as he had always made a point of doing with me? How could I have let my self-consciousness stop me from embracing my dad that day? I'd lived long enough to know life should never be taken for granted. Yet I persisted in living as though there's always another day to do and say the things that are most important. It just never felt like the right time. I never took the time to tell him my life would never be the same without him.

How many of those three thousand people didn't take that moment to kiss their wives and husbands, hug their sons and daughters, or call their best friends before they left home that bright sunny September morning? I thought I was done with mourning my father. But grief has its own course. It can return when you least expect it. Each new loss reverberates with the ones before, teaching new things about life, ourselves and those we have loved. We live like there's always a tomorrow, always another day – to finish growing up, to do things better, to take the time to cherish the people who matter the most. We wait for another time – to tell them, to really show them how much they mean to us.

* * *

'In the final analysis, the questions of why bad things happen to good people transmutes itself into some very different questions, no longer asking why something happened, but asking how we will respond, what we intend to do now that it happened.'
Pierre Teilhard de Chardin

* * *

With both my parents gone for some time, I wish I'd done more for them in life, and so I try to do better by them in death. It's late summer and I'm fulfilling my obligation to go to the cemetery before the High Holy days. I think of all the people for whom Ground Zero is the cemetery where their loved one is buried. Here there are gravestones lined up in a neat orderly fashion with etched inscriptions – Loving Mother, Father, Son, etcetera, leaving no doubt, in contrast to Ground Zero, that this land is holy and belongs to the dead. And unlike the Trade Center site, there's no one in sight, no sound of city congestion or traffic, only me and a lone crow perched on a tree just outside the cemetery wall. I gingerly step between the crowded headstones, then set the handful of small stones I've gathered over the past year on my parents' headstone. I bend down and kiss the short stout granite stone etched 'MAX' in large lettering. Self-consciously I look around to see if anyone is watching, then realize this isn't downtown Manhattan. I talk to my father.

Dad, there were so many things I never told you. I am so much like you. When I look down I see your feet. When I look in the mirror I see your nose. When I clear my throat in a certain way it is the sound of you clearing yours that I hear. Like you, I remember every telephone number after the second call, your telegraphic memory for numbers magically installed in me and in your granddaughter. Every once in a while as I sit at the computer and notice my fingers moving over the keyboard I see yours flying across the obsolescent adding machine. Between nature and nurture the Eisenhower era accountant has spawned a new-age shrink who translates the human condition from your beloved Yiddish into the language of therapy.

I can remember exactly how you smell – the fish reeking on your work clothes, your after-shave, that unique smell of your hands. But tell me Dad, how is that I can remember all this but I can no longer clearly conjure up your face in my mind's eye? Why is it I can remember that you played with the change in your pocket, but I can no longer hear the sound of your laughing voice? Wherever you are, can you understand, like you always did understand everything, just why it is that we cannot bear talking too much about you? For so long I was locked in endless replay of memories of you. Now I'm so sorry but I have to work hard to recapture split-second glimpses of you, the things you said, the things you did.

With memories fading of my father, his death and all that happened in 9/11, the pain and guilt aren't what they were years ago. I know I am fortunate to have this headstone, and this tranquil cemetery to come to. Before 9/11 it never occurred to me to appreciate the fact that I was able to lay my parents to rest in the ground. After the sudden loss of my father I languished in my grief. Until the day I had to look into the eyes of people at St. Vincent's Hospital, people grasping photos and imploring me for 'information' about their mother, father, sister, brother, partner and friend.

Until I sat with all those people who were crying for a body to bury and who had to settle for a piece of paper that verified death, I had little grasp of the particular torture of death without a body. Without being able to see a loved one dead, not being able to watch their body being lain to rest, makes is so much harder to say good-bye and accept the finality of death, to have a sense of closure. The families of those who died in the Towers have created their own rituals. Each year they read out the names of each person, in the tradition that has evolved at the anniversary of September 11th at Ground Zero. This year, as in the past, I anticipate there'll be classical music and people will walk down into the pit. They will hold roses, photos, and signs.

But what ritual can address those of us tied by breath to those who died at the Trade Center? What ritual is there for those of us who inhaled the vapours of humans beings evaporated into the smoke and dust saturated air in the days and weeks after September 11th? Each one of us that lived and worked down there must live with the knowledge that traces of these strangers seeped through the pores of our skin, entering our bodies and souls.

However far away from the disaster we were on September 11th, whatever course our lives have taken, each one of us knows the pain of loss, and most of us will end up having a Bobby Walsh, that dead friend who lives on within us. My father and mother taught me that life is as much about sustaining attachment as it is about letting go. By their example, and their enduring faith in humanity, they showed me the path of caring for the wounded and honouring the dead.

* * *

Over the years, Steve Holland has continued to steadily rise in the ranks of the Fire Department to assume more and more responsibility. Knowing he can't afford to have self-doubt and lingering memories plague him and interfere with his professional functioning, he's committed himself to working through not only the issues the Trade Center raised for him, but also the effects of his childhood traumas and the other forces shaping his personality. He has a better understanding of how he became an 'enabler', that is, someone who is dependent on others being dependent on him in order to feel worthwhile and safe. Steve continues coming to therapy each week in the hour between day and night, and we stand side by side at the window, as the pastel sunset softens the Manhattan skyline. At times he wonders which side of him will prevail, the forceful side he presents to the world or the dark side of buried anxiety and despair. It's my job to help him integrate his strength with his vulnerability, into a more fully realized whole self.

Steve begins today's session, as he does most sessions, bound up with emotion. He explains, 'Something happened at the site. It was bad. I almost lost it, no I lost it.' I know he's referring to Ground Zero, a term he refuses to use. We've talked many times about the ritual Saturday morning trips that he makes down there with the same devotion that he used to go to church on Sundays as a boy. He often says 'I can't say I like it, but I just want to go there.'

Steve can think of nothing in particular that could have sparked the incident. I immediately remind him of the upcoming anniversary and he agrees this must have been what set him off though he says at the time he wasn't conscious of this. He explains that he was working down there with a few guys he likes and trusts. Things were pretty much the same as they've been there for a while. Vendors were selling Big Apple T-shirts, framed photos of the Trade Center along with other souvenirs on the sidewalks. The tour buses and cabbies were honking, and people were setting up good camera shots on the street. That Ground Zero has become a tourist destination was no surprise to Steve. He and I have talked often about the unbelievable commercialization that has arisen there, and about his mixed feelings about the hero-worshipping tourists he encounters whenever he's down there in uniform. He's talked about how uncomfortable he is with the adulation, but agrees nonetheless to give his autograph when asked or to pose for photographs standing by the fire truck. He goes on to say he's been down there at the time of the previous anniversaries but nothing like this had ever happened.

Needing to 'figure out' the reasons for why he 'lost it' that day, Steve wonders out loud, 'You know I didn't mind the vendors and stuff when they were on the other side of the street, where

Century 21, you know the department store, is. If only they hadn't crossed the street.' Meaning if only the vendor hadn't located his cart on the sidewalk that abuts the fenced in gaping thirteen acre hole that is Ground Zero, showing what Steve felt was a lack of respect, an utter disregard for the sacredness of the site. With a trace of sadness he repeats, 'If only they had stayed on the other side,' then goes on, 'There was this guy there, selling hot dogs, Sabretto umbrella up and all, you could smell the pretzels on the side grill. He was right there up against the fence, can you believe it? So people could stare down while munching on their hot dogs. He was acting like it was the circus, or Yankee Stadium.

'I lost it. I started yelling. My guys have heard me yelling before. But not like this. Then I don't know exactly what happened, but as I said, I lost it. Next thing I know, I'm on top of the guy. And yelling like they never heard before. They ran and got Port Authority police. Took three guys to get me off him.'

It may have been only a matter of few feet or yards to most people. But to Steve, this vendor was selling food at the edge of a cemetery called Ground Zero. A cemetery whose future will be configured by the architect Daniel Liebeskind and his winning design for the re-building of Ground Zero. In the time it has taken to dismantle and ready the site and ourselves for moving on and re-building, two wars have begun, George W. Bush completed two terms as president and Barack Obama was elected as the first black president of the United States. The battle that waged for years over Ground Zero, like most battles over land, came down to a conflict between our collective impulse to look to the future and our need to memorialize the past. We had our familiar discourse of money and ideology, but didn't quite know how to think about, much less discuss, our relationship to those who were burnt, buried and pulverized on this land. Does this land belong more to the dead, to the landowners of this property, or to the people of the world that was changed forever by 9/11? More battles are sure to be fought over the final plans. The final design must symbolize our deepest feelings while considering the current and future complex social, political and economic conditions. What will eventually arise from this cemetery has yet to be fully determined, and if successful, the compromise solution will likely feel somewhat unsatisfactory to all parties. In the struggle between preserving the past and looking to the future, between our earth bound nature and divinely inspired aspirations, the Freedom Tower has been conceived, and the 'footprints' of the former World Trade Center will remain where they are, seventy feet below ground. The footprints, as they're referred to, are unlike the human or animal footprints we think of. They are the last vestiges, 'all that's left', as people say, of the buildings of the World Trade Center and the people who died in its towers. No one has the corner on truth. No one really knows what happens to man and his creations when they disappear from sight, and therefore what's the right thing to do and build on the site. But somehow everyone can agree on one thing, the footprints must be saved.

Ground Zero is and will always be a sacred place to Steve Holland, as for so many people connected to the Trade Center disaster. It's an open secret between Steve, Stephanie and me that Steve heard 'something' as he put it, on September 11th. In a couples session some time ago, Stephanie said that Steve had told her that God spoke directly to him that day. She dismissed it as an illusion, if not delusion, arisen from Steve's religiousness, something she doesn't share. Steve confessed that he thinks a divine message was imparted to him that day, telling him that his life must be dedicated to 'doing something' to redeem all those lost lives, including his friend Bobby Walsh, the person Steve feels he most let down on 9/11.

Bobby, who in those last moments called out as he was being crushed beneath the stairwell, waiting to be rescued, who kept thinking about Steve calling out to him before he turned toward the Trade Center. Wherever Bobby Walsh is now, he knows the kind of man Steve is. He knows Steve will always hold himself partly responsible for not stopping Bobby from going into the towers, no matter how much therapy he has. I can only help Steve find a way to forgive himself. Each one of us has a Bobby

Walsh somewhere out there. Someone whose life was doomed, someone whom we have loved but feel we didn't do enough for.

Who's to say, maybe Steve Holland was privileged with celestial communication on 9/11 and perhaps the voices he heard in the breeze blowing through the voids of the mile high mound were real on the morning of September 11th. Like many of us, Steve's position on the existence of God is inconsistent. He balks at organized religion, occasionally blaming his sexual hang-ups on 'the job those nuns did', and limits his church attendance to weddings and funerals. Yet Steve is ironically religious for such an avowedly non-religious man.

He keeps a prayer card in the glove compartment of his car for good luck and for making sure he never forgets. A prayer card from a funeral he had attended for a fellow fireman several months before September 11th, where he sat with his old buddy Bobby Walsh, whom he hadn't seen for some time before. While they were waiting together in the receiving line to give their condolences to the widow, they started shooting the breeze about old times. They were talking about getting together sometime soon, having dinner, a few drinks, with the wives, like they way they used to way back when, when they were young and right out of the academy. As they left the church, both Steve and Bobby grabbed a laminated prayer card the family provided in memory of the man who died.

I suspect Steve will continue to go to Ground Zero, though less often, as the years go on. He'll go very early on Saturday mornings, before the rest of the city has awakened. For now the site is still a thirteen-acre gaping hole in the mammoth canyon of Manhattan's financial district now known as Ground Zero. Steve stands alone at the fence of the cemetery turned tourist attraction, in that no-man's land between the past and present, and wonders what the future will bring. He keeps an ear out for sounds impossible to hear in the din of the work week. As he contemplates the footprints below, he thinks of everything that's happened, and feels inside his pocket to grab hold of his prayer card. For hours afterwards, he can hear the plaintive voice of

Bobby Walsh and the words, 'What's to become of me?' echoing in his brain.

2010

9/11 seems like a long time ago and yet like it was just yesterday. With the end of my story in sight, it would be tempting to spin out a neat and clear cut story of trauma and recovery for Jack Smith, Steve Holland, Patrick Darby, and all the other firefighters and survivors of 9/11. But that would only repeat the cycle of objectification and oversimplification that these men and trauma survivors too often suffer. And it is this very kind of failure to recognize our similarity and connection to those who appear different that is the breeding ground of violence and was the kind of mentality that led to 9/11.

Each of these men continues to quietly suffer while healing and growing in his own distinct way. Each person's response to and recovery from trauma is idiosyncratic, depending on a host of personal and situational factors. These include the extent and duration of exposure to the incident, an individual's history, particularly of prior trauma, the nature of a person's emotional and intellectual resources, and the degree of social support. Most of the firemen, with their highly-developed skills for coping with trauma and with the strong support they get from family and the Brotherhood, have largely recovered from the worst catastrophe they and the Fire Department of New York have ever undergone.

Jack Smith is becoming more and more alive in session and in life. Though most of his acute post-traumatic symptoms have disappeared, every once in a while he has intrusive flashbacks and disturbing memories. He must live with the painful reality of how 9/11 permanently scarred him. On a daily basis he confronts the challenges of retiring from a career that had been his life, and of the pain of loving within the spectre of multiple lost loves.

Steve Holland marches on, having been promoted once again. He holds a position of leadership in a department that is finally recovering its morale and manpower. Our work is an ongoing struggle of faith and doubt. When doubt gets the better of him, he still periodically asks, 'Is this normal? It seems like we've hit a plateau. I'm not sure about this, whether we're going to be able to do it this time,' and I still can't always tell if it's his marriage, the Fire Department or the therapy that he's questioning. Beneath these expressed doubts lie deeper fears and a persistent need to fulfil his mission to 'serve others'.

It's unclear how Patrick Darby's health and early retirement will affect his long term health. He may have flown far a-field but he remains 'a phone call away'. I have every confidence that Darby will remain Darby, the kind of person who lives each day like it's his last. He's hoping and praying, we're all praying, that he will stay lucky, that his respiratory disease doesn't become progressive or life threatening, as is turning out to be the case for a rising number of other Ground Zero recovery workers the more time passes.

No matter how much of a Sisyphus these men may feel at times in their never-ending role of serving others, no matter how worn down or resentful they may get, these men will always define themselves through their responsibility for others. Some people, amateur and professional psychoanalysts alike, might interpret this focus on serving others as pathological, a self-inflicted pain and burden based on guilt, an over-inflated ego, or a perverse expression of personal dependency needs and feelings of inadequacy. Though these interpretations have some validity, they don't tell the whole story. Whatever neurotic function is involved, it doesn't take away from the motivation that fundamentally drives these people – genuine altruism. For Steve, Smitty and Darby, as for their fellow firemen, indeed for all those dedicated to service, being able to help others is what brings personal meaning and fulfillment to their lives. And will thus continue to be these men's source of faith and recovery.

Somehow I find myself returning to the kind of connect-the-dots life that was so thoroughly ingrained in me through my post-World War II education in Yankee New England, where life choices were confined to the five Crayola colours of the rainbow, and the idea of shading, mixing of colours and efficventuring beyond the lines was considered a sign of poor character. And though my days are filled with contemplation of life's big questions with my patients, so much of my life is ruled by the clock. I rise each morning to the alarm after pressing the snooze button three times, make myself exactly one and half cups of coffee, half regular, half decaf, then go to work helping other people discover ways to re-conceive and invigorate their lives.

I come home each night, step out of my professional uniform and slip into the reassuring ease of sweatpants. Every once in a while, after a particularly stressful day, I choose the comfort of my favourite nearly threadbare jeans, those holdovers of my former self from those 'burn your bra' days when we called them dungarees. I slip my hands in the pockets for my paper memory/ talisman of 9/11, when I need that little extra something to keep on keeping on like the way Darby uses his rabbit's foot. I don't think that much about 9/11 any more. Except for when I'm with certain patients. Or on those rare moments when the lights flicker, my subway inexplicably stops between stations, or I hear one too many sirens careening through the streets. I tell myself that at this point in time the psychological imperative of putting it away and resuming life should outweigh the moral imperative of remembering.

Last night I didn't leave my office till almost nine o'clock. I made one last effort to replay a message I'd listened to several times over the course of the day but hadn't been able to determine who it was from. All I could make out was a man saying 'Hello. Liz?', a crackling sound muffling the words, then a redolent second or two of silence before the call was disconnected. Someone's trying to reach me. I didn't recognize the voice as belonging to any of my current patients, but the voice sounded vaguely familiar. It didn't sound like Darby but I thought it might be one of the guys from the firehouse. The voice reminded me of Lt. Ross but I doubted that this practical man, whom I'd heard had been promoted to captain and transferred out of Manhattan, would be inclined to call on me, the lady psychologist from the firehouse who he 'had to help out'. And I doubted it was Sal, who has a therapist. Maybe it was one of the guys who had come to see me. Or maybe Mouse or Pauli or Phil, guys who keep a low profile but who do think about things. Guys who aren't used to anyone taking an interest in them in the way I did, who never came to my private office but spent time with me in the firehouse. It didn't seem too likely that they would pick up the phone and call me at this point, but you never know when someone decides to take that leap.

The idea that I cannot reach someone who's reaching out to me is intolerable. It's hard enough for a person to screw up the courage to call a therapist. People don't call therapists when things are going well. So a therapist not returning a call can be like adding salt to an already open wound. Though not necessarily in desperate straits, whoever that man was, he was calling me for help. How could I simply not respond? But with no name or number to go on, I could only hope he'd call back.

I emptied the trash cans, turned out the lights, and took my ritual last look out the window at the lights of Manhattan as I closed the door and made sure it was double locked. When I got home I decided it was definitely a comfy old jeans night. Only to discover that they had mysteriously found their way into the laundry, taking with them the paper remains of what I'd found at Ground Zero. How could I have let my relic of history bio-degrade in the spin cycle? That night I had this dream.

My washing machine wasn't working, and my laundry had been taken to the Laundromat around the corner from my house. In my dream, I saw a woman pulling my jeans out of my thickly stuffed laundry bag and shaking them as she put them into the washer. She didn't notice the crumpled tissue and piece of paper that I had come to believe was a prayer card falling to the floor. To me that piece of paper was something of the divine that had made its way into human hands, from someone possibly holding onto it for dear life, and then into my hands when I found it outside the Relief Centre of Ground Zero. That wisp of cardboard had helped me find the courage to go back into the firehouse after being pushed out by Robbie Taylor, and that I imagined might have belonged to someone who died there, maybe even Bobby Walsh. That piece of paper was a part of every one and every thing that had vanished with barely a trace left. I was feeling sorrowful and angry at myself for having been so careless with something that I'd been entrusted with.

In my dream the young Arab boy who works there after school was sweeping up, as I've seen him do many times. So preoccupied with the things that daydreaming boys his age are, my little scrap of paper didn't catch his eye. Just as it hadn't caught anyone else's attention when I grabbed it up that day. It was after all only one of literally thousands of pieces of paper that had gone flying with the explosion, some even landing on the sidewalks of Brooklyn. While dreaming of bigger and better things for his future, and still not noticing my piece of paper, the young boy half-heartedly pushed the broom, sweeping the dirt and dust bunnies out the door onto the sidewalk and onto the street, where he knew the passing cars, wind or street cleaners would make it all disappear. My prayer card, or whatever it was, was back on the ground, just like it was when I found it.

Then before either wind or man had their chance at this piece of history, I saw an exotic bird alight on the sidewalk. Larger than the pigeons and sparrows that make this neighbourhood their home, it caught the eye of the Sikh man who runs the news stand next door to the Laundromat. He'd just been listening to a story on public radio about such recent sightings of uncommon birds in Central Park, and went outside to get a closer look. On sensing the man's movement, the bird snatched my paper up and took off, screeching or squawking, the newsstand owner wasn't sure. A woman was jogging by. In my dream it seemed like I was both the woman and myself watching this whole thing. When the bird made its strange sound they looked at each other for a split second, then instinctively turned away, embarrassed by having broken that unspoken rule of New York City life – avoid direct eye contact. His look suggested 'Did you see that?' I, the woman, gave him a look of 'No', then picked up the pace to get across the intersection while the light was still green. The man shook his head as if he was thinking how odd things are here in the States, and went back inside his newsstand.

Then I see the bird flying. It didn't stop at the Brooklyn Promenade where all the pigeons gather. It looked like it was heading towards the Brooklyn Bridge, but then, as though it had suddenly changed its mind, it made a beeline straight to the harbour of lower Manhattan with this bit of memory in its beak. Whatever and all that this piece of paper is, in the dream I'm feeling that its fate is to connect man and nature.

I'm tense but sort of intrigued in my dream, watching, waiting to see what was going to happen. Will this strange creature stop or fly right past Ground Zero? Will the bird drop it into the water or onto the ground? Or will it keep it in its beak and ascend skyward into the celestial drift?

Before I found out the fate of the piece of paper, I woke up.

It doesn't take a PhD to interpret this dream. Set off by the un-recognizable call for help, the dream is an expression of my abiding sense of responsibility. It also reveals my sentimentality and love of nostalgia. Paper represents what makes New York City run. Thousands upon thousands of pieces of paper constitute the raison d'etre for twentieth century life symbolized by those towers. Even in our post millennial, digital age, paper rules. On windy days papers can be seen flying around the streets. Newspapers and advertisements are still passed into people's hands as they come out of the subway, then tossed into trash bins at the corner. The paper that coated the vicinity of the felled Trade Center was the silent ineffable proof of the existence of the three thousand people that evaporated on that morning, and a symbol of earthbound minds transmitting knowledge, reaching beyond the known.

The dream also alludes to religious and cultural differences that became a breeding ground of fear and hatred underlying the terrorist attacks and the subsequent fearful reactive suspicion and discrimination against Muslims and Arabs throughout America. To me, it is the very recognition and appreciation of difference

– race, age, gender, sexual orientation, class, class, culture and religion – that makes New York City tick and, despite what happened, still one of the best places on earth to live.

But on the broadest level my dream is an expression of my faith in the divine spark within and between all things and my belief that we must do our best to keep alive the people and things of meaning that are gone.

* * *

2011

Therapy is about working toward the emergence of a meaningful life story that brings together the past and present in a way that expands one's vision of the future. This allows therapists to be active witnesses in the creating and living through of personal and collective history. Eventually the stories that will emerge out of September 11th will come to reflect more of the people we have become than the people we were at that extraordinary moment in time. In the throes of disaster, time collapses. On 9/11 we were graced with an acute awareness of life in its essence. But Time, that devil angel of the human spirit, has a way of evaporating into the ether, taking with it our glimpse of existential clarity, and leaving disparate bits of memory we collect like beached shells at low tide.

While I remain the same dogged analyst and New Yorker that I was before September 11th, the same chronicler of the seasons in other people's lives, I also know that I, like most everyone, have been irrevocably transformed by the world changing time of 9/11. Yet I still feel the call to dream alongside my patients, family and friends, to awaken memory and instill reverie in others. Needing to feel the world around and within me in search of new memories and dreams, unsure what else to do as this chapter of my life comes to an end, inveterate runner that I am, I take to the road.

Until new paths appear, I stay the course on my time worn trails and make my way over to Cadman Park and onto the Brooklyn Bridge. I love this thirteen-acre park, situated adjacent to the Federal Courthouse and at the base of the Brooklyn Bridge, especially in the early morning. In a few hours it'll be filled with local Brooklynites, and perhaps television camera crews awaiting jury deliberations for one of the famous criminals on trial here, along with anti-terrorist vans and dogs marking their territory on as many as possible of the London plane trees that rise between the old gas posts long ago converted to electric lamps. For now I am alone with the trees and the rare feeling as an urbanite of earth beneath my feet.

My life has been measured in miles of treading steadily on this ad hoc running path that came into being as a footpath to the bridge. This half mile trail was blazed by myself and the few other local joggers thirty years ago, back when you ran because you loved to run, without the benefit of breathable wind and water proof fabrics, Nikes or New Balances, or the burden of 'jogging' for health. As the dirt path weathered, we've had to keep on the lookout for more and more of the tree roots rising to the surface, between stealing glances up through the branches for a glimpse of sky.

I remember the park when it was a favourite cruising spot for gay men and for those without air conditioning to cool off on a hot summer day. That was before Aids and gentrification, before the Red Cross building at the far end of the park went into active service for the first time on the morning of 9/11. Since then everything's changed. An anti-bomb concrete bulwark blocks the iron fence. Now only the homeless, with shopping carts in tow, cruise the park as they root through trash bins for discarded bottles to cash in. There are still young couples, old folks, and the solo reader on benches and blankets in the warmer months. For more years than I care to count I've jogged, bicycled, and thrown balls to children and dogs here. My kids are long gone, but others, far younger, pass their time in the park playing ball, riding bikes.

I enter the park today with some trepidation, for a murder just occurred in this faux European city garden, where the dusty dirt of its once green great meadow and the history it signified has now been replaced with artificial grass. For as long as I have been coming here, 200 trees have encased this park. Two hundred London plane trees that have watched me and that I in turn have watched change with the seasons. Then one day, without warning, there were only 199. One of the mighty planes was sheared to its base and chopped up for mulch. Yet no one protested, no one revolted, or even reported this crime against nature.

Entering the park this morning I'm afraid to look where the electric saw cut smooth and straight with executioner efficiency, severing life's connection with the drone's satisfaction of a job well done, leaving only a stump covered with a few twigs and stray leaves to mark its grave. We runners know its deeply buried roots will never allow sterile erasure of life. Knotty nubs will inevitably break through the earth, cautioning us to not forget that the past will work its way into the present.

Its limbs, whether winter barren, summer green or autumnal yellow, always drew the eye upward. Until it was cut down, I never realized the view it had of New York Harbor, the Brooklyn Bridge, and the World Trade Center on the other side of the river. It watched Engine 224 and Ladder 205 screech around the corner on the morning of 9/11, and return with eight fewer men. It became a witness that had to be silenced, its stump a memorial seat for bearing witness to expendability and the impossibility of time standing still.

Lap 2, only fifteen minutes into the run, my Timex chronograph informs me. A slow day. I run past a bench where twenty somethings are wrapped in each other's arms, swept up in the thought-less touch, smell and breath of each other. I change the station from 'lite' to 'rock' FM, hoping the pulsing music will silence my aching thoughts and awaken my body. This might end up being just one of those 'slogging it' runs. But I have to keep going, I'm determined to keep running to the end. The endorphins and beat of the music finally get me into the contemplative rhythm of running. If I'm called upon to do it again, will I head toward the disaster, or away? I'm really not sure I have it in me to do it again, or to subject my family to the stress it would put on them.

I pick up speed, and as the runner's high takes over, I start to enumerate my share of life's experiences – how fortunate I am, where and how I've taken the leap, feeling regret only for chances not taken. Pushing myself to go another loop around the park, I hear myself counting up miles, men and the many of life's milestones as though they measure a life fully lived. I must complete the distance I'd set for today, then immediately question the meaning of this idea I persist on living by – going the distance. I check my watch, as if it might hold clues. Leaving the answers to life's big questions for another day, I decide in the meantime I should keep track of my mileage and pace myself. I still need to feel that I'm in the race.

My own moments of hypocrisy rarely escape the scrutiny of the analyst in me. I tell my patients, 'Live every moment like it's your last' yet the clock seems to define my every move. I hold high and exacting standards for things like running and work, but I see full well how I allow indecisiveness and lassitude to rule my handling of many details of my daily life. Like the piles of paper that overrun my desk. When all is said and done, what difference will it make if all those papers are filed away? In my mind's eye I see the thousands of pieces of paper, full of words that meant so much to everyone working away in the Trade Center floating like confetti onto our self-important New York City streets.

It's not paper, it's time that's the real enemy. It was one thing to have crows feet borne of laughter and quite another to have one wrinkle after another re-define my face and turn mirrors into a study in self-alienation. Aren't I still that young girl who flirts with ease on a park bench, who can magnetize with my lithe sensuality? Face it, Liz, no matter how great shape I keep myself in, the reality is – that was the past. Now who am I, who have we all become in this post-9/11, post-paper digital world? With no clear answers to any of these questions, what else can I do but keep running? Resolute in making it over the bridge and back before I quit, I make a brief mid-life necessitated pit stop before climbing the stairs to the bridge's walkway.

We Brooklynites swear the Brooklyn Bridge rivals even New York's most famous run, Central Park, for inspirational value. Though only a mile in length, the Bridge's view has no equal. As you ascend from Brooklyn the bridge gives you a vision to your side of the Statue of Liberty, a sliver of New Jersey on pollution free days, and Wall Street, with the space in its skyline where the Towers no longer stand, the spire of the Empire State Building rising between the mass of Manhattan's skyscrapers, and a fan of bridges spanning as far north over the East River as you can see.

This bridge is an ode unto itself. My own offering is limited to tracking her visitors over the decades. In the social downturn of the late sixties and seventies when crime was up and tourism down, few people ventured there on foot. We runners had the bridge to ourselves, but we had to watch our backs as well, for it was too easy to be accosted or mugged with no one within sight or sound. The droves began in the boom of the nineties. Since then, a continuous stream of people, many with cameras and Michelin travel guides in hand, can be seen meandering between those iron lanterns and taking in its views. Wedding parties have posed for photographers, as have models for advertisements. Protestors and walkers for causes have carried balloons and banners across her span, making their way around baby carriages and confused dogs on leashes. Until September 11th when the pedestrian roadway became one of the few escape routes for the mud and dust caked thousands fleeing the disaster. For a month or so after, the bridge was only accessible to emergency vehicles shuttling workers and debris in and out of the site. For the next few years we locals once again had the bridge to ourselves. Fluctuations in weather, economy or social conditions have never and will never deter indomitable foot travellers from making their way over the wooden planks night and day. And now that memories of 9/11 and fears of terrorism have loosened their hold on our psyches, the bridge is once again a top destination spot.

To this day I remain haunted by the question, Why was I and everyone close to me spared? Despite my determination to do otherwise after 9/11, I seem to have resumed life much as I lived it before. Contrary to all that I have witnessed and experienced, my species inherited hubris makes me assume my own survival. Perhaps we humans are simply incapable of fully comprehending our mortality. The bridge has survived. I keep running. The firefighters, police and other first responders keep on fighting fires, protecting people from nature and each other – from invisible terrorist plots at New Year celebrations, car bombs in Times Square, and Thanksgiving Day parades. Therapists keep on opening their doors and hearts to those who seek their help. We go on in our twenty-first century life of yellow, orange and red alert levels. As I make my way over the bridge, I nod, as I've always done, to my fellow runners and to the cyclists crossing from the other direction, to parents pushing strollers, and to the indomitable wheelchair bound persons crossing the bridge on their own steam. I run past the checkpoints of traffic cones and police cars staving off terrorism on the inner roadway, and like everyone else, I no longer even register their presence, much less think about the meaning behind it.

We go on living in the artificial absurd reassurance that all is well, that lightning never strikes twice in the same place, past one 9/11 anniversary after another, and through the endless wars in Iraq and Afghanistan in which so many of our young men and women have been killed and wounded. We Americans believe in 'moving on', we disdain lingering in the past. We tell ourselves we live in the freest and safest country on earth, and the Statue of Liberty reminds us this is true each time we catch sight of her in the Harbor.

I keep running, with time breathing at my back, spotting tourists making their pilgrimage over to Ground Zero, stealing glances at young lovers in romance novel embrace on the mid span of the Bridge. Committed to remembering the missing plane tree. The tree that lived at the crossroads of the era between a nation's innocence and life under the threat of terrorism, felled with the supremacy of the American Empire. There will be a day, as there was for the tree, as for those who died on 9/11 and who die every day around the world, when I too will disappear. When I can no longer take to the road, pound the pavement until my legs magically leave the ground and I can fly with the wind. When that day comes, who among my fellow travellers will notice I am gone?

* * *

In the ten years since 9/11, many other disasters and acts of terrorism have taken countless lives around the world. Each one has its anointed heroes as it briefly crosses the media stage, capturing our hearts and imaginations till the next one strikes. In between it's all too easy to forget how much we depend on firemen, first responders, soldiers, doctors and nurses, to name only some among the myriad invisible heroes, who quietly put their lives on the line to save and care for us every day.

Here in New York, The Fire Department of New York once again, just as the guys predicted, has to struggle for adequate resources to do its job, fighting for its place in the city's budget and on the congested city streets. As for our heroes, all three men, Jack Smith, Steve Holland, and Patrick Darby are now retired. Like Darby, Holland has ended up living far away from the place where these life changing events and our story took place. After taking a prolonged leave earlier this year to help Stephanie take care of her terminally ill mother, who lives outside the country, Holland decided he was ready for a change, and recently put in his papers for retirement. I finally got to meet Darby's wife and kids several months ago when he invited me to his home while I was vacationing nearby. Since Smitty's shoulder injury forced his retirement several years ago he's been talking about moving to the country, far away from the city he fears is a likely target for another major terrorist attack. For now he remains in New York near his daughter, who, like many other New York City children, ended up suffering major post-traumatic distress some years after 9/11. He's gone on to have another child, and with the support of

Fire Department funding for its 9/11 survivors, has managed to make it in for therapy when he can.

As for me, I'm still taking the subway into Manhattan and travelling the world with my patients twenty three stories in the air, blocks away from the once and future World Trade Center. Wondering what's next, in my story and theirs.

I try to make my way over to the firehouse every once in a while, just to check in. Less than a dozen of the original fifty guys in the firehouse from the 9/11 period are still there. Lt. Sal is among them. Happily married and with two children, he's no longer posing for pin-ups, but he still loves to clown around with the guys. The firehouse has continued to hold its memorial each September 11th at the same church, in the last few years gathering after the service in one of the local bars. It gives those of us no longer in the house a chance to catch up and trade stories. Like the city it serves, like so many families, the firehouse undergoes changes yet somehow manages to be its same distinctive self. Policies may change, new guys come in and others leave, but basic protocol is adhered to and its rituals upheld: maintain readiness to respond to the call, welcome visitors, gather around the kitchen table, and 'Keep it in the House.'

The firehouse has tragically suffered the death of two of the men in the story, one in an automobile accident and the other after a long and valiant battle with cancer probably related to Ground Zero exposure. It is a testimony to these men and the very nature of the Brotherhood that the firehouse showed the same profound loyalty and commitment to memory that they brought to the 9/11 disaster. I will be forever grateful to these men for allowing me to help them at such a crucial period in their lives and in our history.

The destruction wrought by incomprehensible evil ripples from one life to another, from one generation to the next, binding together the destiny of individuals and societies. This was the story of one therapist, one firehouse, and a small group of firemen. But trauma and catastrophe are ubiquitous, stress and grief universal. The passing of time has shown us not only the pain but the bonds and enduring memory that comes with sharing such experience.

CPSIA information can be obtained at www.ICGtesting.com
Printed in the USA
BVOW031359281011

274779BV00001B/10/P